TEXAS *Water Safari*

River Books
Sponsored by

THE MEADOWS CENTER
FOR WATER AND THE ENVIRONMENT
TEXAS STATE UNIVERSITY

Andrew Sansom, General Editor

Generously supported by the Texas Natural Resource Conservation Publication Endowment, Meadows Center for Water and the Environment, Texas State University

TEXAS *Water Safari*

The World's Toughest Canoe Race

Bob Spain and Joy Emshoff

Foreword by Andrew Sansom

Texas A&M University Press   *College Station*

Library of Congress Cataloging-in-Publication Data

Names: Spain, Bob, author. | Emshoff, Joy, 1953– author. |
  Sansom, Andrew, writer of foreword.
Title: Texas Water Safari : the world's toughest canoe race /
  Bob Spain with Joy Emshoff ; foreword by, Andrew Sansom.
Other titles: River books (Series)
Description: First edition. | College Station : Texas A&M University
  Press, [2023] | Series: River books | Includes bibliographical
  references and index.
Identifiers: LCCN 2022042431 | ISBN 9781648430589 (cloth) | ISBN
  9781648430596 (ebook)
Subjects: LCSH: Texas Water Safari—History. | Texas Water
  Safari—Biography. | Texas Water Safari (1st : 1963 : San Marcos,
  Tex.; Seadrift, Tex.) | Canoe racing—Texas—History. | Canoes and
  canoeing—Texas—History. | Rivers—Recreational use—Texas. |
  San Marcos River (Tex.) | Guadalupe River (Tex.)
Classification: LCC GV786 .S63 2023 | DDC 797.1/409764—dc23/
  eng/20220923
LC record available at https://lccn.loc.gov/2022042431

Photography Credits:

p. i. Courtesy of Ashley Landis
p. ii. Courtesy of Ashley Landis
p. vi. (*top*) Courtesy of Ashley Landis; (*center*) Courtesy of
  Kevin Bradley; (*bottom*) Courtesy of Ashley Landis
p. xx. Courtesy of Ashley Landis
p. xiv. Courtesy of Eric Schlegel
p. xv. Courtesy of Eric Schlegel
p. xvi. (*top, center, bottom*) Courtesy of Ashley Landis
p. 4. Courtesy of Ashley Landis
p. 222. (*top, center, bottom*) Courtesy of Kevin Bradley
p. 226. (*top and bottom*) Courtesy of Ashley Landis;
  (*center*) Courtesy of San Marcos Daily Record
p. 234. Courtesy of Ashley Landis
p. 235. (*all photos*) Courtesy of Ashley Landis
p. 236. (*top, center, bottom*) Courtesy of Ashley Landis
p. 237. Courtesy of Ashley Landis
p. 238. Courtesy of Ashley Landis
p. 239. (*top, center, bottom*) Courtesy of Ashley Landis
p. 240. (*top, center, bottom*) Courtesy of Ashley Landis
p. 241. Courtesy of Ashley Landis
p. 242. (*top and bottom*) Courtesy of Ashley Landis;
  (*center*) Courtesy of Ann Best
p. 243. Courtesy of Ashley Landis
p. 244. Courtesy of Ashley Landis

Maps by Josh Bailey.

SENATE CONGRESSIONAL RESOLUTION 5

Whereas the fifth annual Texas Water Safari is to be held during the seven-day period commencing on June 17, 1967~ and

Whereas this outstanding sports event has been called "the world's toughest river race" in which men in canoes match their courage, stamina, and skill against 538 miles of winding, twisting rivers and wave-whipped ocean bays; and

Whereas the conditions encountered in the course of this formidable race duplicate in many ways those which challenged the hardy pioneers who followed wilderness waterways to open up a continent; and

Whereas the Texas Water Safari, with its emphasis on courage, skill, endurance, and physical fitness, justly deserves the widespread interest which it has engendered throughout this country and in other nations.

Now, therefore, be it Resolved by the Senate (the House of Representatives concurring), that the Congress extends its greetings and commendation to the Texas Water Safari Association in recognition of its sponsorship of an outstanding annual event which pits the unquenchable spirit of man against nature in a competition which cannot fail to be an inspiration to, and a bond between, all men who admire true sportsmanship. The Secretary of the Senate shall prepare a suitable copy of this resolution for presentation to the Texas Water Safari Association.

{Published in the "Congressional Record-Senate," January 19, 1967, pp. 963 & 964.}

Contents

Part 4. The Rest Is History

Foreword

I was in high school living at the mouth of the Brazos River in Freeport when my Aunt Alice Ann married photographer Pete Stovall. Uncle Pete was an adventurer who taught me how to scuba dive and helped spur my lifelong interest in and love of the outdoors. He ran the very first Texas Water Safari (TWS) in 1963 and I will never forget his tales of the grueling journey down the San Marcos and Guadalupe Rivers to the Texas Coast.

I will leave it to my dear friends Bob Spain and Joy Emshoff, the authors of this narrative of the world's most challenging canoe race, to tell the story, but as our colleague Jim Kimmel described in the very first volume of *River Books* published by Texas A&M University Press and The Meadows Center for Water and the Environment: "Imagine paddling your canoe almost nonstop for 260 miles, down the San Marcos to the Guadalupe, to the mouth of the Guadalupe, and finally across 8 miles of open water of San Antonio Bay to Seadrift."

Bob and Joy are veteran paddlers and certified canoe instructors. Bob is a renowned competitive paddler who helped establish the Texas Paddling Trail program. He was inducted into the Texas Canoe Racing Hall of Fame and continues to compete in canoe races in Texas and around the country, including the Water Safari. He is a former Senior Conservationist at the Texas Parks Wildlife Department.

Thus, it is more than fitting that we are treated here to the fascinating story on these pages of the race itself along with a compelling reminder of the significance of watercourses like the San Marcos and Guadalupe to both the Texas economy and the environment. The very fact that the race commences at Spring Lake on the Texas State University Campus is a metaphor for the interplay of natural resources and outdoor recreation. Spring Lake is a globally significant site which not only provides habitat for eight threatened or endangered species of flora and fauna but is one of the oldest, and quite possibly the oldest continuously inhabited site by human beings in North America.

I have had the pleasure of being in a canoe with Bob and he honored me several years ago by allowing me to fire the starting pistol to start the race below my office in the Old Aquarena Springs Inn, now headquarters of The Meadows Center. I reflected on both the astonishing skill and tenacity of the competitors but also that the watery marathon is another reminder of the urgent need to protect resources like these two lovely Texas Rivers and the springs from which they flow.

After running the Texas Water Safari several times, tragically Uncle Pete who was also a pilot, was killed in an airplane crash but, each year as the race begins at Spring Lake I am reminded of the importance of great people like him, Bob Spain, and Joy Emshoff and of the impact they have on our lives.

—*Andy Sansom*, General Editor

Preface

When I moved to Austin in 1979, I had not heard of the Texas Water Safari. I had participated in high school sports but knew nothing about canoeing. For the next few years, I ran 10k's, played city league tennis, and participated in triathlons, principally in Austin and the surrounding area.

Then in the mid-1980s, my buddies and I decided to do a river trip. I had heard about a canoe livery in Martindale, Texas, that sold canoes and kayaks, so my friends and I bought plastic kayaks and booked a whitewater trip on the Dolores River in Colorado with Tom Goynes.

While I had never done an Eskimo roll (except in a swimming pool), I was off for a whitewater canoe trip. I had heard that there were some Class "IV" and "V" rapids on the river, but "V" is a small Roman numeral—so how hard could that be? Little did I know that a Class "V" rapid was the most difficult! Well, obviously I made it through the trip, but I did swim one rapid and had to be rescued by Marty Pribil, an experienced kayaker. While I gained an appreciation for whitewater, it also "wet my whistle," so to speak, for paddling. Over the next year, I began to paddle more and learned by trial and error how to paddle. However, I would highly recommend instruction to any novice paddler.

In 1988 I entered my first canoe race, the Corsicana Spill, a nine-mile canoe race for recreational canoes near Corsicana, Texas. I was fortunate to have a younger but more experienced stern man, Terry Acker, in the canoe and I think we finished sixth or so, overall. Determined to improve, I trained hard and entered the race the next year with Mike Riley, and we won the race. For the next few years, I began to train with a number of veteran paddlers, and all of them had competed in the Texas Water Safari, "World's Toughest Canoe Race." In 1990 I raced the Safari with two buddies, Russ Roberts and Robert Youens, and we finished fourth overall. I raced again the next year with Joe and Brian Mynar and Joe Burns, and we were second overall. From this point on, I was totally hooked on canoeing and racing canoes. Since then, I have raced canoes in Texas and through my involvement with the United States Canoe Association (USCA), I became more involved with canoeing at the national level.

In 2006 I met Joy at a canoe livery in Austin. She was already an accomplished kayaker who paddled recreationally. By this time, I had become a United States Canoe Association canoe instructor, and she decided to give the Texas Water Safari a try. She asked me to give her a few pointers on the race, so we began to paddle stretches of the Safari course in preparation for the 2007 Texas Water Safari. While she trained for the race, her partner, a college student at Southwest Texas State University (now Texas State University), did not. Well, best laid plans went awry when she and her partner wrecked their canoe on the first practice run. After the mishap, their race was off that year.

The following year Joy and a new partner, Kim Sorenson, finished the Safari in 82 hours and 26 minutes.

In 2016, I had a conversation with Andrew Sansom, general editor of the River Books Series at the Meadows Center for Water and the Environment at Texas State University. He encouraged me to write a book on the race, so over the next few years, Joy and I researched and interviewed countless Safari competitors. Joy wrote the chapter on women of the Safari, and I wrote the other chapters of the book.

Now, fifteen years after we first met, Joy and I still paddle and race canoes, help put on the Texas Water Safari, and are thankful to be a part of the Texas Water Safari family.

—*Bob Spain*

~~~~~~

Yes, it's true, I had to race the Safari before Bob would pop the question. In the paddling community that seems to be the case for a lot of couples! It's paddling that brings us together and keeps us together. It's around paddling that families come together and stay together. Bob and I still love to paddle and continue to host and participate in canoe races in Texas and other states. For the past thirty+ years, Bob has been involved with the Safari as a volunteer and race official and is currently a board member, and today, we both help put on the Texas Water Safari.

In the following chapters, we share stories, photos, statistics, and our favorite tall tales about this incredible race.

—*Joy Emshoff*

Acknowledgments

So many people helped to make this book possible, and it is difficult to list them all. However, Joy and I will attempt to recognize those who made significant contributions.

First, we are indebted to Roger Zimmerman, who for fifty years kept paper archives and an electronic database of the Texas Water Safari. His extensive collection of newspaper and magazine articles, written accounts, and an extensive database of past races has provided vital insight into the early years of the race. This book would not have been possible without his consistent documentation. West Hansen provided a great deal of research materials, including an unpublished manuscript about the Safari, and also taped interviews of past competitors. John Mark Harras provided an excellent spreadsheet that documents all TWS entries for the entire fifty-nine-year history of the Safari. Roy Kleinsasser provided helpful statistical information from the Texas Water Safari archives. He also provided a critical review of the draft manuscript and provided many helpful comments. Tom Goynes, veteran canoe racer, and his wife Paula, provided vital information about the early years of the race and accounts of their race experiences. We are indebted to a number of veteran Safari competitors who provided helpful insight and firsthand knowledge of their races, including: Joe Mynar, Jerry Cochran, Pat Petrisky, John Bugge, and Jay Daniel.

We are indebted to a number of individuals for the photos in this manuscript. The San Marcos Daily Record allowed Joy and me unlimited access to copies of their newsprint images for the entire fifty-nine-year history of the race. Kevin Bradley, a Safari veteran, provided images for the years 1983 to 2005. Erich Schlegel provided images from 2007 to 2009. Ann Best provided images for various years 2007 through 2017, and Ashley Landis photographed the Safari from start to finish, documenting the race from 2012 to 2021. Thanks also to Sandy Yonley and Patti Geisinger who also provided photo images.

We are also indebted to countless Safari board members, competitors, officials, and volunteers who provided stories and information about their personal experiences that helped to document the history of the race. Maps of the race course were created by Josh Bailey.

We are also thankful to all our friends and Safari family who have provided the encouragement and support that have made this book possible. Last but not least thanks to the Meadows Center for Water and the Environment and Dr. Andy Sansom, my friend, for their efforts to conserve Texas rivers and support of the River Books Series. Thanks also to the seven thousand+ paddlers who had the inclination, strength, stamina, and perseverance to race the Texas Water Safari, "World's Toughest Canoe Race."

TEXAS *Water Safari*

Introduction

There is a canoe race in Texas like no other. With a sixty-year history as one of the most challenging ultramarathon canoe races in North America, the race is more like an expedition than a canoe race. Log jams, dam portages, poisonous snakes, nonstop day and night paddling, swarms of mosquitos, swift currents, torturous Texas heat, and 3- to 6-foot waves along the Texas coast are some of the factors that have earned the race its name, the "Texas Water Safari, World's Toughest Canoe Race."

The history of the race is an interesting one. The first Safari was held in 1963, but the idea behind the race began the year before. In 1962 two businessmen from San Marcos, Frank Brown and "Big" Willie George, decided to travel from San Marcos, Texas, to Corpus Christi, Texas, by boat. With approximately 250 miles of rivers and 87 miles of coastal water, and with no motor and only paddles, oars, and a sail for propulsion, they paddled, pushed, and wrestled their heavy boat over fifty-three log jams, dam portages, and rough coastal waves, finishing the ordeal in twenty-one days—no small task!

The following year Frank Brown staged the first Texas Water Safari, which followed the same route that he and Big Willie had endured the previous year. To make the canoe race as difficult as possible, the rules stated that competitors had to carry everything in their boat, they could receive no water until they reached the coast, and if they ran out of food or water,

they could hunt or fish and drink river water. While 127 competitors started the first Texas Water Safari, only four finished—a testament to its bone-wrenching difficulty.

While only Texans raced the first Safari, news traveled fast and the second year drew an international following, including a gold medal Olympian and several pro canoe racers from up North. This trend has continued over the years as some of the finest world-class paddlers and ultramarathon athletes have traveled to Texas to race. Several Texas teams, seeking a win, have recruited elite athletes from not only the United States but also Canada and Central America.

While many canoe races in the United States have their challenges, none can compare to the impediments of the Texas Water Safari. Some would say that the sheer length of the race is what makes it so difficult, while others would say it is the obstacles along the way—I think it is a combination of both. Originally designed as the most grueling boat race anywhere, it has lived up to its billing.

In the early years of the race, the hot Texas weather and the prohibition on receiving any types of assistance from bank crews took its toll on competitors. Heat exhaustion, dehydration, lack of preparation, fatigue, physical injuries, and boat wrecks caused a majority of the competitors to drop out of the race. While the grueling nature of the nonstop race would presumably be a disincentive for most, it has served as an attractant to others. Ian Adamson, a twelve-time World Adventure Racer, has said, "In my experience paddling distance races on four continents since 1984, the Texas Water Safari is the most challenging and diverse nonstop canoe event in the world. No other race combines the diverse conditions, distance. and technical difficulty of the Safari."

Some rule changes over the years, in the interest in safety, have given competitors a better chance to finish. These include a team captain in 1969 to track the progress of the team; water and ice came a few years later, and in 2013 a second team captain was allowed, and teams could receive food and medical supplies during the race. Also, the race course was shortened in 1971 to 260 miles, which has remained the same until the present day.

While the first race had only one class that everyone competed in, through the years additional classes have been added, to include: classes for gender, novice paddlers, boats with specific design features, and classes for solo and tandem paddlers and a multiperson unlimited class for teams with up to six competitors. There are currently ten checkpoints along the route with mandatory deadlines and with a final deadline of 100 hours at the finish line.

With the advent of newer lightweight construction materials, like carbon fiber and Kevlar, and long, skinny 40- to 50-foot canoes and kayaks, present-day competitors have completed the course much faster than competitors racing in the early years of the Safari. Canoes designed and built in Texas, specifically for the race, have pioneered ultramarathon canoe racing and have won most long-distance canoe races in America.

While the first Safari was held in April, the second Saturday in June has become the permanent starting date for the race. Every year at precisely 9:00 a.m. on that day boats line up on Spring Lake on the Texas State University campus in San Marcos, Texas. The lake is fed by the San Marcos Springs, which flows up through the limestone substrate and provides a continuous flow of the crystal-clear water that forms the 80-mile San Marcos River. The Springs are the second largest spring complex west of the Mississippi River and are believed to be the longest continually occupied site in North America. The race course follows the San Marcos River to its confluence with the Guadalupe River, and the course follows the Guadalupe for approximately 177 miles to where it enters San Antonio Bay. The course follows the bay for 6 miles in a southeasterly direction, ending at the Bay Front Pavilion and Park in Seadrift, Texas.

Since the first race in 1963, more than 7,600 entrants have attempted the Safari, but given the hardships of the race, only about two-thirds have finished. While many first-time competitors are "one and done," 60 percent of the finishers are returning racers, some of whom have competed ten, twenty, thirty, or even forty times. About 90 percent of the finishers are men and 10 percent are women. Over the years Safari paddlers have developed a camaraderie with other Safari competitors. Many, like 2014 finisher Kate Tart, refer to their Safari friends as a family:

> What the Safari has given me is more than an accomplishment to list or stories to tell, it has given me a family, my tribe. It has given me friends that have my back, who will show up to help you move in the rain. It has given me women role models for my kids and shown them (and reminded me at times) what badassery looks like. There is the family you are born with and then the family you create, and the Safari has given me a family greater than I could have ever dreamed of.

Joy and I have raced the Texas Water Safari and have also raced or paddled canoes in thirty different states, so we can honestly say that the Texas Water Safari is the most difficult canoe race in the United States, or anywhere for that matter.

In the following chapters, we discuss the high points and low points of the race, elite athletes and novices alike, women who have conquered the race, the large "family" of competitors who come back year after year, perennial volunteers who make the race possible, and many stories and quotes by those who have competed in the race.

We hope you enjoy the book and invite you to drop by the Meadows Center for Water and the Environment on the Texas State University campus in San Marcos, Texas, on the second Saturday in June at 9:00 a.m. to see the start of the Texas Water Safari, the World's Toughest Canoe Race.

PART ONE
The World's Toughest Canoe Race

The Texas Water Safari is about transition.
I am a better version of myself when I cross the finish line.

—*Joel Truitt, three-time Texas Water Safari finisher*

1

Frank Brown and "Big Willie" George

On a summer day in 1962, Frank Brown, manager of the San Marcos Chamber of Commerce, and "Big Willie" George, the owner of a local hamburger drive-in, put in at the headwaters of the San Marcos River—known as Spring Lake—in San Marcos, Texas. It was June 23, and an escort of six Aqua-Maids from the Aquarena Springs amusement park swam along the sides of their 14-foot Lone Star V-bottom boat,

the SMS Aquarena. A crowd of local supporters and the news media watched from the amusement park's glass bottom boats as the two departed on a 337-mile journey to Corpus Christi in a boat with no motor. For the next three weeks, they would have to fight through rapids, portage over logjams—one 2 miles long—ward off huge mosquitoes, fish and hunt for food, and sail and paddle across the coastal bays.

A group of spectators and "well-wishers" launch the "SMS Aquarena" on June 23, 1962. Over the next three weeks Frank Brown and "Big Willie" George paddled and sailed the boat to Corpus Christi. Courtesy of San Marcos Daily Record

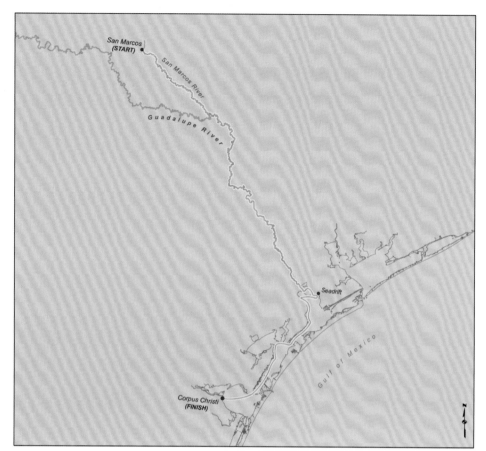

Original route of the 1962 river trip by Frank Brown and "Big Willie" George from San Marcos to Corpus Christi (approximately 337 miles). Courtesy of Josh Bailey

While the adventurers had planned to reach nearby Luling, about 40 miles downstream, by the next morning, logjams and dams slowed their progress to a snail's pace. Because the riverbanks were too steep to climb, and the 133-pound Lone Star boat (not counting the gear) was too heavy to lift out of the river, they had to pull, push, and wrestle the boat over and through the piles of debris, limbs, and logs clogging the river. After three days, they had paddled only 9 miles. According to Frank Brown's own account, "A logjam is a contraption of the devil calculated to spoil rivers and foil the best efforts of men who take them on."[1]

On day five, the two finally reached Luling, where they were greeted by a host of well-wishers, including state representative Henry Fletcher and Luling mayor J. B. Nichols. Already in need of provisions, they bought a tent, patch materials for their air mattresses, soap, suntan lotion, and a 20-pound block of ice.[2] Weary but determined, the two heroes traveled on.

While Frank and Big Willie were "on their own" on the water, they did have a support team that followed on land and handled the media coverage. Frank kept in touch with the city of San Marcos by phone and also sent sketches by mail when they reached towns along their route. An airplane and helicopter checked on their progress frequently.[3] At night, the weary travelers rested in their tent and listened to the owls and other wildlife.

For food, they mostly fished for bass and catfish.

Frank Brown (left) and "Big Willie" (right) talk with a reporter in Victoria, TX. A week later they paddle into Corpus Christi after spending 20 days and 8 hours on the river adventure. Courtesy of San Marcos Daily Record

Approximately 3 miles before reaching Gonzales, they left the San Marcos River and entered the Guadalupe. Big Willie had his best success here when he caught three bass on his first three casts. With only a 1-gallon water container, the two were constantly on the lookout for a camp house so they could fill their jug. When water ran low and no sign of civilization was near, they boiled river water.

At Gonzales, they picked up a hitchhiker—Bill Veidl, owner of KCNY Radio—who rode in their boat to Hochheim. Ready for a change in their diet, the three searched for melons and corn in the fields along the river. On one occasion they found corn, but it was too hard to eat. They also "borrowed" a pet duck. But when they tried to eat it, Frank Brown said, "Not only was it tough as a boot, it was like eating your pet pig in a way."[4]

From Gonzales to Cuero, they hunted squirrels with a shotgun and a .22 rifle. According to Frank's account, squirrel hunting on the river was most successful when squirrels fell on the land, because a dead squirrel sinks immediately in water.

Below Cuero they saw lots of deer and a few coons. They put out throwlines at night and caught a few catfish to supplement their diet. They considered eating a water moccasin, but changed their minds at the last minute. One evening they did decide to eat a softshell turtle, and Frank said it was delicious.[5]

Below Victoria they began to see large gar in the river that must have weighed 50 to 75 pounds, and they encountered large schools of mullet that jumped "6 feet" in the air when their boat passed.

Near Bloomington, the travelers were greeted by two familiar faces, Don Russell and Paul Rogers of the Aquarena Center as well as a friend named Colonel Doughty. They all went to scout the 2-mile logjam below Tivoli that still stood between them and the ocean. While Frank and Big Willie had experienced many logjams along the way, the one up ahead put the others to shame.

When they camped that night, they experienced mosquitoes like never before. In Frank's words, "Usually I'm not one to throw adjectives and superlatives around in a wasteful manner, but the superlative hasn't been born to do justice to those mosquitoes we camped with that night. We had been accustomed to pegging up holes in the front of our pup tent with safety pins, both to keep out bugs and discourage the snakes from sleeping with us, but then those mosquitoes starting unsnapping the safety pins and fighting over Big Willie because he was juicier than I."[6] With little sleep, the two travelers awoke the next morning and decided to take a new route, exiting the Guadalupe River and dragging their boat across a peninsula to Hynes Bay. Colonel Doughty in his cabin cruiser escorted them across the bay to Austwell. The following morning, they rigged sails and leeboards that had been left for them for the *Aquarena* and shoved off for Corpus Christi.

After a frustrating day of tacking back and forth in their sailing boat, Frank and Big Willie came ashore only about 100 yards from the point where they had launched that morning. Unfortunately, the sail had not worked as well as anticipated. After a phone call the next morning, Colonel Doughty returned with his boat and towed them out of the bay to the entrance of the Intracoastal Canal.

While Colonel Doughty tried to persuade them to get a motor, they resisted and continued on. With little food remaining and 100 miles to go, they readied their sail and continued on to Corpus Christi. After an hour or so of paddling, they pulled over and adjusted their sail and leeboards and made better time. By nightfall they made it to the entrance of Aransas Bay. The corn hoe cakes they ate that night would be the last meal of their journey.

On Thursday, July 12, they struck out across Aransas Bay, eager to get to Corpus Christi after now eighteen days on the water. By noon they had drifted 4 miles off course and were out in the middle of the bay. They turned the boat directly into the wind and paddled and sailed, slowly making progress in the right direction. The waves were big, but they inched forward and knew that they had to keep paddling or would be blown backward. By afternoon they passed about one-half mile off the Rockport beach, and at dark they reached the shelter of the canal. The two continued to paddle and sail on into the night, finally stopping by the Dale Miller Bridge near Aransas Pass.

The next morning, Friday the thirteenth, a boat came out to meet them, and a policeman informed them that when they had failed to call in from Fulton or Rockport, a search party had gone out looking for them around Matagorda. They went ashore at Aransas Pass, and Big Willie called his wife and told her to pick up Frank's wife and head for Corpus Christi that afternoon. Frank Brown also called Bob Conwell with the Corpus Christi Convention and Visitors Bureau and asked him to call off the search party and to have an escort boat at the entrance to Corpus Christi Bay.

When they were 6 miles from Corpus Christi, they turned due west and the wind was finally with them. By 2:00 p.m. they reached a buoy, tied up, and waited for the escort boat. When the boat arrived, they immediately transferred their gear to lighten their load. It's a good thing they did, because from there on, their ride was really rough. According to Frank's account, it was "a ride to end all rides."[7]

The huge waves were breaking from the back of the boat, and according to Frank, with each wave, a mountain of water that looked like a twelve-story building lifted their stern. Frank had the boom line in one hand and the rudder in the other, while Big Willie held the boom and shifted his weight for ballast. The two rode the crest of each wave until it passed and then braced themselves for the next one to lift the boat skyward. It was truly the most exciting part of the trip. The waves continued for about two hours until they passed the Corpus Christi breakwater. Then they lowered the sail and the escort boat towed them a hundred yards or so toward the T-head. Proudly, they cast off the tow line and paddled the last few yards.

Frank and Big Willie completed their voyage to Corpus Christi in twenty days and eight hours on Friday, July 13, 1962. Their wives, fans, and city officials greeted them with a golden key to the city of Corpus Christi. That night they were treated to a fish dinner, and I am sure they were glad it wasn't squirrel. When they returned to San Marcos, they were given a hero's welcome on the courthouse lawn, complete with a cake and other gifts.

One year after the historic 1962 river safari, Frank Brown, with the support of the San Marcos Chamber of Commerce and the Corpus Christi Buccaneer Commission, decided to stage a canoe race from San Marcos to Corpus Christi, Texas, following the same route that he and Big Willie had taken on their historic trip. The event was billed as the "Texas Water Safari—The Toughest Boat Race in the World."

"Big Willie" George talking to the competitors at the start of the 2008 Texas Water Safari in San Marcos. He and Frank Brown made the first trip from San Marcos to Corpus Christi in 1962. The next year (1963) the first Texas Water Safari was held. Courtesy of Ann Best

2

The First Race

1963

The first Texas Water Safari was held April 29 through May 10, 1963. According to the race application, it was called "a 500-mile marathon," but in truth, it was actually about 337 miles. As stated in the race application:

> Participation in the TEXAS WATER SAFARI in itself is an honor in that every effort has been made to make it the most rugged event of its kind you are very likely to partake of. So far as is known, there is no boating event in the world comparable.[1]

The rules stipulated a $25 entry fee per team, with no limit on the number of contestants per team. Any type of vessel was allowed, but all boats must use paddles, oars, or sails. All contestants must wear a US Coast Guard–approved life preserver while on the water and must get typhoid and tetanus immunizations. All provisions, equipment, items of repair, and such must be carried from the start. Nothing can be purchased or delivered to the team during the race, but fishing and hunting for food was legal. The only exception was that water would be provided in the coastal segments. To ensure that the competitors

Flyer from the first Texas Water Safari in 1963.

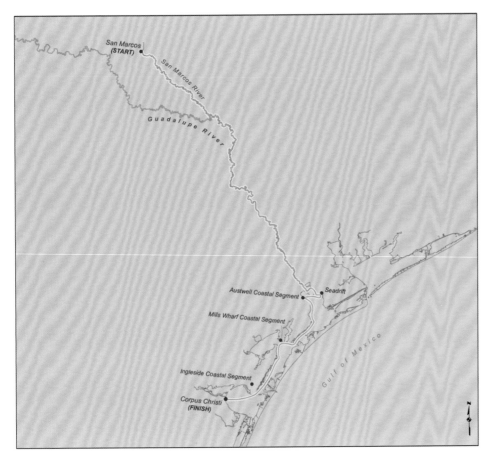

received no outside assistance, monitors would be stationed at undisclosed locations along the route.

During the twelve-day race, the competitors would face dam portages, more than fifty logjams, swarms of mosquitos, hungry alligators and poisonous snakes, 4- to 6-foot waves along the coast, plus fatigue and exhaustion that would certainly take their toll.

While one might think the rugged nature of the event and the rules would dissuade contestants from entering the race, the opposite was true. The promise of extreme conditions and the challenges of competing and finishing were well received, and surprisingly 126 men and one woman signed up to participate. There was one four-person team, thirteen three-person

teams, forty tandem teams, and four solo competitors. All Texans, the field included five engineers, twelve USAF personnel, four farmers, three policemen, two boatbuilders, a hairdresser, four mechanics, two salesmen, a copilot, fourteen students, and seventy-nine others.[2] They showed up in john boats, Grumman aluminum canoes, homemade skiffs, a plywood dory, nine Folbots, a dingy, kayaks, a Polynesian outrigger, and two small barges called "prams."

On April 29, the fifty-eight vessels assembled on Spring Lake for the start of the race. Because the river channel was relatively narrow, race chairman Frank Brown sent out waves of twelve boats every half hour. Only minutes after the start, a waterfall knocked one boat out of the race, sinking it to the bottom.[3] Also, on the first day, Willye Waterman, the only woman in the race, injured her knee when it was pinned between her boat and a rock. Injured but committed, she raced on with her husband, W. J. Even though they were in last place, they were determined to reach the coast where their sailing skills should pay off.[4] Several racers were forced to drop out when they failed to wait for their water purification pills to work properly and stomach cramps and diarrhea set in. By the end of the day, multiple boats were scattered along the banks of the waterway.

While mishaps, equipment failures, lack of boating skills, and physical injuries took their toll on the field, some competitors moved skillfully down the river. The lead boat, #149, paddled by Barney Wiley and Fred Halamicek, continued straight through the night, reaching Gonzales in approximately 24 hours.[5] Two days in, the race lead changed several

Canoes, rowboats, john boats, and other vessels sprint across Spring Lake at the start of the 1963 Texas Water Safari. Courtesy of San Marcos Daily Record

times. James Jones and Lynn Maughmer, two determined policemen from Houston in boat #102, moved methodically up through the ranks and by the third day, they were in second place.[6]

On the fifth day, May 3, the first three boats reached the first coastal segment at Austwell.[7] When each team arrived, their time was taken and the clock would be started again for them on the morning of May 8, when all teams would depart the site together. Although Wiley and Halamicek in boat #149 were leading in elapsed time, they were disqualified when judges charged them with "acquiring additional food," in violation of rules.[8] Over the next four days, the river continued to take its toll, and only sixteen more boats survived past the 2-mile portage through the swamp, making it to Austwell. By all accounts, the swamp was described as the most brutal, snake infested place imaginable. One contestant said, "I was praying a snake would bite me so I could get out of the race honorably."[9]

When each team reached Austwell, they were required to wait in a designated area, roped off from the public until other teams reached the site. Each team's elapsed time was recorded and all the teams would leave the coastal segment in one group. This would allow the boats and planes that were tracking the teams to watch for capsized vessels or contestants stranded in the waters.

The coastal camps along this part of the course must have been a sight, with boats and equipment scattered everywhere, tired bodies lying here and there and equipment lying in disarray along the shore. One account described the area as resembling a prisoner of war camp.[10] Some teams ate food they had brought with them while others fished or scavenged for crabs and oysters in the shallow coastal waters. Solo competitor Roger Zimmerman, in boat #119, had already eaten his two-week supply of dehydrated food in four days and was scavenging the campsite for crabs and oysters.

In preparation for the race, he said, "I ordered dehydrated stew from the Sears and Roebuck Catalog. It was recommended for mountain climbers and I ordered the recommended amount for the length of the 1963 race. Paddlers must eat more than mountain climbers because I was out of food when I reached Victoria."

Desperate for sustenance, he gathered berries along the river and even slipped up on an unsuspecting possum and clubbed it, but in the end, he decided that he could not stomach the marsupial.

Over the first nine days and roughly 250 miles on the San Marcos and Guadalupe Rivers, broken boats and equipment, lack of food, stomach cramps, diarrhea, injury, fatigue and exposure, lack of sleep, and disqualifications had narrowed the field, and only nineteen boats—with Jones and Maughmer in boat #102 comfortably in the lead—reached the first coastal segment at Austwell in the allotted time. After nine days of challenging conditions, they would now have to sail, row, or paddle through high winds and waves on the final leg to Corpus Christi.

On May 8 at sunup, the nineteen boats struck out into the blue waters of Hynes Bay. At this point all contestants were required to follow the directives of the US Coast Guard. Travel would only be allowed from sunup until sundown, so teams would have to reach the next checkpoint at Mills Wharf that day. Cumulative times would be recorded for each team on arrival.

While the obstacles in the San Marcos and Guadalupe Rivers were far behind the competitors, high winds and large waves in the coastal water continued to narrow the field. Only fourteen boats reached Mills Wharf by sunset. At 5:55 the next morning, May 9, 18-knot winds and large waves greeted the teams as

Roger Zimmerman raced the first TWS in 1963 but failed to reach the Ingeleside coastal stopover before sunset and Did Not Finish. He returned and completed the race in 1994, 1995, 2002, 2003, and 2014. Courtesy of Ann Best

they shoved off en route to Ingleside.[11] Rough seas took their toll as masts broke, leeboards snapped, rudders collapsed, and boats capsized.[12] As they neared Rockport, 6- to 8-foot waves tossed the boats around like small corks. By the time the three leading teams—Archie Clark and Vernon Byrd in boat #121, James Jones and Lynn Maughmer in boat #102, and Fred Hurd Jr. and Sam Hare in boat #163—reached the Intracoastal Canal south of Rockport, small craft warnings had been called.[13]

At 3:00 p.m. on May 9, Fred Hurd Jr. and Sam Hare in boat #163 were the first to reach Ingleside. Aluminum canoe #102, which held a large lead in elapsed time, was nowhere to be seen, and if they could not reach Ingleside by sunset at 7:23 p.m., they would be disqualified.[14]

At 5:30 p.m., the radio reported that the two policemen in boat #102 had dropped out of the race. Meanwhile, after washing up on shore about 10 miles away, the exhausted men were still trying to drag the boat to Ingleside. When that proved fruitless, they collapsed on the sand. While the situation would have defeated most mortals, they somehow rose to their feet and gave it one more try. Up ahead was a point of land, and if they could only make it around that point, they could turn downwind. Again, they tried to drag the boat along the shore, but when that didn't work, they decided to sail once more. By 6:30 p.m. they reached the point of land and turned the boat downwind, with time running short. A strong wind caught their sail, turned it abruptly, and the rudder snapped. Next, a large wave struck the boat and the right oar lock broke.[15] Desperate to finish the race, they grabbed the paddles and pressed on. Just when the two men thought that all was lost, they heard music in the distance. Up ahead, the Ingleside High School Band had begun to play to greet the competitors. With only minutes to spare, boat #102 turned toward the music and made it in the nick of time. At 7:12 p.m., with only eleven minutes to spare, the canoe made it to Ingleside.[16]

The two remaining teams, who had survived eleven days of competition, were finally on the last leg of the Safari—some 10 to 12 miles across open water. Since boat #102 had such a large lead in elapsed time, they just needed to finish before sunset to win the race. Sometime around noon on May 10, the two boats floated into Corpus Christi. A welcoming party of Safari buddies who had dropped out of the race, family members, race officials, city dignitaries, and well-wishers were there to greet the heroes. The winning team of Lynn Maughmer and James Jones in boat #102 completed the first Texas Water Safari in 110 hours and 35 minutes. In second place were Sam Hare and Fred Hurd Jr. in boat #163, finishing with a time of 145 hours. Along with the cheers of onlookers and congratulatory wishes, the winning team also received the Argosy Adventure Trophy, a Lone Star boat and motor, a turkey feeder, a pickup camper, a quarter acre of land overlooking Canyon Dam, a Polynesian outrigger, an Alumacraft canoe, and over $6,000 in prize money.[17] The cash prize would be split between the two finishing teams.

3

Tracing the Race Course

In its first two years, 1963 and 1964, the Texas Water Safari followed the original 337-mile course that Big Willie and Frank Brown followed in 1962, running from San Marcos to Corpus Christi, Texas. The race course then changed three times over the next eight years. In 1965–1967, it followed the same route down the San Marcos and Guadalupe Rivers but then turned north, ending in Freeport, for a total of 369

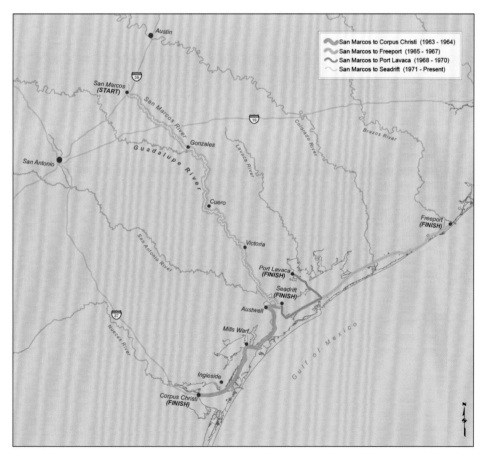

Texas Water Safari courses—1963 and 1964—Corpus Christi; 1965–1967—Freeport; 1968–1970—Port Lavaca; Seadrift—1971–present. Courtesy of Josh Bailey

A Comparison of the 1963 and 2021 Texas Water Safaris

1963 Race	2021 Race
Held April 29, 1963	Held June 12, 2021
Course reportedly 500 miles (approximately 337 miles)	Course is 260 miles
Race Course: San Marcos to Corpus Christi	Race course: San Marcos to Seadrift
12 days to finish	4 days and 4 hours to finish
Absolutely no assistance on river	Team captain(s) provide water, ice, food and/or medical supplies
No check points	10 designated checkpoints
No limit on number of paddlers on a team	Teams are limited to no more than 6 paddlers

miles. In 1968, 1969, and 1970, the race again followed the same river course but ended in Port Lavaca, totaling 309 miles. Since 1971, the Texas Water Safari has begun in San Marcos and ended 265 miles away, in the town of Seadrift. (The only exception was in 1974, when the race was stopped at the Highway 35 bridge near Tivoli due to severe weather.) While the race is much shorter today, and arguably easier, each variation of the course has included a coastal segment that often has become the downfall of even the more experienced teams. This chapter describes in detail the current race course, from San Marcos to Seadrift.

Starting Line: Spring Lake (mile 0)
—Lat. 29.893485; Long. -97.930922

The Texas Water Safari still begins on Spring Lake in San Marcos. Where Aquarena Springs once stood is now the Meadows Center for Water and the Environment on the Texas State University campus. The distance across Spring Lake is only about 500 yards, which can be covered in only a few minutes by the faster boats. At the edge of the lake, contestants reach their first obstacle: Spring Lake Dam. The portage can be tricky, but most make it through unscathed.

Once over the dam, the boats pass under Aquarena Springs Drive and paddle past beds of endangered wild rice that cover the river bottom. The rice (*Zizania texana*) is a federally protected, endangered plant that is found along the first 2 miles of the river and nowhere else in the world.

Just downstream is Sewell Park, and on the left is the Lions Club Tube Rental. The next landmark is Hopkins Street Bridge, with more parkland on the right (west) side of the river. Paddlers then pass under railroad tracks and, a short distance downstream, the river widens and a walkway leads out from the right bank to a small island.

Just past the island is Rio Vista Dam (mile 1.25). In 2006, the city of San Marcos removed the old Rio Vista Dam, which was in need of repair, and built a new one in its place. The old structure had one major slot that channeled a large volume of water over the dam, swamping most canoes that attempted to run it.

Spectators looking across Spring Lake with competitors in their boats assembling for the start of the Texas Water Safari. Courtesy of Ashley Landis

The new dam has three small drops, created by large rocks with a chute in the middle. These state-of-the-art features create one of the most attractive whitewater spots on the river. Rio Vista Dam has become a whitewater mecca where paddlers in squirt boats and all manner of plastic kayaks play below the three drops in the dam complex.

On race day, the city closes the area immediately adjacent to the dam so that contestants carrying and dragging their boats can portage unimpeded by spectators who are waiting to see the crashes that occur

among the racers that choose to run the dam. Running the dam is often a poor choice because competitors often swamp their boat and have to collect their gear, losing precious time to those who have taken the safer portage. Occasionally, someone runs the dam and "crashes and burns."

Once past Rio Vista Dam, competitors paddle under Cheatham Street Bridge and, after a few twists and turns, pass under Highway I-35. A little farther downstream is Cape's Camp on the left and Cape's Dam, which was built from timbers and earthen fill

RIO VISTA DAM CRASHES

In 2012, Curt Slaten in his brand-new carbon fiber/Kevlar, United States Canoe Association solo canoe (USCA C-1) attempted to run the dam. His original plan was to portage and not risk swamping his canoe and losing his gear. However, when he noticed a number of spectators in the spot where he planned to portage, in the excitement of the moment he changed his mind and decided to run it. He made a perfect entry into the slot and crested the dam, but when he dropped into the standing whitewater wave below, water poured over the gunwales and swamped his canoe. Immediately, he was thrown free without injury, but his canoe was not so lucky. The canoe filled with water, turned crossways, and lodged momentarily in the second drop. Then, the enormous force of the water ripped both ends from the canoe. Instantly, his race was over, only a mile from the start.

A similar wreck occurred in 2013, when a tandem team, #1827, decided to run the dam. They, too, swamped their aluminum canoe—it filled with water, floated downstream, and was pinned across the second drop.

This created a dangerous situation because any competitor who also attempted to run the dam could not pass safely through the second drop. Fortunately, there were only a couple of boats behind the pinned canoe and they were directed to portage around the dam.

Thinking that they could free their canoe, the two contestants swam over and began to tug, pull, and wrestle with it, but the canoe weighed tons with the weight of the water. While a large crowd of sympathetic spectators and race officials eagerly watched their efforts, no one was able to provide assistance or the team would have been disqualified. The two wet and frustrated competitors tried desperately to free the canoe, but after twenty minutes or so, Les Sheffield and James Kancewick finally had to ask for help—their race was over.

Les Sheffield and James Kancewick desperately attempting to free their penned aluminum canoe #1827 on the second drop of Rio Vista Dam. Unfortunately, their 2013 Safari was over.
Courtesy of Ashley Landis

in the 1800s.[1] Paddlers either portage the dam and paddle down the old channel or paddle past the dam in the newer channel that winds down and ends in a mill race. At the mill race, paddlers have to portage down Cape Street about 75 yards and then reenter the river at the bridge.

At 4.67 miles from the start, the Blanco River flows into the San Marcos River from the left. At low water, competitors have mistakenly paddled up the Blanco only to run out of water. Proceeding downstream from the junction with the Blanco River, the San Marcos bends right and then left and up ahead you can see Cummings Dam at mile 5.27. This is one of the more dangerous dams on the river. While there have been no fatalities at the dam during the race, over the years several recreational paddlers have lost their lives when they were trapped in a hydraulic below the dam. One-half mile downstream, County Road 101 crosses the river. Also known as Westerfield

Crossing (5.86 miles), this is the first place where some competitors can take on water from their team captains during the race.

Downstream from Westerfield Crossing there are three rapids: Old Mill Rapid at approximately mile 6, Broken Bone at approximately mile 7, and Cottonseed Rapid at mile 9. While all three rapids can be challenging, Cottonseed is the most difficult. It is also one of the best places to witness boat wrecks.

Thanks to the generosity of Harold Perkins and his family, his property is a popular place for family members and other spectators to enter the river and watch the canoes run the rapid. A bend in the river immediately before the rapid obstructs the view of the incoming racers, and several large rocks must be avoided to pass cleanly through without incident. One of these is called "wrap rock" because racers sometimes wrap or pin their canoe against it. While some choose to portage on the right, most competitors take

Team 3734, Brian Frey, Sarah Frey, and Kevin Halbert, portaging Cummings Dam. Sarah and Brian finished in 40th place in 78 hours and 57 minutes. Courtesy of Ann Best

Trey Fly and Beau Brooks in 2007 at Cottonseed Rapid. This rapid can be the downfall of even experienced competitors. Courtesy of Erich Schlegel

In 2004 Bob Bradford (bow) and Bob Vincent, two of the finest veteran paddlers in Canada and the United States, paddling in Cottonseed Rapid. "Wrap Rock" is directly in front of their canoe! Courtesy of Kevin Bradley

Bob and Bob wrap their canoe on "Wrap Rock" in Cottonseed Rapid. Courtesy of Kevin Bradley

Bob Bradford standing near the bow, surveying the damage. Sadly their race was over. Courtesy of Kevin Bradley

their chances and run the rapid. Cottonseed Rapid can be a major challenge for a novice paddler, and even the pros sometimes take a swim or wipeout here. In 2004 veteran paddler Bob Bradford, record holder of the Mississippi River Descent (2,348 miles in 18 days, 4 hours, and 15 minutes) and Bob Vincent, one of finest veteran paddlers from Canada, wrapped their canoe in Cottonseed and had to drop out of the race.

At approximately 10.5 miles from the start is the Martindale Dam. You must portage the dam on the right. Immediately below the dam, only 150 yards or so, is the Martindale low water crossing. At low to medium water you can paddle under the bridge, but competitors must be aware of rocks. Only a little over

a half mile up ahead is FM 1977. The flow begins to pick up here, and once under the FM 1977 Bridge, Shady Grove Campground and Spencer Canoes come into view on the right-hand side of the river. For the next few miles, the river twists and turns on its way to the Staples checkpoint.

Checkpoint 1: Staples Bridge 1 (mile 16) —Lat. 29.782312; Long. -97.83131

Near Staples Dam and the small town of Staples is the first of ten checkpoints that are located along the race course. The checkpoint is set up on Clarence "Shorty" Grumbles's front lawn, which abuts Staples

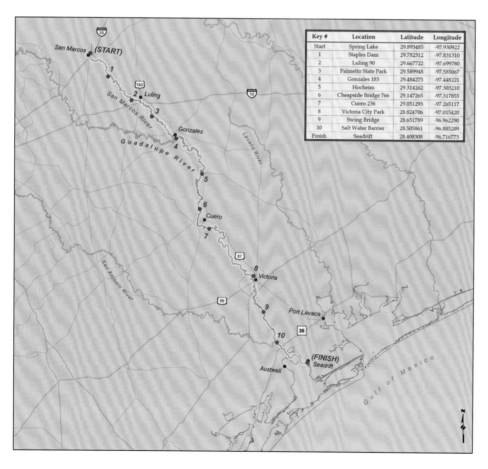

Key #	Location	Latitude	Longitude
Start	Spring Lake	29.893485	-97.930922
1	Staples Dam	29.782312	-97.831310
2	Luling 90	29.667722	-97.699780
3	Palmetto State Park	29.589948	-97.585067
4	Gonzales 183	29.484275	-97.448221
5	Hochheim	29.314262	-97.303210
6	Cheapside Bridge 766	29.147265	-97.317855
7	Cuero 236	29.051293	-97.265117
8	Victoria City Park	28.824706	-97.015420
9	Swing Bridge	28.651789	-96.962290
10	Salt Water Barrier	28.505861	-96.885209
Finish	Seadrift	28.408308	-96.716773

Texas Water Safari course (1971–present) from San Marcos to Seadrift with checkpoints 1–10 noted. Courtesy of Josh Bailey

Staples Checkpoint 1 (mile 16) with checkpoint officials in yellow shirts. Spectators are standing on Shorty Grumbles's lawn. Shorty's porch is on the left adjacent to stairs used to portage the dam. Courtesy of Erich Schlegel

Dam. Each year, Shorty and his family open up their yard to competitors, team captains, and officials. Competitors can portage on either side of the dam or around Mr. Grumbles's house. All teams must reach the site by 3:00 p.m. Saturday or face disqualification.

In the 1990s, I had a chance to visit Shorty's home. There in the living room, he lifted a lid on his coffee table … when I looked down, I could see the San Marcos River. Apparently, he could fish while sitting in the leisure of his home. I understand the trapdoor was later removed and permanently sealed. Maybe Shorty's wife, Norwell, decided that he had caught his limit. Sadly, Shorty passed away in December 2019—the Safari family will miss a good friend.

In between this checkpoint and the next are five bridges. The first is at Fentress, where Highway 20 crosses the river at mile 26, and the next is Prairie Lea Bridge #1, three miles farther down. This bridge is tricky at high water and can be portaged on the right side. There is a small, private bridge a mile farther downstream and another bridge, Prairie Lea #2, at mile 31. The last bridge before the next checkpoint is near Stairtown at mile 33.

Checkpoint 2: Luling Hwy 90 Bridge (mile 39) —Lat. 29.667722; Long. -97.69978

Checkpoint 2 is located just downstream from the Highway 90 Bridge on the left (north) side of the river in a small park managed by the city of Luling. If you

One of the many pump jacks scattered throughout the city of Luling. Adorned with images of cartoon and nursery rhyme characters, the iron structures are remnants of the oil boom of the 1920s. Courtesy of Joy Emshoff

race the Safari, you will be greeted here by Chuck and Ellen Truesdale, the checkpoint officials. They have become a landmark at the site, serving as the checkpoint officials for the past twenty-eight years. Teams must reach the site by eight Saturday evening to avoid disqualification.

This location is also the put-in for the Texas Parks and Wildlife Department's Luling Zedler Mill Paddling Trail. For the next 6 miles, competitors follow the river trail to the portage at Zedler Mill Dam (mile 45) in the city of Luling. On this stretch, competitors may detect a faint but pungent odor of rotten eggs. Permeating from the oil wells that produce "sour crude," which date back to the 1922 oil boom, is an

odor that the locals refer to as the "smell of money." Today the only remnants of the oil boom are the novel pumping jacks. They are scattered throughout the city and are decorated in the shape of animals and imaginary characters such as Santa Claus, an orca, a butterfly, and a cow jumping over the moon, to name a few.

Today, the city is better known for its June celebration called the Watermelon Thump. Each year the city is plastered with signs depicting local schoolgirls running for Watermelon Queen. Even tourists passing through the town can stop and vote in the election. As a fitting monument, the city's downtown water tower is painted like a watermelon.

Team 167 portaging Zedler Mill Dam. The large rocks are hazardous to competitors portaging on the right side of the dam. Courtesy of Ashley Landis

The portage of Zedler Mill Dam is on the right side, with some large rocks that can be treacherous. Some teams with heavier, longer multiperson canoes choose to slide their canoe over the buttresses of the dam, but this can also be very risky. Immediately downstream is the Highway 80 bridge. Another 4 miles ahead is IH-10, and six-and-a-half miles farther is the "Son of Ottine" rapid. This rapid can be run unless the water is extremely low. The next checkpoint is 4 miles downstream.

Checkpoint 3: Palmetto State Park (mile 60) —Lat. 29.589948; Long. -97585067

Checkpoint 3 is located in 270-acre Palmetto State Park, approximately 10 miles southeast of the city of Luling. It is named for the small, palmlike dwarf palmetto (*Sabal minor*), which grows abundantly there. The river dissects the park grounds, and the checkpoint is located on a low-water bridge. Under normal water conditions, water flows under the bridge, but

Jerry Cochran and Erin Magee (not shown) in team 3221 floating under the low-water bridge in Palmetto State Park Checkpoint 3 (mile 60). Jerry's wife Linda and granddaughter Kaley (standing) are looking down at Jerry. Karim Aziz is standing with camera in hand. Courtesy of Ashley Landis

at higher levels, the water flows over the low-water crossing and can be dangerous, especially at night. Because many teams reach this checkpoint on Saturday evening, it is a popular stopover, and twenty to thirty teams might congregate here on the first night of the race. Competitors must reach this checkpoint by 8:00 a.m. Sunday or be disqualified.

Seven-and-a-half miles downstream from the park is Sladen Cemetery Bridge (mile 67). Steep banks and poison ivy make access at this bridge difficult, and it is not recommended. Approximately 9 miles farther downstream is the Highway 90A bridge. For the next few miles, the river widens and the current slows down. There is an old iron bridge at mile 79, and 2 miles downstream the San Marcos flows into the Guadalupe River. Gonzales Dam is downstream at mile 84, and paddlers can portage either side of the dam. The portage on the left was created recently by the city to accommodate a new state paddling trail. The left side portage is longer than the right, but clear of obstacles. However, paddlers must be careful at the put-in, where large rocks at the water's edge can be treacherous.

One mile downstream is the next checkpoint, at Highway 183.

Portaging dams can be a challenge for teams, especially at night. In fact, cuts, bruises, broken bones, concussions, and other injuries have occurred when competitors lose their footing and fall.

During the 2011 Safari, Jay Daniel and Mike Vandeveer were portaging their tandem canoe around the Gonzales Dam, at a time when the only portage around the dam was on the right side. While most portages have impediments and obstacles to navigate, this one can be especially challenging. A concrete apron leads down to the water with some nasty concrete rubble and rusty rebar near the water's edge. On the first night of the race, Mike, the bowman, began to pick his way down the steep concrete apron while Jay followed behind with stern in hand. Without warning, there was a thud and Mike felt the canoe fall to the ground. Because Mike was facing forward, he could not see that Jay had lost control of the canoe and fallen. When Mike looked back, Jay was lying motionless on the ground. While he did not see what happened, he presumed that Jay must have lost his footing by stepping on leaves, mud, or wet concrete. He tried to wake Jay, but there was no response.

Race officials Jack Spencer and Kevin Bradley, who were monitoring the dam, had heard the crash when the canoe hit the ground. Soon after, other competitors began to show up, and after trying unsuccessfully to revive Jay, Mike asked Jack and Kevin for help. With an injured partner, Mike had no choice but to ask for help, and in doing so, forfeited the race.

Jay spent the night in the hospital and made a full recovery. The only thing he could remember was that he was carrying the canoe and the next thing he knew, he woke up in an ambulance. It's been eight years since the accident, and Jay has raced the Safari seven more times.

Checkpoint 4: Gonzales, Highway 183 (mile 85)—Lat. 29.484275, Long. -97.448221

Checkpoint 4 is located south of Gonzales at the Highway 183 bridge crossing on the south side of the Guadalupe River. This a popular stopover for teams to rest or sleep before continuing on downstream. At low flows, the checkpoint is set up on a large gravel bar that forms on the right, upstream side of the bridge. When water flows are higher, the checkpoint may set up under the Highway 183 bridge. Teams must reach this checkpoint by 4:00 p.m. Sunday.

With no public river access for the next 37 miles, teams must stock up on water, food, and/or medical supplies before continuing downstream. The stretch has some gravel bars and sweepers at lower water, but no major rapids.

Checkpoint 5: Hochheim, Highway 183 Bridge (mile 122)—Lat. 29.314262; Long. -97.30321

Checkpoint 5 is located under the Highway 183 bridge. A small, unimproved road, which can be very muddy during rainy weather, runs down to

William Wolfe taking a break at Checkpoint 4, Gonzales Highway 183. He and his partner Callan Price (not shown) finished the 2018 TWS in 79 hours and 3 minutes and were second in the Aluminum Class. Courtesy of Ashley Landis

Lee Harle and Clay Smith coming up the steep bank at Hochheim Checkpoint 5 (mile 122) using Sam's rope, in 2015. Also pictured are their team captains Rob Harle and Morris Snyder. Courtesy of Ashley Landis

the checkpoint. The river access point has steep and muddy banks. The deadline for boats reaching Hochheim is 7:00 a.m. on Monday. Every year, checkpoint official Sam Thiede strings a rope down to the water's edge to help competitors climb up the steep bank to exit the river.

The nearby town of Hochheim is named for Valentine Hoch, a German immigrant who settled the area in 1856. The word "Hochheim," literally translated, means "Hoch's house." The town was part of the Indianola-Austin stagecoach line and prospered in the late 1800s. A post office opened there in 1870 and still operates today. The population grew to a peak of 261 residents in 1904, most German speaking, but numbers have dwindled to a current estimate of only seventy individuals.[2]

The river continues to meander southeast with no major obstacles. There are some small drops and sweeping turns at normal flows. Higher water creates boils and stronger eddies.

Checkpoint 6: Cheapside, FM 766 (mile 147) —Lat. 29.147265; Long. -97.317855

Checkpoint 6 is located 25 miles downstream under the FM 766 bridge. There is a dirt road/boat ramp near the bridge that competitors can walk up or team captains can use to support their teams. In bad weather, cars can park under the bridge or on the road that leads down to the bridge. The checkpoint is named for the small ghost town of Cheapside, which is located north of the bridge crossing. Cheapside was once a small agrarian town that produced cotton, grain, and livestock. According to the Gonzales County Historical Association, the population stood at 150 in 1904 but declined throughout the mid-twentieth century, and today only some old crumbling buildings remain.[3]

There are no major rapids on this stretch, and at normal flows there are some drops and no dams, portages, or logjams. The deadline for reaching Cheapside is 2:00 p.m. on Monday.

Checkpoint 7: Cuero, Highway 236 (mile 160) —Lat. 29.051293; Long. -97.265117

Checkpoint 7 is under the Highway 236 bridge that crosses the Guadalupe River just south of the city of Cuero. For many years, the Texas River Marathon, a 40-mile race held annually on the first Saturday in May, started at this location and finished at the boat ramp in Victoria City Park (checkpoint 8). The Texas River Marathon, often referred to as "the prelim," determines the starting order for the Texas Water Safari that occurs six weeks later. In 2013 the race start was moved downstream to River Haven RV Park and now finishes at the Pump House Riverside Restaurant in Victoria Riverside Park. The new race course is approximately 35 miles long.

Seventeen miles downstream of the checkpoint, FM 150 crosses the river. This is often referred to as the Thomaston crossing, named for the nearby unincorporated community of Thomaston. Founded in 1872 by Nathan Thomas, the community reached its peak of 347 residents in 1904. Today the population has dwindled to an estimated 45 residents.[4]

Downstream from the Thomaston crossing are some rapids and standing waves that form when the flows are normal, but also wash out when the flows are high. The next crossing, 8 miles downstream, is at the FM 447 bridge, or Nursery crossing. The nearby town of Nursery was founded in 1883 by Gilbert Onderdonk, a pioneer horticulturist who located in the area where the sandy loam and clay soils were ideal for a nursery. Through the years he received considerable acclaim for his research on peaches and other fruit trees.[5] He also served as postmaster for the town of Nursery. A historical marker in his name is at the junction of Highway 87 and FM 447.

The deadline for reaching Cuero Highway 236 is 7:00 p.m. Monday.

Checkpoint 8: Victoria City Park (mile 200) —Lat. 28.824706; Long. -97.01542

Checkpoint 8, located in the city of Victoria, is on the left near a boat ramp in the Riverside City Park. The park has about 4 miles of river frontage and is a great place to view boats as they paddle downstream to the next road crossing at the Highway 59 Bypass (mile 212). The deadline to reach Victoria is 9:00 a.m. Tuesday. At this point, competitors have covered a little more than 75 percent of the course. Nine miles downstream, Coleto Creek flows into the river on the right. For the next 9 miles, the river twists and turns on its way to checkpoint 9.

Checkpoint 9: Swinging Bridge / Bloomington (mile 231)—Lat. 28.651783; Long. -96.962229

Checkpoint 9 is on private property owned by the Invista Corporation. Years ago, a suspension bridge crossed the river near a chemical plant owned by the DuPont Corporation, and the checkpoint was near the bridge. While the swinging bridge no longer exists and Invista Corporation now operates the plant, competitors still call the checkpoint "swinging bridge."

The distance to the next checkpoint is 17 miles, and there are no road crossings, but there are a couple

Spectators and race officials gathered at the Victoria City Park boat ramp, Checkpoint #8 (mile 200). Courtesy of Patty Geisinger

Gloria and Steve Reagan in 2019 at the Swinging Bridge Checkpoint 9 (mile 231). For many years they have volunteered to brave the hordes of mosquitos, numerous snakes, and oppressive heat at this checkpoint. They and their group of volunteers also mow the grass, making it a usable site for the race. Courtesy of Ashley Landis

of landmarks—a railroad bridge at mile 236 and a pipeline crossing at mile 237. Over the years, this section has had more than its share of logjams, some extensive. The Swinging Bridge deadline is 8:00 p.m. Tuesday.

Checkpoint 10: Saltwater Barrier (mile 248.5) —Lat. 28.505861; Long. -96.885209

Checkpoint 10 is the last checkpoint in the river before boats depart for the bay and the finish line in Seadrift. The checkpoint is on the right riverbank just before a small bridge. A saltwater barrier, operated by the Guadalupe-Blanco River Authority (GBRA), was installed in 1965 and is inflated with water to act as a dam. When river flows are low, the barrier is inflated to prevent salt water from flowing upstream. Competitors must reach this site by 6:00 a.m. on Wednesday.

The next road crossing is at the Tivoli Highway 35 bridge (mile 251), and Traylor Cut is downstream at mile 255 on the left side of the river. Traylor Cut is a man-made water conduit built in the 1930s that connects the Guadalupe River to the bay to drain portions of the delta for farmland.[6]

The last public access point in the race is at the wooden bridge at mile 256. This is the last time that competitors can take on water, food, or medical supplies or discard any unwanted weight before crossing San Antonio Bay. Approximately 2 and a half miles from the wooden bridge, the Guadalupe River flows into the bay.

The six-man team of Bill Torongo, Nick Walton, Andrew Condie, Ian Rolls, William Russell, and Wade Binion leaving the Saltwater Barrier Checkpoint 10 (mile 248) for the last leg of the race. Courtesy of Ashley Landis

San Antonio Bay is a 55-square-mile area on the Texas coast. It is the last segment of the race and has been the downfall of many teams that never finish or lose hours swimming with their canoes or stranded on islands waiting for better conditions to cross the open water. When the bay is calm, faster canoes can paddle to the finish line in less than two hours, but when strong winds create waves, some competitors can be caught paddling for much longer attempting to reach Seadrift and the finish line. Many boats capsize and the competitors have to swim and end up walking, dragging, and/or floating their boat to the finish.

Finish Line: Seadrift (mile 264)
—Lat. 28.408308; Long. -96.71677

The finish line is located in the small coastal fishing town of Seadrift, named for the debris that originates from the Guadalupe River and accumulates along the shore. The Texas Water Safari finish line is located at Bay Front Pavilion and Park. There is a sign and archway on the shore that reads Texas Water Safari near the pavilion, and a large dock and flagpole along with a marble monument that mark's the finish. The monument was placed at the site by past competitors

Finish line at Bay Front Pavilion and Park in Seadrift, Texas, mile 264. Boats are lined up in the finishing order. Some competitors are still out on the course. Courtesy of Ashley Landis

Finishing marble monument located near the flagpole in Bayfront Pavilion and Park in Seadrift, Texas. It says "Texas Water Safari. The World's Toughest Canoe Race. This is the traditional finish line for the 260-mile Texas Water Safari known throughout the world as the ultimate test of endurance strength and will. Thousands of men and women have run this race since 1963 starting at Aquarena Springs and following the San Marcos and Guadalupe Rivers to this finish line." Courtesy of Ashley Landis

of the Safari. There is an inscription that reads, "Texas Water Safari—World's Toughest Canoe Race—This is the traditional finish line for the 260-mile Texas Water Safari known throughout the world as the ultimate test of endurance, strength, and will. Thousands of men and women have run this race since 1963, starting at Aquarena Springs and following the San Marcos and Guadalupe Rivers to this finish line."

Race officials and spectators begin to congregate at this site almost as soon as the race kicks off in San Marcos. This is a popular place to watch as teams paddle 6 miles across the bay on the last leg of the Safari. Depending on the wind and waves, some may capsize, swim across the bay, or finish by walking on shore and dragging their boats to the finish line.

The boats arrive to a mixture of sleeping competitors, team captains, race officials, family members, and spectators anxiously watching and waiting for their teams to finish. The last official day of the race is Wednesday, but on Tuesday at 1:00 p.m., several hundred spectators as well as competitors who have finished the race gather for the Texas Water Safari Awards Banquet. The banquet is a festive occasion where finishers, past finishers, officials, and spectators tell stories and celebrate. Awards are presented to all competitors that finished the race by Tuesday afternoon. Some competitors receive a well-earned reception when they paddle across the finish line while the banquet is being held. When this happens, the public announcements cease and the paddlers are welcomed with loud applause and congratulatory yells. All teams must finish by Wednesday at 1:00 p.m. or they will be disqualified.

The Texas Water Safari Awards banquet in Seadrift in 2016. Courtesy of Ashley Landis

4

Evolution of the Boats

The race course isn't the only part of the Safari that has changed over the years. When the Texas Water Safari was first held in 1963, there were no classes or specifications for the types of boats that could enter. Competitors paddled, rowed, or sailed various vessels, including canoes, kayaks, rowboats, Folbots, rafts, outriggers, and barges.

Over the years, the boats have changed in style and shape, and new materials like Kevlar and carbon fiber have made vessels lighter, stronger, and faster. Safari six-person canoes, in particular, have revolutionized canoe racing and have won many ultramarathon canoe races in the United States. The chronology of boat design is a testament to the ingenuity and motivation of the competitors wanting to go faster. As Plato once wrote, "Necessity is the mother of invention," and the Safari boatbuilders certainly put this into practice by designing every type of boat imaginable. Through trial and error, boatbuilders have continued to refine their designs in search of an even faster canoe.

In the 1963 Safari, oars, sails, and paddles propelled the winning Grumman aluminum canoe from San Marcos all the way to Corpus Christi. In 1964

Harold and Jay Bludworth, winners of the 1966 Safari, row their way to the finish line in Freeport, Texas. Jay and Harold built the boat that would be the prototype of many rowboats in the coming years. Courtesy of San Marcos Daily Record

and 1965, pro paddlers from Michigan won the Safari in long, skinny racing canoes of their own design. The Bludworth Brothers, Harold and Jay, who owned a shipyard in Houston, designed and built a long, skinny rowboat, in which they won the 1966 and 1967 Safaris. Their rowboat became the prototype of the many rowboats that would follow.

For the next decade, rowing boats dominated the Safari field, winning the race seven times. These boats were homemade and were often a collaboration of several individuals. Bucky and Robert Chatham, Robert "Froggie" Sanders, Charlie Hall, Bud Saunders, Butch Hodges, Howard Gore, Jim Trimble, and Pat Petrisky all had a hand in the evolution of Safari rowboats. During this time of innovation, all boatbuilders were trying to "build a better mouse trap." According to Pat:

> Everything for wood strip rowboats back in the sixties and seventies was homemade. We built the frame to staple the wood strips which became the hull. We boiled the strips in a stainless tube and then wrapped the ribs over the frame and stapled them in place. Then came the long strips that formed the outside hull. There were 1,000 staples to a box and we used five boxes per hull (each had to be pulled [off] to epoxy the next strip). I had skin 1/8" thick on my hands from the staple gun. Aircraft pulleys [were used] for seat rollers, stainless tubing for outriggers, aircraft aluminum for oar shafts, laminated wood oar blades, welded aluminum seat frames, [and] laboratory rubber pump bulbs for bailers.

While rowboats dominated the field in these early years, they had several inherent drawbacks. Their long oars are fast in open water but are also cumbersome. With rowers facing backward, it is difficult to

see obstacles, and some sections of the San Marcos River are too narrow for the oars to pass safely.

In 1968, the Sawyer Canoe Company built a new 24-foot-long by 30-inch-wide tandem racing canoe called the Saber, which would become the favorite craft to rival the rowboats in years to come. A Sawyer Saber Canoe won the Safari in 1971 and 1972 with Pat Oxsheer in the bow and Tom Goynes in the stern.

However, from 1973 to 1976, rowboats again won the top prize all four years. The following year, a Sawyer Saber won the race for the third time. The boat was made of Kevlar, a newly developed bulletproof material that was lighter and tougher than fiberglass. This composite material was developed by the DuPont Company in 1965. Over the years it became a staple in the manufacturing of canoes, kayaks, and even larger boats.

In 1978, a tandem kayak (K-2) manned by Jim Trimble and Pat Petrisky won the sixteenth Texas Water Safari. This was the first and only time that a kayak won the race. They chose a kayak because they knew that racing kayaks were faster than canoes, and if they could solve the stability problem of the long, skinny kayak, they could beat the rowboats and canoes that had dominated the race.

First, they purchased a K-2 trainer hull and outfitted it with decks, seats, and a rudder. They mounted the seats higher in the kayak to make them more comfortable, although this would later prove to be a problem. According to Pat, the first part of the Safari went pretty well, but when they were tired in the latter part of the race, they capsized a dozen or more times. The seats were mounted too high, which caused the boat to be unstable, and Jim's legs kept going to sleep in the tight-fitting bow section of the kayak. While they did win the race, they chose not to try it again in the kayak.

Howard Gore and Mike Wooley rowing to victory in the 1979 TWS. Rowboats like this dominated the race from 1966 to 1979, winning ten times. Note the long cumbersome oars. Courtesy of San Marcos Daily Record

In 1979, Howard Gore and Mike Wooley took advantage of that year's high water, winning the Safari in a rowboat in 36 hours and 40 minutes. This was the third overall win by both men and was the fastest time in the eighteen-year history of the race. It was also the last time a rowboat won the race.

In 1980, a three-person canoe won the Safari for the first time. The canoe was a redesigned Sawyer Saber, adapted to add a third paddler by cutting it into two equal 12-foot pieces. A 3-foot section was

then cut from the middle of a second Sawyer Saber. Once the 3-foot middle section was glued to the 12-foot bow and stern sections, the boat became a 27-foot, three-person canoe. That year, the trio of Tom Goynes, Pat Oxsheer, and Jim Trimble won the Safari in 43 hours and 40 minutes. The same team in the same boat won the Safari the following year.

Tom and his wife, Paula, owned a boat shop at the Shady Grove Campground in Martindale, Texas, where racers like Troy Swift, John Oertel, Pat

Oxsheer, Jay Daniel, and Mike and Jack Spencer were employed. The boat shop and its staff—especially Mike and Jack Spencer—played an integral role in the initial development of newer and faster Safari canoes.

In 1982, the trend for even longer canoes continued as two four-person canoes took the top two spots. The winning canoe was designed by Jim Trimble. He had designed boats with Pat Petrisky in the past, but this time, Jim, an engineer, decided to take a more scientific approach. His idea was to use "a simple sine curve." In laymen's terms, a sine curve shows a smooth repeating pattern. According to Jim, canoes should have fuller bottoms with longer hulls, like a "good cigar."[1] The four-person canoe designed by Jim, called "Locomotive Breath," won the Safari that year.

In 1983, a newly designed International Canoe Federation (ICF) tandem (C-2) canoe won the Safari. While the boat was originally designed to race in international competition, it would become a favorite of Texas racers for many years to come. Canoes of this design successfully challenged the longer three- and four-person canoes, winning the Safari four times over the next five years. The new ICF canoe would become the favorite of many tandem teams and often won the Safari Tandem Unlimited Class, which was created in 1993.

The origin of this ICF C-2 design is an interesting story. It was originally designed by Eugene "Gene" Jensen, one of the foremost canoe designers and racers in the country. During his lifetime, he developed countless designs, many of which are still raced today. In 1981, he designed a canoe to meet the specifications of the International Canoe Federation (ICF), an organization that sanctions Olympic and International canoe and kayak racing. While the tandem canoe met the standard ICF maximum length of 650 centimeters (21 feet and 4 inches), it was more stable

than other ICF C-2s, and therefore paddlers could switch their strokes from side to side to steer. While the newly designed ICF C-2 was not competitive in the 1981 ICF Canadian Canoe Championships, it was perfect for marathon canoe racing. In fact, Mike Cichanowski, owner of Wenonah canoes, began to manufacture the canoe with marathon paddlers in mind. While ICF C-2s are still manufactured by Wenonah today, due to the limited market in the United States, they are only sold in the United Kingdom. Jensen's ICF C-2s won the Safari in 1983, 1985, 1986, and 1987.

In 1984, Roy Tyrone and Jerry Nunnery paddled a United States Canoe Association (USCA) C-2 to victory. This was the first time in the history of the race that a USCA cruiser won the Safari. The victory was significant because unlike the longer, narrower, and faster unlimited canoes and rowing boats that used oars or double-blade paddles, USCA tandem canoes are only 18 feet and 6 inches long by 32 inches wide, and paddlers use only single-blade paddles.

Innovations in boat design continued in 1988 when Mike Spencer built a new three-person canoe that won the twenty-fifth Safari. To build the Spencer three-person canoe (C-3), Mike took the middle section from an ICF C-2 and glued it to the bow and stern sections of a Wabash Valley C-1, creating a 26-foot three-person canoe.

In December of 1988, Pat Spencer bought Shady Grove Campground and the canoe livery from Tom and Paula Goynes, and over the next thirty-three years, no company or individual had a greater influence on unlimited Safari canoes than their boat shop. While the Spencer boat shop built several hundred multiperson Safari canoes, they also designed and built solo canoes, including the Eagle in 1989, the 19-foot 11-inch Extreme in 1992, the 21-foot DSX in 2005, and the Extreme Pro in 2010.

The ICF Safari C-2 won the Texas Water Safari in 1983, 1985, 1986, and 1987. Over the past thirty-five years this canoe is arguably the most popular tandem unlimited canoe that has been raced in the Safari and other ultramarathon canoe races in North America. It is the favorite of Jerry Cochran, Fred Mynar, and other canoe builders in Texas. Courtesy of Ed Jones

Jerry Nunnery (bow) and Roy Tyrone paddle a USCA C-2 to victory in the 1984 Safari. This was the only year a USCA C-2 won the race. Courtesy of Kevin Bradley

SKIP JOHNSON

Skip Johnson is an architect from Houston with a keen interest in canoes dating back to his teens. He built his first canoe when he was sixteen years old, and he has been building them ever since.

I first met Skip in the early 1990s, when he designed a solo racing canoe for me. I had been racing for a few years and wanted to get a solo boat. I saw a long, skinny kayak that had the type of design I was looking for, so Steve Lacy, a master carpenter, and I took some measurements and contacted Skip. I thought I might race the canoe solo, so I asked Skip to flatten the bottom to make it more stable. Once Skip finished the design and Steve built the solo wood-strip hull, a layer of fiberglass was added and I was off to the canoe races. A year or so later, a mold was made from my solo wood-stripped canoe, and Jay Daniel with Rainmaker Enterprises Incorporated began building composite canoes from the mold. A solo canoe of this design won its class in the 1994 and 2000 Safaris.

Over the years Skip Johnson designed a number of long skinny canoes that have won the Texas Water Safari, Yukon Quest, and other ultramarathon canoe races. When I asked Skip about his designs, he was quick to take little credit for himself, giving credit instead to the fine paddlers who raced the canoes. He said, "once a design left my office and the first boat (or plug in some cases) was done, I rarely, if ever, was consulted on subsequent molding, stretching, tweaking, or other modifications that were done." He did say that he was thankful to have been a part of the process that created the long, skinny, multiperson canoes that have raced the Safari.

Milton "Skip" Johnson, architect and boatbuilder, working on one of the many canoes he has designed and built over the years. Courtesy of Skip Johnson

A Spencer C-3 won the Water Safari in 1988, 1989, and 1990. Joe, Fred, and Brian Mynar paddle a Spencer C-3 to victory in 1989. Courtesy of San Marcos Daily Record

In 1989, 1990, and 1991, a Spencer-designed C-3 won the Safari. Then, in 1992, a new C-4 designed by Milton "Skip" Johnson won the race, paddled by Joe, Fred, and Brian Mynar and Joe Burns.

A Skip Johnson–designed wood strip C-4 won the Safari in 1993 and 1994. In 1995, Rainmaker Enterprises Inc. (Jay Daniel) made a mold from the canoe and built a newer, lighter Kevlar C-4, in which Joe, Fred, and Brian Mynar and John Dunn won the race for the third consecutive year.

In 1996, the canoes got even longer when John Bugge designed and built a carbon fiber 36-foot C-5, and he and longtime partner Mike Shively won the race by bringing in three "ringers" from California: Mike Shea, Rich Long, and Jeff Verryp. Carbon fiber, originally used in the space industry, would become the favored boatbuilding material going forward.

The following year, Fred and Brian Mynar, Jerry Cochran, and John Dunn formed a six-person team that included two elite paddlers from up north—Steve Landick and Solomon Carriere. Once again, the team solicited the help of Jay Daniel, who built a new mold and stretched their Skip Johnson–designed C-4 to accommodate two more paddlers. The new canoe had an 8-foot section added in the center. Once the lighter, carbon fiber 38-foot and 6-inch-long C-6 was popped from the mold, the team was ready for the thirty-fifth Safari. With river flows at record levels, the team not only won the Safari but set a record of 29 hours and 46 minutes that still stands today. The canoe also won the Safari in 1998, 1999, and 2000.

With no Safari rules limiting canoe length or the number of paddlers, the canoes continued getting longer in 2001. That year, one nine-person and two eight-person canoes were entered. The nine-person carbon fiber canoe was built by John Bugge. The 55-foot canoe was so long that it had to be hauled in two pieces and then bolted together at the race site.

In 1997 Jay Daniel built this carbon fiber C-6. The canoe was a stretched version of a Skip Johnson–designed C-4. The canoe won the Safari in 1997–2000. The winning 1999 team (bow to stern) Fred Mynar, John Dunn, Chuck Stewart, Donald Baumbach, Joe Mynar, and Brian Mynar. Courtesy of Kevin Bradley

Built in 2001 by John Bugge, this 55-foot, nine-person canoe is the longest boat to race the Safari. It had to be hauled in two pieces and bolted together at the race site. Courtesy of Kevin Bradley

The previous year's winning Mynar team added two new paddlers and were seeking a fifth straight win. Their eight-person team would be paddling a 46-foot canoe that was a stretched version of last year's C-6. Jay Daniel added an eight-foot middle section to the original carbon fiber C-6, and two Canadians, Mike and Fiona Vincent, joined the team.

The other eight-person canoe had a team of seasoned veterans and two "newbies," Reid and Brian McCoy. Reid had one finish and Brian, Reid's dad, had never finished the race. Anxious to give the Safari a try, Reid McCoy purchased a Safari Kevlar C-4. The four-person canoe was designed by Skip Johnson and built by Jay Daniel. To accommodate four more paddlers, Jerry Cochran, Phil Bowden, Pat Petrisky, and other team members added a middle section to the original C-4. The newly designed C-8 was almost 50 feet long and weighed over 300 pounds!

Once the gun went off, two of the longest canoes to ever race the Safari finished first and second overall. For the fifth consecutive year, the Mynar team won the race, followed by the rival Bugge team. The 46-foot eight-person canoe led the race from the start with a winning time of 36 hours and 3 minutes, and Fiona Vincent became the first woman to win the race in its thirty-nine-year history.

The following year, there were no eight- or nine-person canoes in the race. Longer canoes with more paddlers had been a key to success, yet the sentiment among some racers was that while the longer canoes had good top-end speeds, they also had several drawbacks. The boats were especially difficult to navigate down the twisting San Marcos River, were heavier, which made portaging a slower process, and with the added weight of more paddlers, were more likely to run aground on logs.

For the 2002 Safari, Jay Daniel cut out a section from the 2001 winning C-8. The seven-person team won the 2002 Safari handily by more than three hours.

The following year, a six-man team was formed that included Jerry Cochran, Fred and Bryan Mynar, and Chuck Stewart, all past winners, plus Sammy Prochaska and Allen Spelce. Sammy was a veteran with seven finishes, and Allen had ten. While Allen had placed in the top three overall for the past seven years, he had never won the race. Excited about the opportunity to race on a strong team, he contacted Jack Spencer and ordered a new C-6. After a few preliminary drawings, Jack sent the design specifications to Skip Johnson so he could finalize the plans on his computer. Over the next few months, Jack built the new wood-stripped C-6.

Once the gun went off for the forty-first Safari, Allen and his team paddled Allen's new wood-strip canoe to victory in 36 hours and 15 minutes. While that was the last time Allen raced the Safari, he has continued to serve as Texas Water Safari Board member and president until the present day. When asked why he never raced again, Allen said:

> The first time I did the race, our goal was to finish. After that first finish, I went on to win several classes like Solo Unlimited, USCA C2, and Tandem Unlimited. After winning those classes I decided I wanted to win it overall. After a number of second- and third-place finishes to the Mynar and Bugge teams I got a call from Jerry Cochran to ask if I wanted to be on the Mynar team. I said yes. We won it in 2003, eleven finishes in the process, and the daily addiction of training and mental prep work was fulfilled! My firstborn was due that fall of 2003 and I told Kit [wife] if I won the race, I would take a year off. That turned into eighteen years! No regrets. I had accomplished a dream that had chased me daily, and it was fulfilled. I now serve as the president of the Texas Water Safari, and staying involved

allows me to fulfill those urges to race. The Texas Water Safari is more than just a race, it's a passion.

In 2004, Allen did not race, but he loaned his C-6 to the Mynar team, and they won the race again. The following year, a longer C-7 won the 2005 Safari—the same canoe that Jay Daniel modified for the Mynar team in 2002. The winning 2005 team included Tim Anglin, West Hansen, Daniel Cruz, Richard Steppe, Armin Lopez, Jerry Rhaburn, and Leroy Romero.

A rule change by the TWS Board in 2006 limited the number of paddlers per team to six. Seeking yet another overall win, John Bugge designed a new carbon-fiber six-person canoe that was actually a shortened version of his original C-9. He recruited five elite paddlers from Belize and won the Safari. It was his sixth overall victory and twenty-ninth time to cross the finish line.

Known throughout the racing community for his competitive drive, John is also known for the fleet of rock-solid racing canoes he has built over the years. Oddly enough, the first canoe he built was made out of concrete and weighed 300 pounds. Back then, he was a student at Texas A&M University and his civil engineering class built a concrete canoe to compete in the American Society of Civil Engineers National Concrete Canoe Competition, which they won.

When asked how many canoes he owned, John said he really didn't know, but over the years he has built more Safari canoes than any other individual. Only Spencer Canoes, a commercial operation, has built more. His philosophy about Safari boats is simple: He believes that Safari canoes should cruise well while competitors maintain a lower heart rate. Lightweight "skinny" canoes are great for shorter races, but ultramarathon canoes should be designed with good stability and should cruise well with minimum effort.

With a surplus of canoes, John started renting canoes back in the 1990s to Safari competitors who needed a boat. For the 2019 Safari, he rented at least a dozen canoes to competitors.

In 2007, John loaned his six-person canoe mold to Pete Binion, and Pete and his team built a Bugge C-6. That year, Pete and Wade Binion, Amado Cruz, Armin Lopez, West Hansen, and Richard Steppe won the Safari. The following year, Pete rented the canoe to a six-man Texas team, and they won the race. So, from 2006 to 2008, a Bugge-designed six-person canoe won the Safari.

William Russell and his team won the 2009 Safari in a foam strip six-person canoe built by George Melder and designed by Skip Johnson. George built his first wood-strip canoe when he was fifteen and his first tandem wood-strip racing canoe in 2003. When he started racing, he turned to building foam-strip canoes, because foam is lighter than wood. He built the foam-strip C-6 that won the 460-mile Yukon River Quest Race in 2007, and the following year he raced and won the Quest in a C-8 he built.

The 2009 win was a dream come true for William and his cousin Andrew Stephens; they had set a goal to win the race overall following their 2005 victory in the Novice Class. William's advice to other racers trying to "climb the ladder" is that, "You need to buy some solo boats to train in, you need to go tandem unlimited, you need to get noticed, and then you know, maybe you can get in a big boat, because the whole question after we won novice was how do we win the race, overall. That was the goal."

William and Andrew originally raced the Melder-built C-6 in the 2007 Safari. Their expectations were for a high finish or overall win, but the team of William Russell, Andrew Stephens, Jeff Wueste, Jeff Glock, Sammy Prochaska, and Andrew Soles broke the boat in half before reaching the first checkpoint

Canoe #314 is a carbon foam strip C-6 built by George Melder and designed by Skip Johnson that won the 2009 and 2010 Safari. The 2009 team (left to right): Andrew Stephens, Amado Cruz, Daniel Cruz, Armin Lopez, and (not shown) Kyle Mynar and William Russell. Courtesy of Erich Schlegel

in Staples. They didn't win but still managed to finish the race.

After George Melder repaired the badly damaged canoe, William and Andrew decided to recruit four elite paddlers from Belize and go for the overall win in 2008. They ended up in a hard-fought battle with another six-man Texas team and came up just short, finishing second overall. In 2009, Andrew and William recruited Kyle Mynar, Amado Cruz, Daniel Cruz, and Armin Lopez—all four previous Safari winners—to help them win the race, which they did in a total of 42 hours and 55 minutes.

The following year, William was out due to shoulder surgery, but Andrew and an elite team won the 2010 Safari in 34 hours and 40 minutes.

Since the foam-strip, Melder-built C-6 had broken in half in 2007 and had suffered damage in three other Safaris, William decided to contact Jack Spencer to order a new carbon C-6. Given the model's popularity with racers, Jack decided to design a new C-6. After making some drawings, he sent the specifications to Skip Johnson to finalize the plans on his computer. He then fabricated a plug, built a mold, and laid-up a forty-one-foot carbon hull. Once the seats,

SPENCER CANOES

Since 1988, Spencer Canoes has designed and built more custom-made unlimited Safari canoes than any other company or individual. In the early years, Mike and Jack Spencer built racing canoes, until 2008, when Mike left the company and went overseas. Since then, Pat and Jack Spencer have continued to operate the campground, canoe livery, and boat shop, formerly owned by Tom and Paula Goynes.

Located approximately 11 miles from Spring Lake in San Marcos, the campground is a popular access point for both recreational paddlers and Safari paddlers who are training for the race. Over the years, the campground has hosted and sponsored the Martindale Triathlon (canoe, bike, and run), and Spencer Canoes has been a sponsor of the Safari for many years.

When I asked Jack how many canoes he has built over the years, he said he did not know the exact number, but it had to be more than 250. Curious to know what major design changes had occurred over the years, I asked Jack specifically about the Spencer C-6. He said the current C-6 is 4 or 5 feet shorter than the original wood strip canoes that he built years ago. He also said that over the years, he tweaked the "rocker," tumblehome, hull width, seat height, and rigging inside the canoe, and with the advent of carbon fiber, the boats are lighter today. However, he was quick to point out that the basic hull design has not changed over the past ten years.

The boat shop at Spencer Canoes. Note the new carbon canoe (center) with other canoes and molds on each side of the boat shop. Courtesy of Bob Spain

One of the long six-man carbon canoes that has won the Safari twenty times from 1997 to 2019. Courtesy of Ashley Landis

footrests, rudder, and other features were installed, the new canoe was ready for the forty-ninth Texas Water Safari. In an impressive effort, William Russell, Andrew Stephens, and their team paddled the new Spencer C-6 to victory in 2011.

The following year, William and Andrew recruited another elite team and won the race again. Over the next seven years, Jack built three carbon C-6s, sold one, and loaned his mold to Jerry Cochran and Fred Mynar, who built another. During this seven-year period, from 2013 to 2019, a Spencer C-6 won the Safari every year.

During the fifty-nine-year history of the Safari, no other craft has had more overall wins than the Safari

C-6. In 1997, a C-6 won the Texas Water Safari for the first time, and over the next twenty-five years, a Safari C-6 won the race twenty times.

The C-6 has proven itself a winner in not only the Safari but also other ultramarathon canoe races in the United States and Canada. So, what are the drawbacks to this design? There are only a couple available to rent, and the purchase price is $11,000 to $12,000. The canoes are about 40 feet long and therefore difficult to haul. You need special canoe racks and a longer, heavy-duty vehicle to transport them. In fact, they are illegal to haul unless you mount lights on the canoe's stern because it sticks out too far behind the vehicle, and driving in heavy traffic and urban areas is hazardous. For the same reason, steering the canoe is difficult in narrow, winding rivers, and its weight and length make it challenging to portage over and carry around obstacles.

Given these considerations, several top teams had planned to race lighter, shorter canoes with fewer competitors in the 2020 Safari. In fact, two of the top Texas teams and a top team from up north registered for the Safari in C-4s. Regrettably, the Water Safari was canceled in 2020 due to the coronavirus.

The following year, 2021, two elite teams in a Spencer-built C-3 and C-4 entered the race. Each team had both Texans and Michiganders aboard and was vying to beat the C-6s that had dominated the race the past twenty-four years. The two canoes duked it out with a longer C-6 for a day and a half, and the C-4 manned by Kyle Mynar, Tim Rask, Nick Walton, and Tommy Yonley won the race in 34 hours and 46 minutes, marking the first time in twenty-six years that a Safari C-4 had won the race.

PART TWO
Cast of Competitors

We are all connected, we all have different experiences, but that there
exists a silent and heartwarming magic of sharing
stories with those who get it.

—*Ginsie Stauss, twelve-time Texas Water Safari finisher*

5

Bringing in Ringers

The Texas Water Safari has drawn an elite field of paddlers from at least forty-one states, the District of Columbia, Puerto Rico, and nine foreign countries, including Australia, Belize, Canada, Chile, Iraq, Ireland, Italy, United Arab Emirates, and the United Kingdom. While some paddlers have joined teams of their own initiative, others have been recruited by Texas teams in hopes of gaining an advantage. These paddlers, sometimes called "ringers," have helped to raise the competitive standard of the race and have inspired the local paddlers to improve their game.

While recruiting the best paddlers is the best prescription for winning the race, the practice of bringing in ringers is frowned on by some. While it is certainly not against any rule, some people think it's unfair because a "ringer" may be better than everyone in the race, and without the recruit, the team could not win. To put it another way, it's like a major league baseball player joining a team that has all minor leaguers. Others, however, like five-time Safari winner William Russell, hold a different perspective: "Lots of folks in the racing community would talk trash about 'hiring ringers,' but I never looked at it that way. To me the thought was simple. Compile the best team possible. Be with the best and become the

best. Why would someone frown upon me for building a great team? It is a competition after all with the goal of winning. If it was basketball why not get Jordan!"

This chapter highlights some of the elite paddlers from around the world who have competed in the Safari over the years.

Al Widing

In 1964, seven out-of-state paddlers traveled to Texas to enter the "World's Toughest Canoe Race." Leading the field were four ultramarathon paddlers from Michigan: Al and Leroy Widing, Bob Gillings, and Ed Adams.

While all were outstanding racers in their own right, Al Widing's name stands out among the rest. Al won the 1964 Safari along with his partner, Bob Gillings, and won a second time with his brother, Pat, the following year. Al and his two partners are the only non-Texas racers who have won the race without having Texas paddlers familiar with the course in the boat. Al is known not only for his many racing accomplishments but also for his unequaled longevity. Over sixty+ years, Al Widing amassed an

incredible record by competing in more than three hundred canoe races. Also known as "Amazing Al" by his friends, he is an icon of canoe racing.

Over the years, Al started the 120-mile AuSable River Canoe Marathon forty-one times and finished an incredible thirty-three times. In 1999 at age seventy-four, Al and his partner, Bob Bradford, won the Senior Class in a record time of 15 hours, 21 minutes and 22 seconds. Al completed his favorite race for the last time in 2012, with his partner Haley McMahon. He was eighty-seven years old. In 2014, Joy and I raced against Al and his son, Al Jr., in the marathon. Unfortunately, he dropped out that year, and that was the last time he raced a canoe. The sport lost a true canoeing legend when Al passed away on January 11, 2018.

Steve Landick (Safari finishes: 1984, 1992, 1997)

Steve Landick, a Michigander, first came to Texas in 1974 to race the Texas Canoe Marathon. The race was held on the same day as the 1974 Texas Water Safari and followed the original Safari course to Corpus Christi. He won the race that year with ultramarathon paddler and explorer Verlen Kruger. In 1980, Landick and Kruger began a canoe expedition called the Ultimate Canoe Challenge that crisscrossed the North American continent. It lasted three-and-a-half years and covered an amazing 28,000 miles.

Then, in 1984, Steve Landick returned to Texas to test his skills in the Texas Water Safari. He says, "I saw the Safari unlimited race as the 'main event,' It was like I was in the minors and I wanted to race with the big boys."

"I've seen one mistake continually made by out-of-state teams," Landick continues. "A lot of good paddlers have run the Safari, but they just don't give the race—or the local paddlers—enough credit. They can't imagine what it takes to run this race until they try it."[1]

As a warm-up for the 1984 Safari, Steve raced the Safari "Prelim," a 40-mile qualifier for the longer race. To the surprise and amazement of the entire field, he won the race in a Kevlar Wabash Valley "Safari C-1."

Steve Landick and his team captain Peter Derrick in 1984. He came in third overall in a time of 59 hours and 2 minutes. Courtesy Kevin Bradley

Mike Shea (Safari finishes: 1991, 1996, 1997, 1998, 1999, 2001, 2002)

I hardly knew Mike Shea, but I wish I had known him better. From what I've heard and read, he was quite a guy. He first came to Texas in 1988 to race the Texas Water Safari. While he was one of the finest outrigger racers in California, like many nonresident competitors who are unfamiliar with the Safari course, the

Mike Shea taking a break in the 2001 Texas Water Safari. He finished the race in 51 hours and 8 minutes. Courtesy of Kevin Bradley

For the first time in the history of the Safari, a solo paddler was an early contender for the overall win. While he made an impressive showing in the 1984 Safari and led the entire field for approximately 160 miles, he slipped to third overall at the finish—an impressive effort by anyone's standard. Still hungry for a win, he returned again in 1992 and finished fourth overall in a solo boat of his own design in a remarkable time of 36 hours and 8 minutes—a new solo record. In 1997, he joined an elite six-person team and won the Safari in 29 hours and 46 minutes, a record time that still stands today.

rigors of the race took their toll and he dropped out. Being a "never-say-never" kind of guy, Mike returned in 1989 and 1990 to race, but still "no cigar." Mike raced solo in 1991, finishing the Safari in 76 hours and 45 minutes. Over the next twelve years, he raced ten times with six additional finishes (1996, 1997, 1998, 1999, 2001, and 2002), winning the race overall in 1996 in a C-5 with two Texans and two paddling partners from California.

He raced his last Safari in 2002 with partner James "Devo" DeVoglaer. They were fourth overall, winning the Tandem Unlimited Class in 47 hours 20 minutes.

Mike continued to race, but his life was cut short by cancer. Sadly, at fifty-three years of age, Mike passed away on December 6, 2005. In his memory, the Texas Water Safari Board dedicated the 2006 Safari to him.

A friend of Mike's, Rich Long, said of him, "What I remember about Mike was his ability to push you past your limits. Whether calling you out in an outrigger race with his 'male honor code' or somehow talking you into doing a 260-mile nonstop paddling race in Texas [not once, but four times]. He was always looking for the next challenge and not just to do it, but to win it. Besides being the ultimate competitor, he was a kind of modern-day pirate, Adventurer, Warrior & Scoundrel [affectionately of course]. Mike's infectious spirit will continue to inspire us to look beyond our shores, dream big & always fight to the finish."

His former coach, Dennis Campbell, adds, "His work ethic and commitment to excellency were an inspiration to those around him. He loved to compete and to his credit never made an excuse (unlike his coach) if he didn't do as well as expected. He was always the positive, calming influence within the canoe, and everyone respected anything he had to say."

In Mike's honor, the Imua Canoe Club in Newport Beach created the Mike SheaDog—Inspirational Paddler Award, presented annually to the paddler who is an inspiration to his or her fellow paddlers.

Solomon Carriere (Safari finish: 1997)

Solomon Carriere is an elite marathon canoe racer from Cumberland House, Saskatchewan, Canada. Raised in the Canada backcountry, Solomon is a Métis who can trace his roots back to the French fur traders and First Nation Cree Tribe. Living off the land is a way of life for Solomon and his family. With dog sledding and canoeing as major modes of transportation in the backcountry, canoe racing was a natural transition for him. Recognized as one of the finest pro canoe racers in Canada, Solomon has raced and won many competitive marathon canoe races in North America.

In 1984, Solomon was contacted by Butch Stockton, an elite canoe racer from Michigan, and asked to race the AuSable River Canoe Marathon. While Stockton had won the race twice in 1982 and 1983, Solomon had never won the race. At the time he was working in a mine more than a mile below ground and could not take off to race. Faced with a tough decision and given his love for canoeing, he made a quick choice, called his boss, and quit. With only three days to train on the Saskatchewan River, he paddled eight and a half hours a day. To the amazement of the entire field of racers, Butch Stockton and Solomon won the 1984 race in a record time of 14 hours and 20 minutes. Solomon raced the 120-mile marathon eleven times and was the overall winner in 1984, 1993 and 1994.

He was inducted into the AuSable River Canoe Marathon Hall of Fame in 1998, the same year he won the Dyea to Dawson Centennial Race to the

Solomon Carriere in 1997 near Tivoli. Other members of the winning team were Jerry Cochran, John Dunn, Steve Landick, and Fred and Brian Mynar in a record time of 29 hours and 46 minutes. Courtesy of Kevin Bradley

Klondike with Steve Landick. Solomon and Steve Landick were members of the six-man team that won the 1997 Texas Water Safari and set a record that still stands today.

Mike Vincent (Safari finishes: 1998, 2001, 2006) and Fiona Vincent (Safari finish: 2001)

In 1998, Steve Landick asked Mike Vincent if he was interested in racing the Texas Water Safari. Steve contacted Mike on behalf of the Mynar Team, who were looking for a "ringer" to fill the sixth seat in their canoe. Mike was well known as one of the finest marathon canoe racers in Canada and would certainly be a welcome addition to the Safari team. Once Mike learned that there was no prize money to pay for air travel and other expenses, he reluctantly said "no." When Mike's wife learned that he had turned down a chance to race the Safari, she urged him to reconsider. With the encouragement of his wife and

given the chance for a new adventure, Mike called Steve back and agreed to race.

When the gun went off at the thirty-sixth Safari, five Texans and one Canadian (Mike Vincent) took an early lead and held it all the way to the end. Mike says the race was one of the most enjoyable, and he was especially complimentary of his Texas teammates, the "best team I have ever raced with." When asked to compare the Safari to some of the other ultramarathon canoe races he had raced or won, Mike said each race has its challenges, but given the obstacles in the river, the day and night nonstop travel, and sleep deprivation, the Safari is far more dangerous.

After the 1998 race, Mike was asked if he would be interested in returning to race again. While his experience had been enjoyable, he said, "It's been fun but I don't want to come back without my wife."

Three years later, Mike Vincent returned to Texas to race again. This time his wife, Fiona, came with him. An accomplished women's marathon canoe

Mike Vincent won the Texas Water Safari in 1998 with his other team members John Dunn, Tim Rask, and Brian, Joe, and Fred Mynar. Courtesy of Kevin Bradley

Ian Adamson (Safari finishes: 2001, 2003)

In 2001, Texan West Hansen invited Ian Adamson to race the Safari. Ian was truly a "ringer" and elite paddler by anyone's standard and a world-class adventure racer. Adventure racing is a rigorous, nonstop sporting competition where athletes travel over difficult terrain by running, rappelling, paddling, biking, and mountain climbing. The nonstop, multiday events test the navigation skills and mental and physical strengths of each competitor. Known as one of the finest adventure racers in the world, Ian had already won four World

Ian Adamson, eleven-time World Champion Adventure Racer and third place Texas Water Safari finisher in 2001. Courtesy of Kevin Bradley

racer, Fiona would compete with Mike in the enormous eight-person Mynar canoe. That year, the Mynar team won the race, and Fiona is the only woman to date who has won the Texas Water Safari.

In 2003 Mike and Fiona continued their winning tradition by finishing first overall in the 460-mile Yukon Quest canoe race, which is quite an accomplishment for a mixed team.

In 2006 Mike returned for a third time to race the Safari in the Mynar canoe. This time they finished second overall to the rival team of John Bugge and five "ringers from Belize."

Championships, including the 1996 Eco-Challenge in British Columbia, the 1997 X-Games in San Diego, the 1998 Raid Gauloises in Ecuador, and the 2000 Eco-Challenge in Borneo.

Joining Ian and West in the 2001 Safari were two other Safari veterans, Allen Spelce and Jeff Wueste. While an eight-person canoe and a nine-person canoe took the first two spots that year, Ian, West, Allen, and Jeff came in first unlimited and third overall. Given the fact that the first two canoes had twice as many paddlers, the third-place finish by the foursome was certainly an impressive effort.

In 2003, Ian returned again to Texas to race tandem in the Safari. This time, Ian and West Hansen finished seventh overall in 43 hours and 12 minutes. After the 2003 Safari, Ian continued to compete in adventure races until 2007, when he established an unprecedented record by winning eleven World Championship Adventure Races. He also set two Guinness World Records for the longest distance paddled in twenty-four hours in 1997 and again in 2004. He has authored numerous articles on adventure racing and published a book, *Runner's World Guide to Adventure Racing: How to Become a Successful Racer and Adventure Athlete*. He is currently president of World Obstacle Sports Federation and is working to have adventure racing sanctioned as an Olympic event.

When asked about the Texas Water Safari, Ian said, "In my experience paddling distance races on four continents since 1984, the Texas Water Safari is the most challenging and diverse nonstop canoe event in the world. No other race combines the diverse conditions, distance, and technical difficulty of the Safari."

Robyn Benincasa (Safari finish: 2007)

While working as a firefighter in San Diego, California, Robyn Benincasa competed in triathlons and endurance races. Through hard training and natural talent, she quickly became one of the finest adventure and endurance racers in the country.

Robin Benincasa in the middle seat with Bobby Snyder in the bow and Mike Stinson in the stern in 2007. They came in tenth overall and fourth unlimited with a time of 41 hours and 37 minutes. Courtesy of Erich Schlegel

While competing in world class competition with Ian Adamson and a team of elite adventure racers, she won two world championships: the 1998 Raid Gauloises in Ecuador and the 2000 Eco-Challenge in Borneo. She is a ten-time finisher in the Ironman Hawaii World Championships and won the women's solo class in the Missouri 340-mile canoe race in 2010, 2012, 2014, and 2016. Her record finish time of 43 hours and 6 minutes in 2010 still stands today.

She has set two Guinness World Records, including an October 29, 2010, twenty-four-hour paddling record on flat water on Lake San Antonio, California (195.33 kilometers [121.37 miles]), and a twenty-four-hour paddling record on moving water on the Yukon River, Canada, paddling 371.92 kilometers (231.10 miles) on June 26, 2011.

In 2007, she ventured to Texas to race the Texas Water Safari, competing on a three-person team with Mike Stinson and Bobby Snyder. They finished the race in tenth place in 41 hours and 37 minutes. That same year, she was diagnosed with osteoarthritis, which required several hip surgeries over the next few years.

Determined to continue her long-distance adventures and not let the physical condition cut short her future activities, she has continued to compete. Robyn also founded the Project Athena Foundation, an organization that helps women with physical and traumatic challenges fulfill their goals and dreams.

In 2013, Robyn set yet another Guinness record when she paddled a stand-up paddleboard with an elongated kayak paddle 146 kilometers (91 miles) in twenty-four hours in Huntington Harbor, California.

While continuing to work as a firefighter, Robyn published a best-selling book in 2012, *How Winning Works: 8 Essential Leadership Lessons from the Toughest Teams on Earth*. She has also become a highly sought inspirational speaker.

Carter Johnson (Safari finish: 2007)

In 2006, Carter Johnson raced the 460-mile Yukon Quest Canoe Race, winning the solo class in a record time of 44 hours, 56 minutes, and 34 seconds. Ready for yet another challenge, he decided to test his marathon skills in the Texas Water Safari. He contacted Mike Shea, a local California legend, who had finished the Safari multiple times. Carter had a great deal of respect for Mike and considered him as tough as nails and faster than anyone in California. When he sent Mike an email about the race, Mike's response was something to the effect of, "It is too emotional an experience to share unless face to face."

When Carter finally had a chance to talk with Mike in person, he got little encouragement and was told, "You better be OK with spiders the size of your fist crawling all over your face." After further consideration, Carter decided to give the race a go.

He came to Texas in 2007 with high hopes for a good overall finish or maybe a solo win, although he had one thing working against him. While most elite paddlers pair up with Texans who know the course, Carter chose to paddle solo. Richard Ameen, who had raced the past three years, volunteered to be his team captain.

On race day 2007, Carter sat on the starting line ready for the 260-mile adventure. Once the gun went off, his immediate plan was to blast off the line and beat the long boats to the first portage at Spring Lake Dam. His plans soon changed when a C-6 crashed into his solo boat, costing him valuable time. While he was able to survive the mayhem, he was passed by thirty or forty boats on the lake. After a quick portage, he began to skillfully maneuver his way through the boats on his way to the first checkpoint at Staples Dam. After 16 miles of paddling, he was in third place overall. Through the night and the next day,

he continued a pace of slightly over 7 miles per hour. During this time, he began to slowly close the gap on the second place Cowboys' six-person canoe. Somewhere slightly before the Cuero 236 Checkpoint (mile 160), he passed the Cowboys. Now in second place, Carter began to pick up the pace and lengthen his lead on the third-place Cowboys.

When he reached the Saltwater Barrier Checkpoint (mile 248), he was informed by Richard Ameen, his team captain, that he had a chance to break the solo record if he could paddle to the finish in 2 hours and 30 minutes. After making a quick calculation, he knew that he could not cover the remaining distance in that amount of time. Wanting to simply get it over with, he blasted out of the checkpoint en route to the finish.

By the time he reached the seawall, with a mile or so to the finish, he had already paddled 2 hours and 45 minutes. While he thought his chance for a solo record was over, Richard yelled from the shore that he could still break the record. Exhausted and completely spent, Carter gave it his all and reached the finish line in second place overall with a new solo record of 36 hours and 3 minutes, five minutes faster than the old solo record that was set by Steve Landick in 1992. No solo competitor had ever finished second overall in the forty-five-year history of the race. While his team captain had given him some misleading splits during the race, it actually motivated him to push hard and break a record.

Since his amazing effort in the 2007 Safari, Carter has continued to excel in canoe and kayak races across the country. In 2008 he set a solo record in the Missouri 340-mile canoe race, and in 2010 he finished second overall in the Yukon River Quest, only one minute behind the winning six-person team. The following year he set a Guinness record by paddling 280 miles in twenty-four hours on moving water on the Yukon River in Canada. He also set a second Guinness record in 2013 by paddling 156 miles on flat water in twenty-four hours in California.

Nick Walton (Safari finishes: 2018, 2019, 2021)

Nick Walton lives in Eaton Rapids, Michigan, and like many Michigan canoe racers, he cut his teeth on the Michigan Canoe Racing Association pro circuit. He entered his first canoe race at age thirty-one and has never looked back. Now forty-nine, Nick is one of the finest marathon canoe racers in the United States.

From 2010 to 2019, he raced the annual 120-mile AuSable River Canoe Marathon. During this ten-year period, Nick placed in the top ten every year and was second overall in 2013 and 2014.

Nick has also won the USCA C-1 Class at the 70-mile General Clinton Canoe Regatta in New York State several times and has placed third with Ryan Halstead at La Classique Internationale de Canots de la Mauricie in Shawinigan, Quebec, Canada. These two races, along with the AuSable River Canoe Marathon, are the three most prestigious canoe races in North America, sometimes called the Triple Crown Races.

When I asked Nick what race he was most proud of, he said there were two. In 2013, he had his best year canoe racing, winning seven races on the Michigan circuit. Shortly before the AuSable River Canoe Marathon, his partner was hurt and could not

Nick Walton walking up the steps at the finish line after winning the 2018 Texas Water Safari with his team, in a time of 36 hours and 45 minutes. Courtesy of Ashley Landis

race. With only a week until the race, he recruited eighteen-year-old Canadian Christophe Prouix. With only a week to practice together, Nick and Christophe finished second overall in 14 hours and 32 minutes. That was Nick's fastest marathon finish.

Later that year, Nick, Andy Triebold, Matt Rimer, and Steve Lajoie raced the 90-mile Adirondack Canoe Classic in New York State in a voyager C-4. The foursome won the race in 11 hours, 6 minutes, and 29 seconds. The winning time was the fastest ever recorded.

In 2018, Nick traveled to Texas to race the Water Safari. Like many elite paddlers, he was recruited to race in a Safari C-6. Once the gun went off, the team of Nick Walton, Andrew Condie, Ian Rolls, Wade Binion, William Russell, and Amado Cruz led the race from start to finish. With the second-place team only five minutes behind, the race was the most competitive in Water Safari history. The following year, Nick returned to Texas with fellow Michigander Bill Torongo. Racing with Bill and four Texans, he won the race a second time. He won a third time in a C-4 in 2021.

Bill Torongo (Safari finish: 2019)

Bill Torongo came to Texas in 2019 to race the Texas Water Safari with Nick Walton and four Texans, winning with a time of 34 hours and 27 minutes. Like Nick and other elite racers from Michigan, he honed his skills on the Michigan pro canoe racing circuit. Always a top competitor and frequently the overall winner, Bill has raced the Triple Crown pro races in New York, Michigan, and Quebec, Canada, multiple times. Over the years, he has been a frequent competitor in the United States Canoe Association National Championships and has won the Men's USCA C-2 Class and numerous age class championships.

In 1993, I was at the forty-eighth AuSable River Canoe Marathon in Michigan supporting one of the teams. My job was to provide food and water during the race, and according to the local vernacular, I was called a "feeder." Anyway, I was able to watch Bill Torongo and his partner, Jeff Kolka, lead the race through the first thirteen checkpoints, setting new records and winning prized money at each site. Then, near the end of the race, a Canadian team of Serge Corbin and Solomon Carriere passed Bill and Jeff, who finished in second place. Bill and Jeff returned

Bill Torongo in 2019 with his first place trophy. Bill and teammates Andrew Condie, Ian Rolls, Wade Binion, Nick Walton, and William Russell were first overall in 34 hours and 27 minutes. Courtesy of Bob Spain

the next year and again finished second, but their time of 14 hours and 8 minutes is still the fourth-fastest time in the seventy-five-year history of the race.

At age sixty, Bill is still one of the fastest marathon racers in the country. When asked how many times he has competed in the Triple Crown races in Grayling, Michigan, Cooperstown, New York, and Quebec, he said, "I think I've been in 36 Michigan marathons—dropped out of a few. [I] did the 70 in New York 20+ times and have around 20 finishes in Shawinigan. No wonder my shoulder hurts."

Ben, Mike, and Mary Schlimmer (Safari finishes: 2018, 2019)

In 2018, brothers Ben and Mike Schlimmer, known as two of the finest marathon canoe racers in the country, raced the Texas Water Safari in a six-person canoe. In an impressive effort, they finished second overall in 36 hours and 50 minutes behind another six-person team. With only five minutes separating the two top teams at the finish, it was the most highly contested win in the fifty-seven-year history of the race.

According to Ben Schlimmer, canoeing is a family affair that started with his grandfather, a scoutmaster who taught canoeing to Boy Scouts. Growing up in a big family with three boys and three girls, there was always someone to paddle with. Ben started canoe racing in high school and has been racing ever since. Both he and Mike are frequent competitors in the AuSable River Canoe Marathon. From 2008 to 2016, they raced the marathon eight times and finished in the top ten every year. In 2015, they finished the 120-mile race third overall in 14 hours and 49 minutes.

Team #123 in 2018 (left to right): Clay Wyatt, Logan Mynar, Kyle Mynar, Ben Schlimmer, Mike Schlimmer, and Fred Mynar. They were second overall in a time of 36 hours and 50 minutes. Courtesy of Ashley Landis

Ben and partner Trevor Lefever won the "Rat Race" in Athol, Massachusetts, four years in a row. This unique race is more like an obstacle course than a canoe race. Because all competitors draw for a starting position, there is no guarantee that you will be near the front at the start. You could have 200+ canoes in front of you, and it is the only race where recreational canoes purposely crash into other canoes like bumper cars.

In 2019, Mary Schlimmer, younger sister of Ben and Mike, came to Texas to race the Safari. In a record-breaking performance, the fastest time ever by a women's team, she and partners Virginia Condie, Kaitlin Jiral, and Morgan Kohut finished fourth overall in 37 hours and 31 minutes. Mary now resides in Michigan, where she competes in the Michigan canoe racing circuit. She has won many Women and Mixed Classes in canoe races, including the 70-mile General Clinton Canoe Regatta Women's Solo Class and the United States Canoe Association Women's C-2 Class with Sarah Lassard. Mary, Ben, Mike, and their brother, Joseph, were all members of the 2019 US Dragon Boat team that won many gold medals at the International Dragon Boat Federation Championships in Pattya-Rayong, Thailand.

Team #40 in 2019 (left to right): Kaitlin Jiral, Mary Schlimmer, Morgan Kohut, and Virginia Condie. They finished fourth overall with a time of 37 hours and 31 minutes. They have the fastest time for any women's team and are also the highest placing women's team in the history of the Safari. Courtesy of Ashley Landis

Team #10 at Cottonseed Rapid in 2004 (left to right): Lee Deviney, Alex Lisby (DNF), Jeff Glock, Daniel Cruz (DNF), Armin Lopez, and Peter (Fuzzy) Churchman (DNF). With three paddlers dropping out, they finished in sixth place in 37 hours and 58 minutes. Courtesy of Kevin Bradley

The Belize Connection

In 2003, Lee Deviney, an experienced paddler with four TWS finishes, heard about a competitive 170-mile, staged race in Belize. The race was called the Ruta Maya Belize River Challenge and was billed as the toughest canoe race in Central America. While the race was fairly new, its reputation had grown along with its cast of elite paddlers. In an attempt to put together a crack team to race the Safari, Lee

recruited a few "ringers" from Belize who had won the 2003 Ruta Maya Belize River Challenge.

On June 12, 2004, at 8:45 a.m., Daniel Cruz, Armin Lopez, and Alex Lisbey, all three from Belize, and Lee Deviney, Jeff Glock, and Peter Churchman, all three from Texas, sat on the starting line of the Safari.

While the team had early aspirations of winning the race, their luck quickly changed when Peter "Fuzzy" Churchman, the stern man, began to complain that he was not feeling well. While Lee

Deviney, the captain, felt that it was nothing serious, to his surprise, somewhere near Slayden Cemetery Bridge, Fuzzy, in an unsuspected turn of events, jumped from the canoe. With no one in the stern seat, Armin Lopez in seat five crawled back to the stern seat and began to steer. With one paddler out of the race, the team began to struggle to hold their position. Their luck went from bad to worse when they flipped the canoe and Daniel Cruz suffered an injury to his ribs during the mishap. While he continued to paddle for a while, he had to drop out somewhere near Cuero—now there were four! As a final blow to the team's string of bad luck, Alex Lisbey mysteriously got out of the boat near Victoria. Deviney, Glock, and Lopez struggled to keep up in their long, heavy six-man canoe. While they paddled desperately to hold their position, they slipped to sixth overall and finished in 37 hours and 58 minutes.

While the race had not worked out as planned, the reputation of the paddlers from the small Central American country of Belize had spread throughout the paddling community, and they would continue to be highly recruited by top Texas teams.

In 2005, Armin Lopez and Daniel Cruz returned to Texas to race and brought along two new paddlers from Belize: Jerry Rhaburn and Leroy Romero. The four paddlers along with a trio of Texans paddled a seven-man canoe to victory in 36 hours and 56 minutes.

Over the next fourteen years, eleven different paddlers from Belize traveled to Texas to race. During this time, they amassed an incredible record, with five different paddlers winning the race multiple times. The most impressive was Amado Cruz, who won his first Safari in 2006. Over the next thirteen years he competed in the Safari eight times, winning

Belizean "ringer" Amado Cruz drinking from the Argosy Adventure trophy after winning the 2018 TWS. Looking on are the other team members (left to right): Tommy Yonley, Ian Rolls, and William Russell. Courtesy of Ashley Landis

seven of those races. Other Belizean paddlers with multiple wins include Daniel Cruz with six wins, Armin Lopez with four wins, Efrain Cruz with two wins, and Jerry Rhaburn with two wins.

Safari veteran William Russell said that, "Paddling with Armin [Lopez], Amado [Cruz], and Daniel [Cruz] was one of the highlights of my life. Over the years they taught me a great deal about paddling and racing. We raced many races together all over the place. I have been lucky to race with truly some of the best racers out there and I have never met anyone who could match up in terms of the full package like they did. Witnessing their incredible strength, unmatched toughness, and competitive drive was something to behold. Actually being on a team with guys like that was a dream."

Andrew Stephens (bow) followed by Amado Cruz, Leroy Romero, Armin Lopez, Felix Cruz (all Belizeans) and William Russell in the stern. From 2003 to 2019, eleven different paddlers from Belize have raced the Texas Water Safari. Courtesy of Erich Schlegel

6

Women of the Safari

Joy Emshoff

On April 29, 1963, Willye Waterman looked around at the 126 men she would be competing against in the first Texas Water Safari. She wondered how she and her husband, Jim Waterman, would fare in their Folbot in the twelve-day race to the coast. Well-versed as a sailor, she had high hopes of crossing the finish line in Corpus Christi. Unfortunately, the rigors of the race took their toll and she and Jim dropped out at Cuero.

Willye raced again next year with her husband and Bob Smith. She was the only woman entered. The team finished the race that year with a time of 172

Willye Waterman raced her first race in 1963 but failed to finish. She returned to race with her husband Jim Waterman and Bob Smith in 1964. They came in fourteenth place with a time of 172 hours and 42 minutes. She was the first woman to complete the race. Courtesy of San Marcos Daily Record

hours and 42 minutes, fourteenth overall and in last place. She entered again in 1965 in a four-person boat that was wiped out in flood waters near Luling. While that was her last race, she remained an avid supporter of the Water Safari and wrote and published a detailed magazine chronicling the race for the next two decades.

It was 1975 before the next women raced in the Texas Water Safari. Carol Keirnan and Kathie Derrick, *née* Bellman, each entered as part of a mixed team. Their teams were two of only nineteen that finished out of forty-three entered. Since then, women have participated in the race every year, in growing numbers. In total, about 10 percent of competitors have been women. Finishing the Safari have been 498 women racers, and thirty-two women (through 2021) have completed the race solo, some several times.

In 1976, five women finished the race. Nova Hall and Carol Keirnan were the first women's team to race USCA C-2, and Nancy Wattner, Laura Hanks, and Kathie Derrick also raced that year. Kathie Derrick was the first woman to ever finish the Safari solo, with a time of 76 hours and 13 minutes. Kathie would eventually complete the race ten times.

Fiona Vincent is the only women to finish first overall. In 2011, she won the race with her husband Mike Vincent, Donald Baumbach, John Dunn, Brian Mynar, Fred Mynar, Kyle Mynar, and Chuck Stewart in a time of 36 hours and 3 minutes. This was her only year to race.

Marie McKay is another who helped establish a place for women in the early history of the Safari. She first won Women's Solo in 1986 with a time of 85 hours and 5 minutes. She would go on to win

Kathie and Peter Derrick in 1997. They finished tenth overall, second mixed, first masters with a time of 43 hours and 9 minutes. Courtesy of Kevin Bradley

Fiona Vincent, first women to win the TWS first overall and mixed. She was part of an eight-person team in 2001. Courtesy of Kevin Bradley

Marie McKay in 1996, happy to have finished the race! She and her team of Lee Deviney and Robert Youens placed seventh overall with a time of 56 hours and 26 minutes. Courtesy of Kevin Bradley

Lee Deviney, Marie McKay, Robert Youens at Cottonseed Rapids in 1996. They won second mixed and seventh overall with a time of 56 hours and 26 minutes. Courtesy of Kevin Bradley

Teddy Gray (bow) and Celeste Wilkinson in 1986. The old swinging bridge is in the background. Courtesy of Kevin Bradley

Dianna Finstad (bow), Teddy Gray (center), and Donna Bugge (stern) in 1991. They finished thirteenth overall, first women's team with a time of 57 hours and 43 minutes. Courtesy of Kevin Bradley

Women's Solo two more times in 1990 and 1992. She also raced mixed four times and finished the Safari seven times.

Teddy Gray also started racing the TWS in 1986. She raced and won the Women's Class in that year with Celeste Wilkinson with a time of 72 hours. She competed again in 1991 with Donna Bugge and Dianna Finstad. Teddy had another first place finish in the Women's Class in 1997 with Cindy Meurer in a time of 47 hours and 35 minutes. Teddy has five Water Safaris under her belt.

Cindy Meurer raced in six Safaris, completing all six. She and her partners West Hansen, Jack Kraus, and Jeff Wueste won the Mixed Class and placed fourth overall in 1996 with a time of 51 hours and 46 minutes. As mentioned, in 1997, she won the Women's Class with Teddy Gray. In 1998, she won the USCA C2 Class with Grady Hicks with a time of 56 hours and 38 minutes and placed eighth overall. In 2000, she won the Women's Class again with Ginsie Stauss, with a time of 46 hours and 55 minutes.

Cindy Meurer (*center*) with her mom Barbara and her dad Larry in 1996. She raced in a four-person team with West Hansen, Jack Kraus ,and Jeff Wueste. They came in fourth overall and first mixed with a time of 51 hours and 46 minutes. Courtesy of Kevin Bradley

Mick Edgar is in the bow, Donna Bugge in the middle seat, and Robert Youens in the stern in 1993. They finished fifth overall, first mixed in a time of 44 hours and 59 minutes. Courtesy of Kevin Bradley

Another woman with an impressive Safari record is Donna Bugge. In 1989, Donna placed second overall and won Mixed with her then husband, John, and Russ Roberts, with a time of 48 hours and 4 minutes. In 1995, she paddled with John, Robert Youens, and Mike Shively. They finished the race in 38 hours and 23 minutes, winning Master's and again placing second overall. She last raced in 2000 with John, Pat Petrisky, Richard Steppe, Ginger Turner, and Mike Shively, placing third overall with a time of 36 hours and 49 minutes. They also won Mixed and Master's that year. She raced the Safari a total of eight times, with six finishes in the top ten, and was twice thirteenth place overall.

The race she is most proud of is her 1987 finish with Teddy Gray. She had attempted the race the previous year but had to pull out at Cheapside after vomiting for twelve hours. This time, the lights on the boat did not work. After attempting to fix them with no luck, they went on into the night. They mostly paddled alone, only occasionally being able to piggyback other racers with lights. They finished the race in thirteenth place overall, fourth Unlimited with a time of 50 hours and 54 minutes.

As Donna says, "The race changes people. It gives paddlers such a feeling of accomplishment, it makes you feel stronger and teaches humility. I was very lucky to have raced with some great paddlers."

~~~~~~

Erin Magee has raced the Safari more than any other woman. She is in the Hall of Fame with twenty-one finishes, as of 2019. She also holds the distinction of having finished the race solo more than any other racer, man or woman, sixteen times. She became the oldest woman solo finisher in 2018, with a time of 56 hours and 7 minutes and in fifty-first place. That record was broken by Salli O'Donnell in 2019 and again in 2021 at sixty-one years of age.

Erin understands how the race can be life changing. "I came to understand that the water wasn't going to treat me any different than Fred Mynar or Jerry Cochran, and I had to stand up to the challenge of working with the water and boat on its joint terms, not me thinking I was 'special.' Once I stopped wanting to be special, I could get on with my life as a whole much more successfully, on and off the water."

She also shared this life observation: "I never learned anything about how to improve or change my river skills by speed paddling a solo boat. I learned a lot by

Erin (Bowden) Magee in 1994. She raced with Phil Bowden and Ron Henk, coming in eighth overall, winning first mixed with a time of 51 hours and 21 minutes. Courtesy of Kevin Bradley

taking the advice of those that excelled beyond my ability or that observed me while paddling—my friends that knew my goals and that I wasn't reaching them.

"I'd been training and racing for five years and a very observant fellow racer, with good communication skills, pointed out to me that in our numerous runs from San Marcos City Park I slowed down after Westerfield Bridge exponentially all the way to Cottonseed Rapid. It wasn't something I would have ever picked up on because the place I did not want to be was Cottonseed. I spent four years justifying portaging Cottonseed. The bottom line was I couldn't afford to break or damage the boat. I would rather spend the time portaging and avoid all the anxiety of having to run it or think about running it. That fifth year I could see that to make big gains, I needed to do things differently. I would have to at least consider running Cottonseed. Each run from Westerfield Bridge I would think about whether I should or should not run it and I slowed down getting to that point. I did a 50/50 split of running it very conservatively with a super high heart rate, or portaging it to be prudent for long term goals, with less anxiety.

"When my training partner pointed out I was losing speed for 3 miles dreading Cottonseed, his suggestion was to 'race to Cottonseed' and once there do whatever my preference was taking whatever time needed. But don't waste time going slowly to get to where I really never wanted to be.

"It was good advice for racing . . . but it was great advice for life. What I learned out on the water is the opportunities you miss going slowly to what you want no part of will be lost on you as present opportunity. You'll never see opportunity dreading disaster. In life it taught me to commit to and pursue goals realizing the less time I spent reaching a goal, the more likely I was to achieve it, and the more likely I would be to have opportunities beyond it.

Erin Magee in 2015. She came in thirty-first overall, winning first women's Solo with a time of 59 hours and 22 minutes. Courtesy of Ashley Landis

"Five years after I began racing to Cottonseed, I had a fellow female racer that wanted some input on how to achieve her goal of finishing the TWS. I told her about 'Racing to Cottonseed' and how to apply the advice in the small picture to achieve the big goal. She finished the TWS as the first woman in a USCA C1.

"The ability to pass forward what you can't pay back is never ending in this sport and in this race . . . it keeps you in touch with where you once were on the skill set, while making you humbly grateful to be where you are in life, as a whole."

Erin feels that people of Safari are adventurers at heart. She feels that they value experiences as much, or possibly more in some instances, than possessions.

Of the race itself, she feels "it's the best/worst thing to happen to paddle sports in Texas, it's true. And even more often I hear from participants . . . it's the training that brings me back, the race sucks, it's horrible, but the training—that is a lifestyle and it keeps them coming back to race. We've glamorized the race."

Ginsie Stauss has finished the TWS twelve times, as of 2021: five solo finishes and seven team finishes. She has also volunteered as a team captain in nine Safaris. Ginsie has a true love of adventure and the river. In her words, "Until recently I would declare the Safari as something I did to test myself, to get off the grid, to push myself more than, or in a different way than, regular life. After much reflection over the past two years, I can now recognize that the river is the reason and the Safari has been my way of escaping to the river. Getting out there anywhere on the race's 262 miles is my true joy. Realizing that when I connect with a river, I learn organically by witnessing nature's miracles and feel a peace from within. Training for the Safari allows me to paddle on the course, scouting the same sections many times over the years, witnessing the changes in the river. Over the course of a year I would behold the trees changing with the seasons and birds migrating. I am still now learning the names and habits of all the different birds. I've seen a few snakes and many alligators, all sizes. The Safari has connected me to other paddlers, who introduce me to different rivers, boats, sections of rivers, different people and ways of life. All of this is still a way to get out of my own head, and challenge myself, it all works together to help me stay strong, while under the purview of training for the race. The families growing up surrounded by the Safari are a part of this joy as well. We are all connected, we all have different experiences, but that there exists a silent and heartwarming magic of sharing stories with those who get it."

As Ginsie says, "The River calls us back, year after year regardless of the pain."

Ginsie Stauss in 2011. She won second women's solo, thirty-ninth overall with a time of 79 hours and 22 minutes. Courtesy of Ashley Landis

Holly Orr has thirteen finishes: three solos and ten team finishes. Holly has held many records over her racing career. Some have now been broken, but others remain in place today.

Holly began her Safari career in 2002. Two years later at age twenty-one, she won the Women's Solo Class in 49 hours and 26 minutes, a truly impressive effort. The following year, she and Sandy Yonley and Mary Tipton won the Women's Class in 48 hours and 26 minutes. She won the class again in 2005 and a third time in 2007, setting a record of 44 hours and 50 minutes. Four years later, in 2011, she completed the race tenth overall in 55 hours and 42 minutes in a six-woman canoe along with Sandy Yonley, Virginia Parker, Jamie Norman, Natalie Taylor, and Samantha "Sam" Binion. She paddled solo the following year in a USCA C-1 and set a record of 68 hours and 28 minutes. She broke that record in 2014 with a time 57 hours and 49 minutes.

Holly Orr in 2014. New woman's C1 record with a time of 57 hours and 49 minutes, twentieth place. Courtesy of Ashley Landis

Bow to stern—Amy Boyd, Debbie Richardson, Rebekah Feaster, Melissa James, Holly Orr in 2017. They were the first women's team, fifth overall in 43 hours and 13 minutes. Courtesy of Ann Best

To Holly, the Safari means "Friendships. Nature. Challenge. I love being outside and the challenge of the race. In some ways it is an escape from all other distractions of this world. A time to simply focus on the beauty God has given us through and around the river. I deeply treasure the friendships that have been developed through the Water Safari. It also provides good motivation to stay physically fit and healthy."

One of Holly's favorite stories is from her race in 2011. "I was in the six-girl canoe near the end of the race, 3 o'clock cut to be exact. We had to carry our boat around a downed tree and there was a 5ish foot alligator swimming around where we needed to reenter the water. There was no stepping into the boat from the 6-foot drop to the water. All of us stood there looking dumbfounded at this gator blocking our way and, in our sleep-deprived minds tried to think of another way to get into the boat without getting into the water. Sandy yelled at us, "What are you doing, we need to go!" as she boldly did a cannon ball jump 10 feet away from the gator. We couldn't let her get eaten alone so we all jumped in the river after her and never saw the gator again. However, I am pretty sure we set a record for reentering the canoe that day!"

Through her hard work and determination, Holly continued her love of paddling and nature into her professional career, where she makes boat covers, teaches paddling, guides trips down various rivers, and rents boats for pleasure paddlers and racers.

~~~~~

Sandy Yonley is a second-generation Texas Water Safari veteran. Her dad, Tom Goynes, is an icon of the race. In fact, we have dedicated a chapter to him called "Old Man River." Sandy raced her first Safari at fourteen years old in a three-person boat with her

Sandy Goynes Yonley in the bow with her dad Tom Goynes in the stern in 1998. They won second mixed and first parent-child with a time of 59 hours and 18 minutes. Courtesy of Kevin Bradley

parents, Tom and Paula. At the time, she was the youngest TWS finisher. Sandy recalls she and her mom argued a lot—in fact their team's name was "Mumbles, Grumbles and Stumbles."

Just as Tom and Paula met through the Safari, so did Sandy and her husband Tommy. Sandy says, "The litmus test for Dad to see whether we could get married was if we could complete the Safari together. We barely made it the first year we raced together. Nevertheless, we did finish, so marriage approved. After our second Safari together, I swore 'never again.' But then he got fast so I agreed to race with him a third time." Sandy says they had an amazing race that

The first and only six-woman team in the history of Safari, in 2011. Bow to stern is Virginia (Parker) Condie, Holly Orr, Sam Binion, Jamie Norman, Natalie Taylor, and Sandy Yonley. They came in tenth overall with a time of 55 hours and 42 minutes. Courtesy of Ashley Landis

year, 2012. They finished fourth overall, the highest a mixed tandem team has ever finished with a time of 43 hours and 5 minutes. Sandy feels it was the "perfect race" for her, and after that she was happy to retire. She is still always on the riverbank cheering on her family and friends. "Sure, it's a competitive race. For some it's an adventure race. For me it's just a part of our annual schedule and a family event. I grew up with the competitors' kids. Now a lot of those "kids" are racing. Many of my close friends are from the Safari community.

"As for the race itself," she says, "I think you don't really know what you are doing until you've done five Safaris. It takes a while to learn how hard you can push yourself. When you start out, typically there's a lot less strategy involved (especially when you start at age fourteen). However, once you start getting competitive, the race turns into a constant strategic planning session. How can I take a better line in the current to gain time on my competition? Whose wake can I ride so I can catch up to the next boats? How hard can I paddle during the heat of the day?"

Sandy's advice if you are thinking about doing the race is to just do it! "Life is short. Don't put things off that you'll regret. The TWS is a lifelong adventure. And who knows, it might start a family tradition."

Sandy has raced eleven times and she says she will probably race again someday.

~~~

Jeannette Burris came to racing in a very roundabout way. She started sprint triathlons at age fifty and was joined the following year by her oldest daughter, Jennifer. They enjoyed the events before and after the races, but their age kept them in different groups so they were never together while racing. Jennifer then found an adventure race hosted by canoe and kayak racers Debbie Richardson and Janie Mize Glos—something they could finally do as a team.

After a couple of races, they joined a large group of women on an overnight kayak and camping trip on the Colorado River. During this camping trip they met several other—in Jeannette's words—"crazy" women who raced canoes. After some discussion, they decided to give racing and the Colorado River 100 a try. The race was only eight weeks away, so they rented a canoe, borrowed paddles, and received some much needed instruction from Debbie and Janie, since neither of them had ever paddled a canoe before. They worked hard and finished the 100 miles in a little under 20 hours for third place in the Tandem Women's Division.

Jeanette's journey into paddling and the Texas Water Safari has been an emotional one. She tells her story: "When starting this new hobby years ago, my husband who was neither a paddler nor a fan of camping, referred to all those doing so as 'river

Left to right, **Max Hambly, Mike Tecci, Jeanette Burris, Chris Paddack, John Hoffart, John Qualls, Joe Graef (TC) in 2017, fourth unlimited, eleventh overall with a time of 45 hours 6 minutes. Courtesy of Ashley Landis**

trash.' He supported me as I trained long hours for four more CR 100s, 3 Texas Winter 100s, and 5 Texas Water Safaris. He supported me as I went on week-long paddle and camp trips down the San Marcos and Guadalupe Rivers, and he supported me when I cooked for or volunteered at other races. He was always willing to allow me this time with my 'river trash' friends who were becoming a big part of my life, becoming family to me. When you've spent so many long hours together in the confines of a canoe and you've put yourself thru all kinds of struggle to complete an ultramarathon race together, you create a bond that is hard to explain to others.

"After a few years of this activity, my husband was diagnosed with cancer, which he battled for five years. During those years he saw how my 'river trash' friends supported me as I battled his cancer with him. He had visits, phone calls, and lots of prayers from the 'river trash' and came to know and love them as I did. During the last years of his life that term became one he used with love and respect for the big-hearted people of my paddling community. He recognized their commitment and love to each other, and it was extended to him many times over. 'River trash' was always spoken with his special smile in his last year, and since his passing that 'river trash' has helped me get through some of my hardest days.

"Though this story is my story, what you hear again and again from others is how much help they've received from this paddling community. I guess in addition to creating strong muscle, paddling also creates big hearts and turns people into RIVER TRASH."

~~~~~

Myla Weber also has very strong emotional ties to the Safari. She has nine finishes: two solo and seven teams. She says, "My first solo was something I had to do for myself, and it had nothing to do with competition with other paddlers. In 2010, I was diagnosed with stage 3 breast cancer. I spent the remainder of that year and most of the next having surgery and completing rounds of chemo and radiation. During that time, I watched my oldest daughter, Courtney, train to race solo C-1 in 2011. She was determined that if I could survive what I was going through, she could survive C-1, and she did! In 2012, I decided if I could survive cancer, I should do the ultimate challenge—safari solo. So many things during that race screamed at me to quit.

"Physically I was not strong enough, but mentally I somehow thought it would 'put me back together.' Before I made it out of Spring Lake, a tandem team broke the rudder off of my Landick ll boat. At Cummings Dam, I dropped my boat and put a hole in the bow with no way to fix it. The first night my lights ran for five minutes and quit due to faulty wiring and again, no way to repair. Alone in the dark is one of the worst feelings I can remember. Sometimes it was okay, I could sing songs, but sometimes I had to pull over and cry until another boat would come along and allow me to tag behind. I slept at night more than I wanted because I could not see. By the time I made it through the lower jams I had convinced myself I was going the wrong way and would never see Salt Water Barrier. Tears again. Then Wade Binion's words seeped into my mind, 'Follow the bubbles,' and somehow, I made it out. But this voyage would not end without insult added to injury. I had trouble in the bay. I walked all I could as my pump stopped working and I did not have the energy to empty it. With water sloshing in my boat and hurting feet, I threw my shoes to the waves, tied my boat to the grass, crawled into my spray skirt and dared the alligators to come and get me! The next morning

as the sun came up, the first thing I saw were those horrible shoes washed back to me! I bailed the boat, threw those shoes under the spray skirt, and paddled to the finish."

~~~~~

Melissa James's story is one of strength and determination. Including this first run, she has raced the Safari seven times, with five finishes. In 2013, in an aluminum canoe, her partner dropped out at Saltwater Barrier due to a heat stroke. In 2014, again in an aluminum canoe, her partner dropped out at Gonzales. "We put a log in the front and I kept going—but I was crushed. My whole race just changed. Between Gonzales and Hochheim, I saw a man on a boat dock who asked me if I was OK, and that made me stop paddling. I went for my dry bag and unhooked it, getting ready to open up my cell phone and get my TC to come pick me up, I was ready to quit. Then I thought how lame that would

be to quit there, so I clipped my dry bag back to the boat and paddled on to the checkpoint to get out there. Then, I got clipped by a sweeper, just before the Hochheim checkpoint. I traded the big log for three large rocks in the bow, and this was a game changer! My speed almost doubled. I had lost a lot of time, going really slow with the big log, so I had to keep focused if I was going to make it to Seadrift by the cut off. I knew where to go through the logjams, my only concern was the bay. On the way to Salt Water Barrier, sleep deprivation set in. I started hallucinating the people in the trees scene, my TCs were in the trees too, cars parked on the left side of the bank, and someone behind me kept asking to borrow my paddle, over and over again.

"As it turns out, going aluminum solo is not optimal in a choppy bay. I couldn't control the boat from the stern, so I had to walk the boat up the spoil islands. Once I reached the barge canal, my choices were to paddle from the front seat to shoot across, or swim it. I made it across, sitting in the bow. I

Melissa James in 2019, paddling with her partners Nathan Hudgins (not pictured) and Jeremy White (not pictured). They finished thirty-eighth overall with a tme of 50 hours and 56 minutes. Courtesy of Ashley Landis

remember looking at my watch and seeing 12:45 p.m. and still had a ways to go. I wasn't going to make the cut off.

"The whole race, I had to believe that I was going to make it to the finish line by 1:00 p.m. Wednesday. I thought I was going to do it, but . . . 101 hours later, I finally reached the steps. I was shocked to see a large group of people gathered at the sea wall to watch me come in an hour late! At least three racers were ready to give me a patch at the finish line. My life was forever changed by that moment when I felt so much love and support by the safari community."

~~~~~

Janie Glos first raced the Safari in 2010 as part of the Hippie Chicks Team, along with Debbie Richardson and Ginsie Stauss. She says her funniest story was when the Hippie Chicks tried to cross the bay at the

end of the race. "We had some spray skirt malfunctions so we all three were holding it up around us with our teeth. Even doing that and with both pumps running we couldn't keep the water out. We got to the other side and walked for a very long way. We finally reached the tip of the spoil islands, where we could see the barge canal. Sammy Prochaska was already there and had been for quite some time. We decided to stay put since it was getting dark and the bay was not calming down. We were pretty sleep deprived and not thinking clearly. We decided to make a little camp, rolling around some logs and clearing an area to lay down our space blankets. Deb decided to gather all our remaining food and ration it out. My little ration was a half round of Bonnie Bell cheese and a Triscuit cracker. I can't remember what they ate but it wasn't much. I told Deb I was hungry and she said no more because we didn't know how long we would be there. We had plenty of food but could only think about being there for days. We finally all three laid down and were cold so we spooned; we had to be quite the sight. When dawn arrived, we had been joined by more boats. Everyone was just waiting for a break to cross. It was a little calmer at daybreak so everyone started trying to make it across. We finally made it and pulled the boat up on land and drug it all the way to the finish. It was a great finish and we won the Women's Division.

"What does the Safari mean to me . . . there is so much to say about this and hard to put into words. The biggest thing is probably the sense of community like a family. When I moved to Austin in 2008, I was alone and didn't know anyone. I knew Deb's name from adventure racing in Houston, so we connected and she introduced me. The rest is history—everyone was welcoming, and I found a place in Austin. Although I haven't raced in a couple of years, the people I met are still my closest friends.

The other thing that stands out is a sense of pride and accomplishment. Even though I've done other types of races/events, this is the one people want to know about. Texas Water Safari stands out as the race to do." Janie has completed the Safari four times: three in a team, one time solo.

Another of Janie's fellow Hippie Chicks is Debbie Richardson. Debbie has completed twelve races: eleven with a team and once solo. Debbie believes that women who race the Safari can be strong and fierce and yet keep their femininity. She says she has learned something every year from the race. "It strips you down to the core of your being—makes you more aware."

Debbie says she looked at her first race as just a race—she just wanted to finish. She remembers the pain and difficulty and remembers thinking "never again!"

"Time went by and I started thinking, how can I do better and not have issues. So I overhauled

The "Hippie Chicks" (bow to stern) Debbie Richardson, Janie Glos, and Ginsie Stauss in 2010. They came in thirty-third overall and first women's in a time of 70 hours and 48 minutes. Courtesy of Ann Best

everything, looked at the physical perspective and had a mental shift . . . maybe a five-person team."

Now Debbie says she tries to be present and enjoy the moment. "You don't look back in a race, you let it go. You can redo and rethink in practice. That's how life should be, let stuff go, focus."

~~~~~

Virginia Parker has finished the Safari nine times, with one solo finish and eight team finishes. She holds the current Women's Solo Record for fastest time of 40 hours and 17 minutes. In 2019, she and Mary Schlimmer, Kaitlin Jiral, and Morgan Kohut finished fourth overall with a time of 37 hours and 31 minutes, breaking the record for fastest women's team and the highest place an all-women team has achieved. Virginia feels that not only does the race keep her

in shape, it gives her a connection with nature and a higher power. "There is a calm that comes with being on the river; it is so powerful and vulnerable . . . the fascination that comes with watching it change and move each year is incredible. Winter is my favorite time to paddle because the wildlife is so much more visible without the tree cover and it's fun to see the animals along the riverbanks getting a drink of water: everything depends on it.

"I met the father of my two beautiful children and found my dream job at San Marcos River Foundation because of the Texas Water Safari. I have met some of our truest and best friends through the years. The bond that forms with people you've raced with is something you can't explain to someone on the 'outside' . . . anyone who has finished the TWS knows what I'm talking about. There is a lot of competition, secret planning and big talk amongst the racers, but

Virginia Parker in 2016. She came in seventh overall, first women's solo with a time of 40 hours and 17 minutes, setting the new women's solo record. Courtesy of Ashley Landis

at the end of the day it's one big family and any one of the racers would give you the shirt off their back if you needed it. The friendly competition and boat analysis consumes more time than most people would allow . . . I can't get enough."

~~~

Many racers are "one and done." Linda Cochran is one of these folks, and she has become a key volunteer year after year supporting the race. Her husband, Jerry, has raced numerous times, and she is always there to support him. Without people like Linda, the race simply could not continue.

Jerry, Lillie (*center*), and Linda Cochran in 1994. They came in tenth overall and second mixed with a time of 54 hours and 4 minutes. Lillie became the oldest female finisher at sixty-six years of age. Courtesy of Kevin Bradley

In 1994 she raced with Jerry and Lillie, her mother-in-law. Lillie still holds the record for the oldest female finisher. She was a few days short of sixty-seven when the team finished the race.

Jerry had tried to compete in the Safari with his mom a few years before, but they weren't able to start because she suffered a heart attack. A couple of years later they tried again but weren't able to finish. As Linda recalls, "He asked me to go with them because he seemed to think we'd all have a better chance of finishing with three of us. Honestly, I'm not sure that I could have finished without her, she was such a strong competitor, and neither she nor I wanted to 'embarrass' Jerry. Our daughter, Marianne, was our team captain. I'm really glad that we did it, but don't care to compete again."

~~~

To Safari team captain and former racer Kate Tart, the race is so much more than just a weekend in June. To her it's a community, a lifestyle, a family, a challenge, and a test.

"As exciting as race day is, Safari starts long before June. In order to compete in a race like this it takes months and months of training. Every weekend you will find groups of people, teammates and competitors, coordinating shuttles and training runs. You will find those that will be competitors come race day, jumping in to fill seats in boats for a training run. Even for those racing solo, this isn't a solo sport. Yes, you alone are the one that can power the boat down the river, but it takes a community to get you to that point, and to shuttle you, help feed you and take care of you during the race. In a world that seems convinced every situation is a win/lose scenario, the paddling community sees life as a win/win scenario. Don't get me wrong, these are some of the most competitive people I know, but they want to beat you on your best day. They will support you, push you, encourage you and likely believe in you more than you believe in yourself.

"While the race does test your physical strength, more than that, it tests your mental strength. It tests your willingness to not give up, to push on, to push through the pain, to embrace suffering. And if you can, if you can push through the pain, push past what you think are your limits, you get to cross the finish line. There is no prize or award waiting for you. But what is waiting for you is weeks and months after, when you come face to face with an obstacle or challenge, it seems smaller than it would before the Safari. Overcoming that obstacle seems more feasible. If you can drag a boat through knee-deep mud while an alligator watches you after having paddled for forty hours, addressing the challenge at work seems a lot less intimidating. And accomplishing a goal, any goal, now seems more feasible. If you have put in all the hours and gotten up early on Saturday mornings to be on the river before the tubers, and sacrificed time away from your family and spent date nights rigging boats all to get you to Seadrift, then that next goal seems feasible, the mountain to climb it a little less steep. Finishing the Texas Water Safari changes the lens through which you see the world and life and offers more perspective in terms of what matters in life and what you can accomplish.

"What the Safari has given me (and my family) is more than an accomplishment to list or stories to tell, it has given me a family, my tribe. It has given me friends that have my back, who will show up to help you move in the rain. It has given me women role models for your kids and shown them (and reminded me at times) what badassery looks like. There is the

Kate Tart (*center*) with her husband Nate on the left and (TC) Dwight Tart on the right. They came in thirtieth overall, fourth mixed with a time of 60 hours and 31 minutes in 2014. Courtesy of Ashley Landis

family you are born with and then the family you create, and the Safari has given me a family greater than I could have ever dreamed of."

～～～～

For many, the Safari can be a place of personal accomplishment and reverence. One of these stories is told by accomplished Safari veteran Ann Best. "'I want to throw his ashes out here!,' my 2003 tandem partner Julie Basham yelled from the bow. We had swung wide into the bay around the 80-hour mark and had just turned toward the finish line. I stopped the boat about 100 yards off the seawall and removed the teal Nalgene container that had held her Dad's ashes for the last 262 miles. He died that spring and she asked me if he could join us on the race. I passed the container up to Julie on the face of the paddle. She said a few quiet words and set about opening the container. She couldn't get it open with her blistered hands and neither could I.

"We paddled to the finish line, where her family was waiting. It took both of us to get the lid off of his resting place. She turned toward her family and threw his ashes out in a big arc over San Antonio Bay. Days earlier at check-in, Cindy Meurer had smiled kindly as she reviewed and approved the last item on our list of contents. Julie's Dad."

Ann Best holds the record of being the first woman to ever paddle the race in a USCA C-1, in 2007. However, her adventure began a decade earlier in a conversation with veteran paddler Bill "Polecat" Stafford.

"In 1998, after several weekends of mucking out Polecat Stafford's house after a historic flood on the Guadalupe, Polecat repaid the volunteers with a day on the river near Thomaston. Since there weren't enough canoes for the group, Polecat sent me to the barn to fetch a narrow white boat that looked more

like a sculling rig than a canoe. While zigzagging my way down the Guad in the strange boat, I asked Polecat what it was doing in his barn. He told me he'd paddled it solo in the Safari.

"'You should do the Safari,' he said. That's the day I learned that a woman hadn't run the race in a [USCA] C-1 yet. Years later, John Mark Harras would wisely recommend running it tandem first. The Safari bug hit me in the fall of 2002, when I found someone as novice as myself to agree to the 2003 dance. I remember thinking, both of us can paddle—how hard can it be? We bought the heaviest tandem unlimited we could find and started training.

"At the Safari seminar, we sat at the feet of Cindy Meurer, who both fascinated and horrified us with her female-friendly intel about the race. Among other things, she described how a careful modification to your tights would allow you to answer the call of nature discreetly, without putting on a show for the rest of the field. Over the next few years, I would meet a handful of women who I grew to admire: Erin Magee, Teddy Gray, Ginsie Stauss, Julie Morgan, Holly Orr, Joy Emshoff, and more. Whether paddling with me, offering shuttle help, sharing advice and lessons learned, or bringing grace in the face of hardship, each of them inspired me in different ways.

"I completed my second Safari in 2007, in a [USCA] C-1. I did it because no one else had done it and because it seemed to me the purest way to run the course. Even though I don't remember most of it, that Safari journey is my most prized possession. My fondest training and race memories are of having poison ivy, uninterrupted, for more than 100 days; being shocked by the electric fence at Staples bridge; the kindness of the young men who offered to carry my boat as I stumbled through logjams on the final night of the race (I did not accept); waking up underwater near the saltwater barrier after falling asleep

Ann Best in 2007. She came in seventieth overall, first women's USCA C1 with a time of 74 hours and 47 minutes. She was the first woman in the history of the Safari to finish in a USCA C1. Courtesy of Erich Schlegel

while paddling; and how much the Safari boosted my street cred among stodgy corporate coworkers.

"Canoe racing is the great equalizer. It doesn't care who you are, how old you are, what you do, where you live, what you drive, where you came from, or how much money you make. Everyone has the same chance on the water. I have never been particularly competitive—so for me, Safari is about community, adventure, digging deep, doing the thing that scares you, and finishing what you started. You'll never know what you are capable of until you try."

~~~~~

Brenda Jones calls herself the "Reluctant Paddler." She says she never had aspirations to paddle in a canoe race, much less the TWS that lasts multiple days in the Texas heat. She doesn't feel that she is competitive by nature. She was raised by a father who was a safety consultant for IBM, and he taught her to see the danger and risk in everything. "Playing it safe was how I lived—and I liked it that way." Her sister, Donna, was more attracted to adventure. "She helped me support my husband and son in their first race effort in the 2009 TWS, still considered one of the lowest water years on record. It took them 95.5 hours to finish and it was a brutal struggle every inch of the way. After watching them endure the horrible conditions in the heat, mosquitos, snakes, mud, log-jams, alligator gar (jumping in the boat), snake close encounters, throwing up from who-knows-what, and then finally crossing an open, angry bay, Donna had the nerve to cheerily declare, 'Let's do it next year!' Meaning, with me!"

"I thought she was out of her mind and remembered a training run, my first, that I had done a few months earlier with my husband; it bordered on terrifying. I felt that if she only knew how awful it actually was, she would give up on the idea for sure. I reluctantly agreed to do a few training runs with her, knowing full well she would hate the experience and agree with me that the idea was ridiculous. We ended up training for six months in flood conditions with what seemed like weekly near-death experiences. Donna was still more than excited about the prospect of doing the race while I was filled with dread every time we sat in the canoe. We started training without knowing the dangers of high water and sank or damaged our boat on multiple occasions. Each time required an expensive, time-consuming boat repair. We even dropped the boat off the top of a dam a couple of times while trying to portage. I was secretly hoping that maybe the boat would not survive the drop. After several months of training with no drop in my sister's enthusiasm, I felt obligated to race since there would not be enough time for her to find a new partner this close to the race.

"Eventually race day arrived and we began doing what we had practiced all year long. It was every bit as awful as I thought it would be, and more. The pain from continuous paddling and frequent portages started soon and was relentless. Blisters on our hands, and more surprisingly, our butts hurt with every stroke. We had to climb over logjams, some of them in the dark. The jams were infested with snakes, huge hand-sized spiders, and the occasional alligator. There were so many fears to deal with at one point I just thought that I couldn't be any more dazed or afraid than I was at the moment. After paddling a couple of days and nights we began to experience hallucinations, which were amazing and concerning all at the same time.

"With every passing hour, I reminded my sister that I hated her, in a loving way of course. It was like a dream and I couldn't wrap my head around the insanity of it all. We met many great people along the way that helped to guide us through a lot of it and we appreciated that more than they will ever know. The hard work eventually paid off and we reached the finish line during the awards banquet. As we approached the finish line, crowds of faster racers, supporters, and the curious were gathered to cheer us on.

"As we crossed the finish line, something just clicked . . . I got it! I finally understood why people love this race! I was a changed person. I had accomplished something I never believed I could. I accomplished more than I ever thought possible and would never look at a difficult challenge the same way again. In short, I think that the TWS changes the way you handle difficulty and the way you look at life. Never again will I say 'I am so tired,' because you will never know what 'tired' feels like until you know the 'tired' of a TWS.

Brenda Jones going solo in 2013. She finished fifty-second overall, second women's solo in 84 hours and 57 minutes. Courtesy of Ashley Landis

"I have gone on to do the TWS almost every year since and have ten attempts and six finishes. Each one of them is so special. I am so grateful for the gift my sister gave me for insisting that we do this race. This year I am applying the same pressure to my daughter to race with me and Donna, in a three-person canoe. My daughter is by far worse at these types of things than even I was, but I see the value in what the race did for me and I want my daughter to experience the life-changing power of doing something hard and terrifying. I want her to feel that deep satisfaction of finishing something extremely hard that seemed impossible. I will be forever grateful for the gift of the Texas Water Safari."

~~~~~

Pam LeBlanc competed in the Safari for the first time in 2019. She has done ultramarathons, extreme sports of all kinds, and has lived quite the adventurous life. Her account of the Safari is one I want to share:

"Until the 2019 Texas Water Safari, I'd never paddled more than sixty consecutive miles. Ever.

"My paddling experience generally consisted of a few recreational trips in West Texas, when I loaded a tent, sleeping bag, and a bottle of wine into the big belly of a borrowed aluminum canoe and hoped for the best. I'd drifted around Lady Bird Lake in a rental boat a few times, too, but that hardly counts.

"'I don't do sleep deprivation,' I told Safari veteran Curt Slaten ten years ago, rolling my eyes when he suggested I sign up for the Safari. 'Stupid. No way I'd do that race.'

"Then in 2018 I spent five days following the Safari for the Austin American Statesman, where I worked as a staff writer. I gawked at five-person boats bristling with pee cups, little containers of Ibuprofen,

and bottles of something called Spiz. I eyeballed the inspiring messages ('Pain does not live in this boat') scrawled inside the canoes. I chuckled at paddlers wearing white tights and baggy shorts. I watched people flip boats at Rio Vista Dam, saw JT Van Zandt's partner ditch the race at Hochheim, and sat horrified as West Hansen puked his guts up on the side of the river in the dead of night.

"Despite all of that, when Sheila Reiter and Heather Harrison invited me to join their three-woman team a few months later, I agreed. Three weeks have passed now since Team That's What She Said finished the race in 53 hours and 15 minutes (an easy year, they tell me), and I've had a little time to think about what happened. The things that stick in my mind most about my rookie experience. The training. It wasn't just the race, it was the months leading up to it, and the time spent driving up and down Interstate 35 with a torpedo strapped to the roof of the truck. I loved those weekend runs, and everything that happened on them: Sheila using her paddle to fend off a water moccasin trying to slither into our canoe, logjams rife with bobbing logs, palm-size spiders, dead and bloated farm animals and debris, and complete exhaustion at the end of every session. Each time I thought to myself, 'That was 30 miles, how the heck am I going to do 260'?

"Friends pitched in with helpful advice. Sheila coached me how to pee in a cup in a moving canoe. Debbie Richardson suggested I precrush potato chips so I could eat them faster. Jimmy Harvey loaned me a paddle. West Hansen told me I could do it. But Jeff Wueste summed it up best: 'The boat's going to Seadrift. Just stay in the boat.'

"In reality, the race sucked just as much—possibly even more—than I expected. Anybody who tells you otherwise is lying. One of our team captains quit in a huff the night before the race. The start felt like trying to escape a burning building while carrying a wet sofa. We lost a paddle in the first mile.

"On Day 2, the heat index climbed to 110. I felt like crap. I couldn't eat. Even cheeseburgers and breakfast sandwiches the crew tossed at me made my stomach churn, and all the icepacks in the world couldn't cool me off. I focused on balancing on my seat as gently as possible and not puking my guts up.

"Somehow night finally fell, and I stayed alert enough to experience what everybody warned me about—hallucinations. Trees along the banks morphed into leering clowns, walls of spray-painted graffiti and a cast of cartoon characters.

"I'm not going to lie, things got tense in our boat a few times, too. We snapped at each other. Then made up.

"Eventually, the sun rose again. I still felt terrible, but I was able to keep paddling.

"We got to the saltwater barrier, then to Traylor cut, where we received the happy news that the bay was 'like glass.' Or had been. Or perhaps, 'was like glass earlier but might have a few ripples now.' Which apparently is the code for 'gird your loins, girls, it's going to be brutal.'

"We got out into the chop, and I swear the waves were 2-foot-high, probably not bad by Safari standards, but the wind forced us to paddle like someone had turned the dial up to 11. We chugged as hard as we could for an hour, got to a spit of land, and realized the wind had shifted.

"I was wrecked. My teammates pulled me through—who would EVER do this race in a solo boat has to be nuts—and we ended up on a small deserted island somewhere, where I flopped out of the boat, lay prone on the beach while a fully grown alligator swirled in the coffee-colored water just offshore, and I prayed that it would all end quickly.

I couldn't stand up. Someone poured water in my mouth. I expected a helicopter to haul me away.

"But Seadrift lay on the horizon, and I needed that finishers' patch, so we clambered back in the boat and pointed into the wind.

"To prevent flipping, we braced during the bigger waves and paddled during the smaller ones. The spray skirt kept our boat from filling with water, but by now, it seemed, it had filled instead with pee. We reeked.

"About a quarter of a mile from Seadrift, we noticed another boat coming in from another angle. And they were moving quickly. Heather and Sheila hollered, and we began paddling frantically, as fast as we could. I had no idea a nearly dead person could temporarily revive, but it happened. I must have been faking my sickness.

"We blazed across that last bit of now much-calmer bay. I thought my heart would explode, but it didn't. I kept yelling 'Dig deep,' and the boat seemed like some giant being had smacked it with a giant cue stick. In the end, that other boat beat us to the finish by a few seconds, but that didn't really matter.

"I got to that rickety set of steps, staggered my way to the top, and walked (that's using the expression loosely, I was not really vertical) with assistance, to a camping cot, where I laid down and someone removed my shoes. I remember feeling grateful that all the skin on my feet didn't peel off with my shoe as I expected.

"My head buzzed. I had a horrific rash on my ass and one-inch strips of sunburn around each ankle, on the skin between the tights and my shoes. Someone put a grape in my mouth. I shut my eyes.

"Three weeks out, my brain has done a good job editing out the worst of the race, but leaving those memories of the stars at night, fog swirling on the water's surface, and the paddlers who ran alongside us

Left to right, Heather Harrison, Sheila Reiter, Pam LeBlanc in 2019. They finished forty-sixth overall, third women's unlimited in a time of 53 hours and 10 minutes. Courtesy of Ashley Landis

for long stretches. I can still hear the roar of cicadas and tree frogs, and see the cardinals that guided us down river.

"People ask me now if I'll do the Safari again, and I'm not sure. I might, given the right conditions. (OK, I know the water was high and the jams were mostly clear and conditions will never be as good as they were in 2019.) I want to know how it might feel to race a bigger boat, maybe a four- or five-person canoe. I loved the training. I loved the community.

"And a part of me loved the horrible race, too.

"It made me feral, like a wild animal jamming through the jungle, scampering over whatever popped up in front of me, not caring about the soul-sucking mud and serpents and the squalor and the heat. It gave me something—besides that colorful little patch that finishers earn—too. It gave me a shot of self-confidence that nobody can take away.

"Because if I can do the Texas Water Safari, I can do anything that life throws at me."

7

Old Man River

In 1963 a twelve-year-old boy named Tom Goynes read about the first Texas Water Safari in the *Houston Chronicle*. Little did he know that the Safari and the San Marcos River would come to play a major role in his life.

Four years later in 1967, he entered the race with his brother, Jim, and a friend, Richard Page. While the team dropped out before reaching Luling, the experience gave Tom motivation to enter again the following year. This time he and Jim finished in 79 hours and 22 minutes, and at seventeen years of age, Tom became the youngest person to complete the race. For the next two years, Tom moved up in the field, and he won the race for the first time in 1971. Over the next fifty years, his name and the Safari would become inseparable. During this time, he raced with several partners and family members, including his wife Paula (three times), and his daughter Sandy (five times). He also raced with Pat Oxsheer several times and in 2003 had amassed an incredible record of twenty-five starts and twenty-two finishes. He was first overall seven times, and in 2012 he was inducted into the Texas Water Safari Hall of Fame.

Since 1967, Tom has been active with the Safari as a competitor, as chairman of the Texas Water Safari

Tom Goynes: campground owner, canoe racer, friend of the river, conservationist, Texas Water Safari Hall of Famer, and good guy. Courtesy of Ann Best

Board (1978–1989), and as a volunteer, continuing to help out with the race every year. While he is well known throughout the racing community for his many accomplishments, he is known by a much wider audience for his unyielding efforts to conserve and protect the San Marcos River.

In the 1970s, Tom formed the River Recreation Association of Texas, commonly referred as the River RATs. Its original purpose was to promote safe paddle sports, conserve rivers, and protect river access. Tom became the first president, and I suppose the appointment was for life, as he still holds that position today.

In 1972, Tom and Paula moved to San Marcos and began renting and selling canoes at the Pecan Park Campground. That same year he organized the first San Marcos River cleanup. Now, forty-nine years later, the cleanup still occurs every March, run by the city of San Marcos and Eyes of the San Marcos River along with the San Marcos River Foundation and local businesses. Tom's influence and contacts within the racing community have brought many marathon canoe competitors in to help clean up the river. The cleanup is the oldest annual river cleanup in Texas and surely one of the oldest in the nation.

After running the campground and canoe livery at Pecan Park for several years, Tom and Paula decided to own their own campground. After looking for suitable property along the river, they purchased the

Tom and Paula Goynes (blue shirts) working the finish line at the 2017 Safari. Also shown: Chris Issendorf (center/green shirt) and Tommy Yonley (no shirt). Courtesy of Ashley Landis

Trash from the Annual San Marcos River Cleanup. Courtesy of Paula Goynes

Shady Grove Campground a few miles downstream, near the town of Martindale, in March 1979.

Operating their own campground and canoe livery gave Tom a chance to keep a watchful eye on the river. Over the next few years, their business grew along with the popularity of the river. In 1987, Tom and Paula sold the canoe livery operation to their good friend Duane Te Grotenhuis. Duane and his wife, Evelyn, and more recently his son, Alex, have continued to operate the business as T-G Canoes and Kayaks until the present day.

By 1988, Tom and Paula's booming campground and canoe and kayak business continued to grow, and

with eight employees, it became the largest Perception kayak dealership in the country. By this time, Tom began to spend so much time in the office that he had little time to get outside and enjoy the very thing that caused him to move to the area in the first place.

He says, "One morning in the fall of '88, as I was jogging on Highway 1979, I told God that I was ready to give Him complete ownership of 'my' business (I had become a Christian in 1981). Until that time I was hanging on pretty tight to that business, having built it from the ground up into the mess that it had become. Anyway, after making coffee in the office, Mike Spencer walked in and asked if I knew

TOM'S CONSERVATION EFFORTS

Listed below are several examples of conservation efforts Tom has worked on:

- **Worked with the Sierra Club in the 1970s to try and ban glass containers on the San Marcos River**

- **Worked with the Texas Parks and Wildlife Department (TPWD) to establish an upper Guadalupe Canoe/Hiking Trail, which was part of the "Pathways and Paddleways Program"**

- **Testified numerous times over the years to create a Water Oriented Recreation District (WORD) on the San Marcos River, similar to the district on the Guadalupe River in Comal County**

- **Worked with TRPA in the 1990s to seek better water quality on sewage treatment in San Marcos and testified on water right applications**

- **Worked with TRPA to purchase and preserve thirteen acres of land on the Brazos River near Navasota for recreation**

- **Worked with the Martindale City Council to ban the use of small disposal containers within the Martindale City limits. The ban is currently in place, as of this writing**

of anyone who was selling riverfront (property). I almost dropped the pot."[1]

A few months later, Tom and Paula sold the business to the Spencers and were out on the streets, so to speak. After a long vacation in 1989, Tom attended the Dallas Theological Seminary for a semester, but then decided that he could do more good on the river than attending classes.

In January 1990, the Goyneses moved back to the Martindale area and bought property on the river, calling it Pecan Park Retreat. The name changed about ten years later to its current name, San Marcos River Retreat. Again, Tom became immediately immersed in conservation work and turned in the city of San Marcos for dumping poorly treated sewage into the San Marcos River. Tom and Paula's new campground catered to youth and church groups, and Tom began holding short worship services on Sundays.

During the 1990s, Tom and several like-minded individuals formed the Texas Rivers Protection Association (TRPA). Tom became the first president and served in that capacity for thirty years. He is also past president of the San Marcos River Foundation (SMRF) and continues to work with the foundation on conservation efforts of mutual interest.

Over the past forty+ years, Tom has been an active steward, working tirelessly to conserve and protect the San Marcos River. While his efforts have been unwavering, the benefits sometime take years to accomplish. Conservation initiatives often lack wide public support and tend to take a "back seat" to other initiatives with measurable, economic benefits. Also, it can take several sessions before proposed changes to the state laws receive serious consideration on the floor of the state legislature.

Tom's efforts to conserve the river have been recognized and applauded by many who enjoy, appreciate, and use the San Marcos River, and his accomplishments have received special recognition by several conservation groups over the years.

In 2000, Tom Goynes, received the Evelyn R. Evans Award from the Texas chapter of the Sierra Club. The award commemorates the conservation efforts of Evelyn R. Evans, a Fort Worth environmentalist who worked to save the Brazos River.

Tom and Paula Goynes also received the Lifetime Guardian Award in 2011 from the San Marcos River Foundation. The award is presented annually to an individual(s) who has made "a significant contribution towards protecting and preserving the purity and flow of the San Marcos River for future generations." This is what the foundation had to say about Tom and Paula: "This river has been so lucky to have people like Tom and Paula Goynes living near it. . . . They have genuinely spent their lifetimes taking care of this river now and for the future."

Whether he is organizing the annual cleanup of the entire river, testifying before the legislature in support of river conservation, heading up the Texas River Protection Association, or working to create a state recreation district to monitor and regulate recreational use and tubing on the river, no single individual has done more to conserve the San Marcos River than Tom Goynes.[2]

8

Unsung Heroes
The Volunteers

Since the first Safari in 1963, the competitors and especially the finishers have been revered by others in the paddling community. They are considered heroes and are featured in newspapers, interviewed on television, and seen in videos and documentaries and on Facebook and YouTube. While they certainly deserve recognition for even competing in the race, there is another group that receives little public credit—the many volunteers, without whom the race would not be possible.

Robin Reeves, eight-time Safari race chairman (in cowboy hat), receives an appreciation award wooden paddle from Bob Spain. Courtesy of Ashley Landis

The Texas Water Safari is a 501c3 nonprofit organization with no paid employees. Instead, there are five board members who host the race: Harvey Babb, Jerry Cochran, Jay Daniel, Allen Spelce, and yours truly. Assisting the board each year are several key officials: the race chairman, head race judge, rescue/search boat director, social media director, SPOT tracking director, sweeps judge, and communications director.

Various other race officials and volunteers fill important roles, including staffing checkpoints, registering competitors, monitoring the race course, setting up the awards banquet, compiling race results, searching for stranded teams, and other tasks as needed. Each year, a host of seventy to eighty volunteers work day and night for 100 hours to make the race possible.

Checkpoint Officials

While all race officials play an important role, one group of particular importance is the checkpoint officials. They staff the checkpoints 24/7 until all the contestants have passed down the river. Many perform this duty year after year, and for some it's like a family reunion.

In 1971, Chuck Truesdale agreed to enter the Safari with Jamie Hallmark. Jamie had completed the 1968 TWS but Chuck had never been in a canoe and had no idea what he was getting into. On the first practice run, after four hours of paddling, Chuck said, "Jamie how many hours would it take us to finish the race. He [Jamie] replied, 'A lot.' The next practice run I said, Jamie what did you mean when you said, 'A lot,' last week? That's when I found out the whole story about the length of the race."

Chuck and Jamie raced the 1972 Safari and made it all the way to Hochheim, when fatigue and lack of water took its toll and they dropped out. Here is Chuck's account of what happened: "Back in those early years of the race there were no team captains, no water, no ice, or food provided from the bank. Everything had to be taken in the canoe. River water had to be purified with Halazone tables. It was like trying to drink bleach. Each time I started to dip water out of the river we would paddle past a dead bloated cow, pig, and even one dead horse. As a result we put off drinking and hit the wall at Hochheim on Sunday afternoon where our race ended."

Over the next few years, Chuck and his wife, Ellen, returned to watch the race, and then in 1990, they followed the team of Judy Hallmark and Debbie Brown all the way to Seadrift. Apparently, that rekindled Chuck's desire to race again.

The following year Chuck and Ken Watts raced an aluminum canoe with Ellen as team captain. They finished in 91 hours and 42 minutes. The following year Chuck raced again with his 1972 partner, Jamie Hallmark, for a second time and they finished twentieth. While that was the last time that Chuck raced, his interest in the race continued.

The following year, Chuck and Ellen traveled to San Marcos on Friday to watch the race. That year Chuck was asked to check in canoes and Ellen was asked to sell T-shirts. Later that day they were asked to travel to Luling on Saturday and staff the checkpoint, which would become an annual event for the Truesdales for the next twenty-seven years and counting.

Every year at the Safari prerace registration, Chuck and Ellen return to help out. Since Chuck has performed the job for almost three decades, he admits that he has seen it all. Here is what he had to say in 2019: "Over the twenty-seven years that I have seen many interesting and strange things that have been taken in canoes during the Safari. Before

team captains could provide food, I once checked in a 50-quart ice chest filled with apples, oranges, and bananas. A few years back I checked in a volleyball that looked like Wilson in the movie *Cast Away*. I heard at Seadrift that it ended just like the movie. The one thing that left me baffled to this day was the huge, heavy, stainless steel pressure cooker that I checked in for a pair of racers six years ago."

Since 1993 Chuck and Ellen have manned the Luling Highway 90 checkpoint every year. Their contribution and unselfish dedication to the Safari is extraordinary, and, apparently, they have no plans to give up their post in the foreseeable future. Chuck said, "Our family, church members, and friends all know where we will be every second Saturday in June, and we plan to be there as long as the Lord is willing and the creeks don't rise."

If you choose to visit the small city park on Highway 90 near Luling on the second Saturday of June, you will see Chuck and Ellen at work.

Twenty miles downstream of the Luling checkpoint is Palmetto State Park. Located on a low-water bridge in the middle on the park is checkpoint #3. Over the years the checkpoint has been one of the most challenging for competitors and checkpoint officials alike, given the low concrete bridge that crosses the river. When the river flow is low, water flows freely under the bridge and teams can paddle up to the bridge and portage or float their boats under. However, when water flows are high, teams must portage the bridge and swift waters can pin canoes against it. On more than one occasion, competitors have been caught in swift-moving water and had to be rescued or lost their boats. Because

Ken Thigpen (*right*) (checkpoint official), and Richard Ameen (*left*) at the Palmetto Checkpoint #3 in 2015. Water is flowing over the low water bridge they are standing on. Courtesy of Ashley Landis

many competitors reach the checkpoint in the dark and choose to sleep, competitors, team captains, and spectators hang out at the site. Managing the site is not a small task for the checkpoint officials.

Ken Thigpen first manned the site as checkpoint official in 2002. Since then, he has worked the checkpoint seventeen times. Ken and his team of officials have done an outstanding job of checking through canoes and keeping a watchful eye on competitors and bystanders. On more than one occasion, Ken and his team have had to rescue competitors at the low-water bridge.

During the fifty-seventh Texas Water Safari in 2019, flows at the bridge were at dangerously high levels. Swift water was lapping up and sometimes over the low-water bridge. Competitors who paddled all the way to the bridge risked being swept under it,

and to make matters worse, a downed tree with a root ball partially blocked the right side of the bridge. If approaching canoes failed to either go far left or go to the far-right bank and portage, they would be forced to paddle straight into the middle of the bridge and exit the canoe in the swift water.

Race officials were especially diligent to keep a watchful eye on competitors approaching the bridge to prevent any mishaps. It is a good thing they did. Saturday afternoon about three thirty a fourteen-year-old girl lost her footing while wading upstream from the bridge. Apparently she was visiting the park with her family and was not part of the Safari crowd. As the swift water pushed her toward the bridge, race officials Richard Herbert and Bear Bryant saw the girl and rushed to the bridge to lend a hand. While she struggled frantically to gain her footing, she was

Downed tree with root ball partially blocking the portage, at the bridge at the Palmetto checkpoint in 2019. Courtesy of Ashley Landis

swept farther downstream toward the bridge. Just before she was swept underneath it, Richard and Bear grabbed her and pulled her to safety.

Aware of the potential problems at the bridge and in an effort to prevent Safari competitors from being swept under it, Ken and his team stationed race officials upstream to warn them.

Most of the boats had passed by early Sunday morning, and things were beginning to wind down for race officials who had been up all day and into the evening. At approximately three forty-five Sunday morning, Eddy Amaya and Gary Campbell were paddling kayak #6468 in the Tandem Unlimited Class toward the bridge. Earlier in the race, they had collided with the "wrap rock" in Cottonseed Rapid and knocked a hole in their kayak. While they made a temporary fix with duct tape, water continued to pour in and every hour or so they had to stop and dump the water. To further slow their progress, their lights were not working well, and in the darkness they could not see clearly what lay up ahead. As novices, they were unfamiliar with this section of river and did not know about the low-water bridge.

As they approached the bridge, they continued to paddle in the middle of the river. Though the checkpoint officials were yelling to portage right, it was too late. Unable to see clearly, they hit the root ball, spun their canoe around, and the swift current pushed them straight into the middle of the bridge. Sensing danger, Gary Campbell in the bow bailed out just as their boat hit the bridge. While Gary was able to scramble

Kayak #6468 stuck under Palmetto low water crossing bridge in 2019. Courtesy of Mary Wilson

up on the bridge, Eddy Amaya was not so lucky. He was swept into the bridge and grabbed the lip with his arms. Luckily race officials Roy Kleinsasser, Lance Bielke, and Bear Bryant were able to grab Eddy as he was going under the bridge. By this time, Gary had joined in to lend a hand. As they held onto Eddy and Eddy held onto the bridge, more officials rushed over to help out. With a firm grasp on his life jacket, the officials pulled him to safety. Ken Thigpen and his team of checkpoint officials were awarded the Brad Ellis Spirit Award that year.

Checkpoint #5 near Hochheim is 62 miles downstream from Palmetto State Park and under the Highway 183 bridge that crosses the Guadalupe River. For the past sixteen years, Sam Thiede has been the checkpoint official at the site. After completing his last Safari in 1995, Sam continued to support the race, first as a race official or team captain and from 2004 through 2021 as the checkpoint official. Like all Safari officials, Sam is a volunteer who receives no pay but returns year after year because he loves the race. Since all checkpoints are manned 24/7, they all have their challenges. Hochheim is no exception. The checkpoint is approximately 122 miles from the start, it is out in the middle of nowhere, and the road and parking area under the bridge are so muddy when it rains that some team captains choose to walk down from Highway 183 to avoid getting stuck.

Every Saturday afternoon, following the race start in San Marcos, Sam parks his vehicle under the bridge near Hochheim and sets up an easy chair that doubles as his bed. As a veteran of nine Safari finishes, he is a good source of information for new team captains unfamiliar with the race or needing directions to the next checkpoint. For the next day and a half, until the Monday 7:00 a.m. deadline, Sam mans the station around the clock.

Sam Thiede checkpoint official (dark T-shirt on right) at Checkpoint #5 near Hochheim. Gib Hafernick, TWS veteran (in light shirt on left) and Ann Andrisek, volunteer (center with sun visor), talking with Sam. Courtesy of Ashley Landis

When asked why he returns every year to the Hochheim checkpoint, the Safari veteran said, "It's payback, and I get to see my friends one time a year."

One unsung hero who gets little attention or recognition is the sweep judge. The sweep judge is responsible for following the race course and shutting down the checkpoints when the checkpoint timed deadlines are met. Their duties are many and varied, including hanging around the back of the pack, waiting hours for boats to make the timed checkpoint cutoffs, acting as cheerleader for lost or disappointed team captains and tired and weary competitors, tracking down team captains who forgot to sign at checkpoints, and collecting the unwanted or lost items that are left along the race course. They never get to see the top teams during the race or the finish in Seadrift.

Given the nature of the job, you would think that most individuals who volunteer as sweep judge would be "one-and-done," but not Mary Wilson. Every year since 2004, she has returned with a smile and a quick "one-liner"—along with her iconic hat with a stuffed toy fox draped across it—to keep things lively. She says, "Having been in the race two times, I can definitely identify with the issues many of them face. I also love telling them jokes and lightening their mood! My job as Sweep has multiple parts to it, other than accountability of all boats at all times—but I feel that otherwise, my most important job is to encourage the paddlers, team captains, and supporting spectators. The paddlers I 'sweep' down the river are the stragglers, the ones that might not finish. I don't leave the course until all the boats have finished the race, so with my slow boats, I'm there at the finish encouraging them and celebrating their hard-fought finish with them. What keeps me coming back year after year is that I feel I need to be there for the paddlers, to

Mary Wilson in 2013, sweep judge. She raced twice, finishing in 1992 with a time of 74 hours and 15 minutes. She volunteered as sweep judge in 2004 and has returned every year since except one. Courtesy of Ashley Landis

encourage them, to keep them paddling and smiling somehow, if not to get their minds off their mental and physical pain but for just a minute. I also feel that all the repeat race officials and the TWS Board are like a big family that have a reunion once a year and I wouldn't miss it for the world! I love being the Sweep Judge! Broom in hand, fox on my hat—I'm ready for the next one!"

Team Captains

In the early years of the race (1963–1970), competitors could not receive any type of support while on the river, although water was provided by the race organizers in the coastal segments. Racers were on their own to either treat the river water or scout the riverbanks for water faucets. Starting in 1969, teams were allowed to have one team captain (TC) but still had to fend for themselves for drinking water while

on the river. During this time, the common practice was to treat river water with water purification tablets (Halazone). Given the fast pace of the race, competitors did not always wait for the pills to work properly, drank the water, and got sick.

Sometime in the 1970s, race organizers started allowing TCs to provide water to contestants during the race. Given the hot Texas temperatures in June, this rule change was a welcome benefit, since heat and dehydration often took their toll on competitors. Sometime later, ice was legalized, and this was a great addition to the race as well. This allowed competitors to get a cold drink of water, and the ice could be used to soothe sore, aching muscles and injuries. In 2013, the rules changed again, allowing each team to have a second team captain. The rules also allowed not only ice and water but also allowed food and medical supplies to be procured at any time during the race.

Today, as in the past, TCs play a vital role in the

performance of their team. Having an experienced team captain is an asset to any team. Most TCs are spouses, other family members, friends, or past racers. Some never race but serve as team captain year after year.

Sandy Sherrod has never raced the Safari and has no plans to do so. While she does not race, she still shows up every year and follows the race from start to finish. During the past twenty+ years while Vance, her husband, has raced, she has faithfully supported him and his team. One year when Vance chose not to race, she volunteered as TC for Samantha "Sam" Binion.

"I've officially been team captain 13 years and helped other years for a total of 21 years," Sandy said. "I continue to help because it's fun and the people are amazing. We have formed so many friendships over the years. It's great to be around strangers willing to help and trust. It's such a great social activity and everyone is always willing to help with everything."

Since 1998 Janet Ward has been a team captain for her husband, James, every year, except during the three years when they raced together. According to Janet, the race is one of the highlights of the year. "For us, the race was like Christmas in June," she says.

(*Left to right*) Sandy Sherrod, team captain, husband Vance, Samantha "Sam" Binion and husband Wade, at the finish line in 2012. Sam and Wade finished twelfth overall in 48 hours and 32 minutes. Courtesy of Ashley Landis

Janet Ward, team captain, and husband James in 2016. James finished solo in 60 hours and 7 minutes. Courtesy of Ashley Landis

When her coworkers ask what she is going to do for a vacation she proudly answers, "I am going [to] sit under a bridge on the bank of the river, swat mosquitos, and wait for a man in a boat. They don't get it."

Ham Operators

Long before cell phones were in common use, the internet had been developed, or a Global Positioning System receiver had been invented, the Safari relied on amateur radio operators, also known as "ham radio operators," to communicate and track the progress of canoes competing in the race. The hams received no pay and supported the race because they enjoyed the work.

Beginning in the 1970s, a group of ham operators from Houston began to track the progress of the competitors during the race. The Houston Hams asked William "Bill" Lynch Jr., communications chairman for the San Antonio Repeaters Organization, to coordinate the hams on the northern section of the river. He provided hams from San Antonio and Austin and developed schedules and procedures for the checkpoints needing coverage. "Over the next two years," he says, "we gained experience with the project and some Hams began building or acquiring innovative equipment so they could work from the low terrain that rivers tend to be."

The Safari was a family affair for Bill, and every June, he and his wife, MaryBeth, and their two kids loaded into their van and followed the race from start to finish, checking on all the radio operators along the way. Even with radios, the reception along the river is limited because the river is the lowest spot on the land. To remedy this, Bill always parked his van on the highest spot he could find near the river and carried a walkie-talkie down to the checkpoint. With the van serving as a command station, he could communicate via walkie-talkie with all the operators downstream. According to Bill, these challenges made the Safari "a marvelous opportunity for us to acquire and develop equipment mixes to better prepare for the disasters we periodically covered."

One of the ham operators is Lee Besing, who keeps track with his son David of the canoes and kayaks at the first checkpoint, Staples Dam. For the past sixteen years or so, they have manned the station, keeping track of the boats as they paddle downstream. Lee first became interested in citizen band (CB) radios back in high school. In 1974, he became a ham operator and joined React International, a nationwide voluntary service organization that mobilized for emergency and catastrophic events as well as public events like the Multiple Sclerosis 150-mile Bike Tour and cross country trail rides. Apparently, the Texas Water Safari is a good opportunity to test their communication skills.

While some ham operators may volunteer only a year or two, others return year after year. None, however, can match the record of Eric Olson and his wife Sharon. In 1978 Eric became the ham operator at the Luling Highway 90 checkpoint. The following year his wife joined him at the site. For the past forty-two

years the couple has volunteered to man/woman the radios at the Luling checkpoint. When I talked with Eric about his forty+ years of service as a volunteer, he admitted that he had missed a year or two along the way, but it was only because his son or another family member got married. He also said that ham operators often volunteer to help out during natural disasters such as floods and hurricanes, and the Safari is a good chance to practice their skills.

For the past thirty+ years Harvey Babb has served as communications director for the Safari. He is also one of five board members who host the race. When asked how he got into amateur radios, he said it was while in college at East Texas State University. He said, "The Water Safari seemed like a fun application for the radio. I was a tech geek from way back, so that's what pulled me in."[1]

When he first started with the Safari, he operated out of his car, but in 1996 he married his wife, Pat, and the two have continued to coordinate the radio communications ever since. The Babbs operate the Safari radio command station out of Pat's motor home. Pat said, "That's something we joke about. He always says that he married me for my motor home."[2]

Like clockwork, the Babbs travel to Seadrift on Sunday following the race start and park their motor home near the seawall in Seadrift, erect a tall antenna, and set up the radio command center for the Safari. While neither Harvey nor Pat desire to race down the river, they have a deep appreciation for the accomplishments of those who race.

"These guys do something really incredible for these days that they're on the water. You can really see how it affects them. It sounds kind of corny, but it really is a life-changing experience for them. It's a wonderful tradition."[3]

While ham radios were the only means of communication in the early years of the race, sometime in the late 1980s clamshell or flip phones also aided in the tracking of Safari competitors. While advances in cell phone technology improved communications along the river, there are some locations where cell coverage is still very limited.

Further advances in technology gave rise to a new way to track boats during the race. Just as Global Positioning System (GPS) devices are used for car navigation, GPS trackers use the same technology to track the location of canoes and kayaks during the race. Beginning in 2012, SPOT trackers were carried on each boat during the race to track their progress. The following year, Jeff Snider, SPOT tracking director, developed a program that allowed race officials and the general public to track the canoes and kayaks on cell phones and computers. This application not only aided officials in keeping track of the teams during the race but also allowed the general public to watch the progress of the race remotely.

With the recent evolution of social media, the progress of the race is followed on the internet and is shared with a much bigger audience in other states and other countries. Through the years the acclaim of the race has grown along with the number of entries. In 2019 a record number of 392 competitors raced the Safari, with 330 finishers.

PART THREE
Our Favorite Stories

There will always be memories of the hours that you were dead tired.
The hallucinations of people you saw on the banks that didn't exist. The objects
floating in the water that took on different characteristics, and the canoes
being lifted and rolled by gars, alligators, and any other objects
just below the surface (especially at night).

—*Don Montier, 1967 Texas Water Safari finisher*

9

Tall Tales and Hallucinations

During the past thirty-five years, I have been involved with the Safari as a spectator, volunteer, race official, competitor, and for about fifteen years, a board member. I have witnessed extraordinary accomplishments and heard legitimate tales and testimonials from competitors, and I've heard other stories that I simply take with a grain of salt. While it's true that extraordinary things do occur during the race, I know that storytellers, in the excitement of the moment, tend to embellish their stories. Someone once said, "I would tell a person the truth two or three different ways

before I would lie to them." But seriously, some stories —even those believed to be real by the observer—are so unbelievable and unexplainable that they must surely be hallucinations.

There is one section of the Safari course in the lower Guadalupe River that is often referred to as "Hallucination Alley." While there are no set boundaries, generally speaking, competitors often experience hallucinations in the section beginning at Checkpoint 8 in the Victoria City Park at mile 200, and Checkpoint 10, Saltwater Barrier, at mile 249. By the time

Safari competitors have hallucinated and described various apparitions including "a 747 jet, Mickey Mouse playing a guitar, a naked lady standing in the water, a tiny circus, and imaginary people standing on the bank." Courtesy of Joy Emshoff

some competitors reach this area, they have been paddling for several days and are sleep deprived and exhausted.

Competitors have described all manner of objects that they claimed to have seen while hallucinating. Some are so bizarre that I will name a few: a giant Godzilla, a funeral procession, huge parade balloons with faces of family members painted like clowns, tiny mannequins in the trees, a 747 jet in the water, Mickey Mouse playing a guitar, a naked older lady standing in the water, a tiny circus, and imaginary people standing on the bank.

"Hallucinations can't be all bad," said one Safari competitor. "I thoroughly enjoyed our stay on the mosquito-infested spoil bank. My partner found a couple of soft rocks to rest on and I went over to talk to a very attractive blonde female. We talked at great length about sex and she laughed at all my Aggie jokes and discussed the possibility of continuing a relationship should I survive the last three miles of this damn boat race. I think I showed my 'macho image' when I informed this sweet young thing that we had just paddled around four hundred and fifty miles of river and a few miles of salty old bay water was nothing to be frightened of. So much for hallucinations!"[1]

Following are some of the best stories I have heard from competitors—some true, some surely imaginary. You be the judge.

Eric and Matt

In 2011, Eric Whicker and Matt Sandel were paddling their first Safari in aluminum canoe #41 in the Novice Class. Somewhere between Hochheim and Cheapside, Eric started feeling strange and told his partner that he couldn't describe the feeling, but the sense that things were going to get weird was undeniable. With no sleep for more than forty-eight hours, he was having trouble distinguishing objects and told Matt he would need help steering the canoe.

While he knew that Matt was in the bow, instead of Matt, he saw a brown blob with a light radiating from it. He also had the feeling that there had been a third person in the canoe, but he couldn't remember who it was. His depth perception worsened, and he could not distinguish whether an object, like a stump, was 5 or 25 feet away. Eric continued to hallucinate throughout the race, but to their credit, he and Matt finished in 83 hours and 7 minutes. He still claims that he never slept.

Nate and Kate Tart

While most hallucinations occur during the race, oddly enough, one occurred after the 2010 Safari. That year Kate Tart drove her exhausted and sleep deprived husband, Nate, who had just finished the race, to a restaurant to eat.

According to Kate, "Nathan's novice year had the best stories—at least in terms of hallucinations—and not just during the race. They finished Monday afternoon and Nathan was set on crab legs for dinner. So after a shower and change of clothes, we drove to Port Lavaca. The sun was still up and Nathan was still on a race high, so he hadn't slept yet. We ate dinner and then when we headed back to Seadrift, the sun had set and it was dark. As we were driving through Port Lavaca, Nathan freaked out that I was getting ready to run into a Porsche sitting in the middle of the street. After freaking out that I was getting ready to get into an accident, I realized there was no Porsche and not to trust Nathan. After convincing him there was no Porsche, he then responds with, 'So I guess there is no mariachi band playing in the middle of the street either?'"

Pat and Tom and the Canadians

In the early 1970s, Tom Goynes and Pat Oxsheer raced and won the Texas Water Safari several times. In the 1971 race, Tom and Pat were trying desperately to catch two Canadian racers who were in the lead.

Tom recounts: "So anyway, it's June, 1971, I'm paddling down the Guadalupe River below Victoria in very hot conditions with no ice. The Canadian team is about ten minutes ahead of us (at least according to a drunk fisherman) and my partner is starting to act a little strange."

"Now let me say right here that Pat Oxsheer is the reason that Goynes and Oxsheer won three Safaris (not to mention a couple more with Jim Trimble). Pat is as strong as an ox and full of sheer brawn (pun attempted). But all of us have our limits. And, on this particular occasion, Pat had been pushed too hard. I realized that we had a problem when he starting yelling at folks on the bank who weren't there. He would become quite animated and get really angry at those scumbags. I asked him what they were doing and he said they were digging shortcuts, then letting the Canadians use said cuts, but then covering them up by the time we got there. No amount of reason would help to convince him that wasn't happening, so I played along—hollering at the top of my lungs with my partner. I have often wondered if anyone might have heard us as we slowly progressed down the creek—and what they may have thought."

Later, Tom and Pat actually caught up with the Canadians, Luc Robillard and Denis Theberge, and the two boats paddled together for a while. Then the Canadians paddled away in the dark and their boat light disappeared. Normally that would mean that they were far ahead, but in this case, they had turned their light off to sneak away, which would later be their downfall.

By this time Pat had recovered some, but occasionally he would carry on a one-way conversation with his wife, Barbara, who he said was on the bank. After a while Tom and Pat paddled around a right-hand bend in the river where a large elm tree had fallen into the water. Tom and Pat knew about the downed tree, but Denis and Luc did not. During daylight it would be easy to avoid, but at night, it was trouble. When the two Texans rounded the bend and slipped past the tree, they saw an overturned Sawyer Saber canoe, life jackets, and paddles floating in the water along with the two spent Canadians. When Tom asked if they needed help, they said "NO." After leaving the river, Pat and Tom paddled across a rough San Antonio Bay in a winning time of 57 hours and 38 minutes.

While Pat and Tom were paddling and swimming across the rough bay, the Canadians' troubles continued.

The previous year, Luc Robillard raced the Safari and, by all accounts, was leading but got lost and never finished. This year was more of the same. Confused and lost, Luc and his partner, Denis, decided to sleep until morning and paddle when they could see better. The next morning, they paddled into the barge canal, which is against Safari rules. When they found a cabin on the shore, they stopped to get directions. No one was home and the door was unlocked, so they walked in to make a phone call. No one knows who they called. At this point I am not sure how many Safari rules they had broken, let alone civil laws like trespassing and breaking and entering the house. However, they were good house guests, since they paid for the food they found in the fridge. They decided to leave the race course, walk to a nearby road, and stop a passing car for directions.

A local stopped, picked them up, and drove them to the Safari finish. By this time Tom and Pat had finished the race, cleaned up, eaten, slept some, and were waiting at the finish line. While they had expected to see the Canadians paddle across the water, to their surprise, the team drove up in a pickup instead. Normally, they would be disqualified immediately, but the race chairman, Lawrence Hagan, was not around and the local official was puzzled as to what to do. Feeling sorry for his fellow competitors, Tom Goynes asked the race official if he could

Tom Goynes in the stern and Pat Oxsheer in the bow, racing a Sawyer Saber in 1971. They won the race in 57 hours and 38 minutes. Courtesy of San Marcos Record

Two Canadians, Denis Theberge (bow) and Luc Robillard (stern), in the 1971 Texas Water Safari. Courtesy of San Marcos Daily Record

drive the northerners back to their boat so they could paddle to the finish. Once Tom received permission, he and his wife, Paula, loaded the pair in their Ford Econoline van and drove them back to their canoe.

By this time, the cabin owner had returned home and discovered that someone had been in his cabin. Maybe it was the money lying in the kitchen, food missing from the fridge, or the muddy tracks on the floor that gave it away. So, he called the sheriff and reported it. About this time, Tom and Paula dropped off Denis and Luc, and the cabin owner saw them drive away.

Since the Ford Econoline van, equipped with curtains and a "Peace" sign, was obviously not local, the cabin owner alerted the sheriff. It did not take long for the sheriff to track down the van at the finish line, but fortunately the race chairman vouched for Tom and Paula. However, he was not so lenient on the Canadians, who were disqualified immediately on arriving by canoe. The two headed north and never returned to race again.[2]

Six Men in a Boat

Boat #314 was one of three six-person canoes entered in the 2007 Safari. All competitors in the canoe were seasoned paddlers who had raced the Safari multiple times—except for Andrew Soles, a newbie from up north. While he was a rookie in the race, he was arguably the fastest paddler in the boat—some would call him a "ringer."

The other five paddlers were Jeff Wueste, Sammy Prochaska, Andrew Stephens, William Russell, and Jeff Glock. Wueste, the stern man, had a perfect record of nine finishes out of nine starts. Sammy Prochaska had eleven finishes, two of them overall wins. The other three in the canoe had two to three finishes each.

As expected for a six-person canoe, the team took an early lead, and their first several portages went off without a hitch. Everything seemed to be clicking, and once past Shady Grove Campground, they had completed 12 miles with only 248 more to go.

In an attempt to catch the boat up front, they continued to pull hard on their double-bladed paddles. As they approached a blind, right-hand turn, they were moving well at top speed. While they were familiar with most sections of the river, they had run this section only once prior to the race. In the heat of battle, they forgot about the downed tree that blocked the river bank to bank, out of sight and just around the corner. Unable to stop, they hit the tree and four men were thrown free, while Jeff Wueste and William Russell in seats five and six were swept

downstream with the boat, where the current was flowing under the tree's trunk. Jeff was able to pull himself on top of the tree, but William was trapped just above the surface against the trunk. Quick thinking and the brawn of a highly motivated pull-up allowed him to scramble on top of the tree to safety. The force of the water pinned the boat against the tree and in an instant, the 40-foot boat was torn into two pieces—seemingly their race was over.

Once team #314 swam to shore, to their disappointment, the trailing ninety-four canoes began to pass them, one by one. With all hope of winning the race or even finishing gone, the six paddlers pulled the stern and bow portions ashore and began to assess the damage. Since there was poor land access at this location and Staples Checkpoint was only 4 miles away, they decided to try to piece her together and paddle to Staples.

The canoe had broken in half between the second and third seats, and unless they could overlap the stern section inside the bow section, they would not be able to make it float. With no tools to work with, they decided to lift the canoe and ram the stern section against a nearby tree. They were able to jam the stern section inside the bow portion, but it also ripped out the footrest for the third seat when the stern slid farther forward than expected.

They lashed sticks to the gunnels in the bow and stern. Duct tape was added to seal the overlap, and "she was as good as . . . ," well, maybe she would float. By this time, an hour had passed and all the canoes in the race had also.

Once back in the canoe, they had one major problem: water was pouring in to the area where the bow and stern overlapped. Instead of six paddlers, only four could paddle while the other two bailed continuously. They made it to the checkpoint, and after docking the broken canoe at Staples, Jeff Wueste spotted board member Jerry Cochran on the bank.

Feeling a bit defeated, Jeff walked over to Jerry and said, "I guess this is going to be on my perfect record of finishes, right?"

Jerry, with his normal dry sense of humor, answered, "Wasn't it the bowman's fault?" This would later become a point of humorous banter between Jeff Wueste and Jeff Glock, the bowman, when each blamed the other for the boat wreck.

For most, a canoe broken into two pieces would certainly cause a DNF (did not finish). But the team found some wire to strengthen the makeshift gunnels and secured the seal between the bow and stern, and they were off to the races once more.

I can only imagine how difficult it was to keep the canoe afloat with the bow and stern flexing back and forth and water continuously pouring in; steering the canoe must have been a nightmare. On every portage, the boat would flex, and any semblance of the makeshift duct tape seal was broken. The team decided to reevaluate their situation at the Palmetto Park Checkpoint at mile 60.

Their team captain, Jimmy Harvey, was a veteran with five Water Safari finishes, and he had a plan in mind. Fearing that the team would pull the canoe ashore and drop out at Palmetto, Jimmy tossed all their water jugs into the boat and to their surprise, retreated to his truck and drove away. While his departure must have made some team members more than a little irritated, it forced them to continue on to at least the next checkpoint at the Gonzales Highway 183 gravel bar.

The leak between the two portions of the hull had become so bad that four of the competitors bailed water while the other two paddled. But the team, against all odds, committed to finishing the race. As they paddled on, one thing gave them hope: they began to catch and pass slower boats. On one occasion they paddled up to a man in a solo canoe, and he began to give them pointers on how to paddle. Amused by his offer to help, the team carried on in search of the next boat.

By Monday morning, under normal conditions, boat #314 would be lying on the shore near the flagpole in Seadrift and the competitors would be getting a few hours of well-earned rest. But not today. The crew was now on the lower coast, and after a rough night in floodwaters, they were relieved to see what lay ahead. With more than 250 miles behind them, they had only one major obstacle left—San Antonio Bay.

When canoe #314 reached the bay, they finally caught a break. There was not a whitecap in sight. Ordinarily that would mean the crossing could be completed in two hours or so, but without a canoe

After 58 hours and 50 minutes, six-man team #314 completed the TWS in forty-second place. With the team safely on land, the canoe is broken into two pieces. Courtesy of Erich Schlegel

cover, no functional pumps, and a boat cobbled together with duct tape, bailing wire, river mud, and ingenuity, it could take forever. After paddling and bailing for 250 miles, I am sure the team was prepared to swim her in, if need be.

While following the shoreline is the safest route, the veteran paddlers knew that waves constantly pounding against the sides of the canoe would swamp the boat. Instead, they paddled straight into the open water and eventually made a left turn toward to the finish line. While the plan was good, the execution was difficult. With water pouring in the two-piece hull faster than four bailers could keep it out, the canoe slowly swamped. They made it past the barge canal and from that point on were able to float and swim her in. To their relief, the crew spotted the pavilion and flagpole at the finish line in the distance. At this point, they knew they could make it.

Against all odds, on Monday, June 11, at 7:50 p.m., boat #314 and its six-man crew completed the World's Toughest Canoe Race. In doing so, they passed fifty-two canoes, finishing in forty-second place, averaging 4.4 miles per hour, clocking in at 58 hours and 50 minutes—a truly incredible effort.

Black Helicopters and the Nekid Man

I served as head race judge for the fortieth Texas Water Safari, coordinating race officials, making sure the rules were followed, and sending out a search team if someone became lost, injured, or otherwise in trouble. By day three—June 11, 2002—the faster teams had already finished, some teams had dropped out, and a number of others were still out on the course. I was not aware of any major problems or injuries, and everything was running smoothly.

A grueling battle was underway between the two teams that were leading the Novice Class. Sleep deprived and with many miles to go, it was going to come down to which team would crack first. George Melder and Allen Chellette in canoe #24 were in the lead, but the two were having problems much greater than their close competition.

Maybe it was the fast tempo, the heat, or the hours without sleep, but Allen was convinced that he and George were paddling upstream. George tried to convince him otherwise, but Allen would have no part of it. To further confuse the situation, Colin Grimshaw and Julie Morgan in canoe #25 were disoriented and paddling upstream straight toward George and Allen. As Colin and Julie approached, they informed the novice team that they were paddling the wrong direction. This heightened Allen's objections, but George continued to paddle downstream, in the right direction. Later, Colin and Julie turned around and eventually finished the race. George and Allen would not be so lucky.

Sometime around sunrise, the Water Safari safety director Robert Youens woke up from a few hours of much needed sleep. With things well in hand

at Seadrift, Robert began surveying checkpoints upstream from the coast. Upon reaching the Tivoli Checkpoint, the wife of a competitor approached Robert with tears in her eyes. She told Robert her husband was way behind schedule, and he assured her that it is not uncommon for teams to stop and sleep.

Back on the river, about midway between Swinging Bridge Checkpoint (mile 231) and the Tivoli Checkpoint (mile 251), Sandy Goynes and Tommy Yonley were paddling downriver and saw something hanging from a tree that looked like clothing. As they

Tommy Yonley (bow) and Sandy Goynes (stern) paddling in the 2002 TWS. Tommy and Sandy paddle downstream to get help to rescue Allen Chellette who is hallucinating and has walked off into the swamp. Courtesy of Kevin Bradley

got closer, they recognized a Texas Water Safari competitor T-shirt and stopped to inspect it. "Help Me" was written in mud on the T-shirt.

They paddled to the bank, and Sandy exited the canoe, climbed up the bank, and looked around. She ventured into the waist-deep weeds and yelled out, but no one responded. With no sign of a stranded boat or competitors, Sandy was puzzled about what to do. After talking it over with Tommy, she and Tommy decided to paddle downstream and get help. Before leaving the site, Sandy removed the T-shirt from the fence and marked the spot where she found it with an empty Cheetos bag.

Sandy and Tommy paddled a short distance downstream and saw an aluminum canoe on the shore with a person swimming in the water. It was George, who let them know that he was fine, but his partner Allen had been acting strange. Shortly before Sandy and Tommy arrived, Allen had told George that fields of marijuana were growing near the river and drug runners in black helicopters were after him. When George tried to calm him, Allen resisted and left the canoe, informing George that he was "walking over the hill to get a Whataburger."

Unable to reason with Allen, and not knowing what to do, George paddled away to get help. Shortly thereafter, he had second thoughts about leaving his partner and decided to pull over to wait for him to return. Convinced that George was lucid, Sandy and Tommy decided to head downstream and get help.

By this time, Robert Youens had determined that the distressed wife's husband was in canoe #24, and that is the same team that had been leading the Novice Class at the Swinging Bridge Checkpoint. Because canoe #24 had not arrived at the Tivoli Checkpoint and was long overdue, Robert and I agreed to declare an emergency. With the concurrence of the TWS Board, we sent out a search team. We also alerted the US Coast Guard, a local fire department, and the Calhoun County Emergency Medical Service.

While most rescues on the river are done by veteran race officials in canoes, given the nature of this emergency and knowing that a motorboat could safely and quickly cover more river, Robert enlisted the help of a volunteer with a motorboat. He surveyed the spectators on the bank to see if anyone had medical training. One man said, "Yes, I am a fireman and EMT," and volunteered to go along. Little did Robert know that the EMT had an ulterior motive.

After boarding the borrowed motorboat, the boat captain, Robert, and the EMT traveled upstream in search of the missing novice team. After traveling for miles, the rescue team encountered Sandy Goynes and Tommy Yonley, who relayed their encounter with George, who was waiting in the river for Allen, who was hiding on land from the imaginary black helicopters. Shortly thereafter, they found George still waiting in the river. He reaffirmed the story, and the rescue team continued on to search for the lost competitor.

Here is Robert's description of the rescue: "Once the Cheetos Bag was located, our rescue crew discuss our options. It is getting dark, the surrounding area consists of swamps 18 inches deep and we are looking for a man, deep into hallucinations, who doesn't want to be found. The fireman suggested floating silently with the current to see if we might hear him. I agreed, so we listened. It was not long before we heard a scream coming from the swamp. I asked the boat captain to take me to shore.

"As I waded through the swamp, I spotted him in the twilight. The young man in his twenties was strong, lean, and without a stitch of clothing on. As he peered in my direction, he had the look of a 'mad man' in his eyes. Waiting for him to divert his attention in the opposite direction, I made my move. I rushed the man from behind and tackled him around the shoulders, submerging us both in the swamp. As we struggled, I screamed 'help, help . . . ' The fireman came crashing through the swamp. Just as he approached, the man ceased to struggle, and the fireman fell to his knees and began to cry. An amazing reunion . . . the fireman was the nekid man's father.

He hadn't informed me for fear that he would not be invited on the rescue."

As a fitting end to the story, Allen and George returned to race the Safari in 2004 and win the Novice Class in 44 hours and 3 minutes—a record that still stands today.

In the 2002 Safari, Allen Chellette, in a state of delirium, abandoned the race and wandered off into the swamp. Allen, fearing for his life, had begun to hallucinate and was convinced that drug runners in black helicopters were after him. Courtesy of Joy Emshoff

10

River Critters

The San Marcos and Guadalupe Rivers are important resources for wildlife, both land-dwelling creatures living along the banks and those that live in the water itself. Over the years, many competitors have had encounters with these denizens, especially alligators, snakes, and gar. Since the first Safari in 1963, there has never been a reported injury from an alligator, although paddlers have been bitten by snakes. Gar are not aggressive and show no defensive behavior, but they have, on rare occasions, caused injuries while trying to escape from unsuspecting paddlers.

Alligators

While it is true that alligators can and have preyed on human beings, causing major injuries and even death, it is rare. In fact, there has been only one reported death caused by an alligator in Texas.

Over the years I have seen a number of alligators in the Guadalupe River, and there have been many gator sightings by competitors during training runs and the race itself. Generally speaking, most gators are observed on the lower Guadalupe River and in coastal waters, and the sightings decrease as you move upstream. While alligators are rare in the San Marcos River, I saw one back in the 1980s while on a training run in or near Palmetto State Park. I had noticed a fishing line downstream on the right bank that was moving back and forth in a jerking motion. Obviously, there was something on the line.

I learned years ago that it is a "no-no" to mess with a fisherman's line, but curiosity got the best of me. When I reached down and grasped the line, I could feel the weight of what I expected to be a big catfish or gar. But, to my surprise, an alligator two to three feet long was hooked on the line. After I took a good long look, I lowered the reptile back into the water and paddled away. I often wondered what the fisherman must have thought when he learned the same thing.

Over the years, many Safari competitors have seen gators, but few can match the experience that Geoff Waters faced in May 2006.

Geoff was soon to make his first solo attempt, and he was determined to learn the route through the San Antonio Bay to the finish line. Nighttime, high waves, strong winds, disorientation, and swamped canoes have been the downfall of even the most experienced competitors over the years. Determined not to make the same mistake, Geoff traveled down to the coast for a practice run. He was new to the Safari crowd and had no paddling partners to shuttle his kayak, so he decided to paddle from the finish line in Seadrift

The American alligator (*Alligator Mississippiensis*) is the largest reptile in the United States, with a population of approximately five million that are found in the southeastern states from North Carolina to Texas. Males are slightly larger than females and can reach 14 feet in length and weigh 1,000 pounds. Alligators have extremely rough skin with armored, bony plates on their backs called osteoderms or scutes. They are carnivores that eat, fish, frogs, turtles, lizards, snakes, birds, mammals, and other alligators. They have seventy-five to eighty teeth that are replaced throughout their life. Alligators can live fifty or more years. Courtesy of Texas Parks and Wildlife

(mile 260) upstream to the wooden bridge near the mouth of the Guadalupe River and then paddle back to Seadrift.

After paddling across the bay in the direction that he thought was the mouth of the river, he ended up at Austwell. He changed his course, paddled around Foster's Point, and eventually saw a line of trees that marked the mouth of the river. With the river less than a quarter mile away, he saw his first alligator, a baby, on a muddy beach. Amused by the small gator, he felt no threat and thought it was kind of cute.

"Fifty yards later," he says, "I passed a clump of reeds on the muddy beach and saw three eight-foot alligators just as they saw me. The alligators all launched themselves into the water, and from about 100 feet off the bank, I saw three torpedo wakes heading straight out from shore toward me. I gunned it, while starting a mental countdown in my head. The wakes disappeared as the water got deeper, but I was prepared for something to hit the boat or bite my paddle. After about 10 long seconds, I started to think, 'it should have happened by now.' I didn't exactly relax, but I began to think it was a case of me startling the alligators and them feeling safer in the water."

Up ahead, Geoff could see the mouth of the river and was surprised by how narrow it was. Feeling relieved that the gators were behind him, he paddled into the river. However, up ahead he spotted two sets of eyeballs that immediately disappeared below the water. While one gator apparently swam away from his kayak, again he saw a torpedo-like wake as the second gator rapidly approached his boat. Wanting to put distance between him and the gator, he pulled hard on his paddle—only a thin layer of fiberglass between him and the largest, most ferocious reptile in North America.

As the water settled down and he continued paddling upstream, the river narrowed. He considered turning around and returning to Seadrift, but it was too narrow to swing around the 14-foot boat. Every 100 yards or so, he saw another gator enter the river from the bank or submerge itself below the turbid water. On one occasion he heard a hissing sound, presumably a gator, hidden in the vegetation on the bank.

At this point he began to consider his options. Should he continue and take out at the Highway 35 bridge and hitchhike back to Seadrift? The other option would be to turn around and paddle through alligator alley again. After deciding on the latter, he

Geoff Waters paddling his kayak in the 2016 TWS. He finished nineteenth overall, second solo unlimited with a time of 45 hours and 9 minutes. Courtesy of Ashley Landis

found a wider section in the river where he could safely turn around without crowding either bank and potentially surprising a sleeping gator.

On his return trip, he paddled along with no interference. He was pleased to see only two or three gators along the way, and they quietly submerged below the water. At this point, he was almost to the bay. Feeling relieved that he had seen his last gator, he felt he was "home free."

The story doesn't end here.

"I was starting to internally sigh with relief, when a HUMONGOUS alligator came up out of the water directly in my path. His whole head, neck, and front legs down to the elbows were above water. He (or maybe she) was facing slightly downriver, looking at me out the side of its eye. This alligator's head was as big as the cockpit of my kayak, and from looking at pictures of alligators online afterward, I'm estimating it was 13 feet and 600 to 700 pounds."

"I was close and had been pulling hard to get back to the bay. I had a second to decide what to do . . . back paddle to come to a splashy stop nose to nose? There wasn't room to go around. It came up, paused for a second, then seeing a red kayak coming toward it (rather than another alligator), it started to go back under. My reaction was to quit paddling and brace for impact. Whatever happened, I desperately wanted to remain upright, or failing that, scramble up the overgrowth while the alligator chewed on my kayak. Like I said, the alligator was starting to go back under, and his head had just gone under as he nosed over and dove. My bow hit the back of his neck/shoulder, and as he dove, the scutes on his back went bump-bump-bump against my hull. There was one final big bump as he pushed off the bottom of my kayak with his back foot, and then it was over.

"I paddled the rest of the way to the bay, and all the way to Seadrift, with my mouth hanging open."

Alligators normally avoid humans, but encounters have become increasingly more frequent as human and alligator populations continue to grow. Texas has an estimated population of 250,000 to 300,000 alligators; Louisiana has the largest number of alligators with an estimated population of two million. However, Florida has the most fatalities caused by alligators. Of the reported thirty-one fatalities in the United States over the past seventy years, twenty-seven were in Florida, two in South Carolina, one in Georgia, and one in Orange, Texas, in 2015.

Snakes

You have probably heard the adage, "The only good snake is a dead one," and I understand why some people feel this way. Because many harmless snakes have a similar look and color as dangerous ones, it can be difficult to tell the venomous from the non-venomous. So, I certainly agree that it's smart to avoid them. There are several water snakes in the genus *Nerodia* for example, that can easily be mistaken for cottonmouths, and in a quick encounter, only experienced, trained eyes can tell the difference. These nonvenomous snakes will strike when threatened, and they have teeth that can break the skin.

Over the years I have seen a number of snakes on the water, and as a trained biologist, I have noted that most are nonvenomous. However, I have seen cottonmouths as well. I have also heard a number of Safari stories of run-ins with both types of snakes. Fortunately, in most cases, the encounter simply gave the individual a renewed sense of awareness or woke them from a drowsy state.

In 1972 Chuck Truesdale and Jamie Hallmark teamed up to race the Safari. Jamie had completed the race in 1968, but Chuck was a total novice. In fact, Chuck said, "I had never been in a canoe in my life

The western cottonmouth (*Agkistrodon Piscivorous*) is a venomous snake found in the eastern half of Texas. They are sometimes called "water moccasins" and, as the name implies, they are found in or near streams, swamps, and coastal marshes. Adults can reach 5 feet in length but most are 3 to 4 feet long. Young cottonmouths and young copperheads look very much alike. Juveniles are tan with broad, jagged, mahogany crossbands that contain a light brown vertical inner core. Adults turn darker with age and the bands become obscure.

Cottonmouths have a small heat sensitive hole or "pit" in front of each eye. The "pit" is used to locate prey species. Cottonmouths have large retractable fangs that inject hemotoxic venom into their prey. Hemotoxic venom destroys tissue and prevents blood clotting. Their bite can be fatal, and medical treatment should be sought immediately. Courtesy of Texas Parks and Wildlife

and didn't know the bow from the stern." Anyway, on a training run, they came to one of the many logjams, which Chuck hated. He said, "One Saturday as we were portaging a huge logjam I heard what I thought was a 22 shot. I looked around and couldn't see anyone anywhere. Then I looked down and saw that a cottonmouth had struck at me, missed, and had his fangs stuck in my wooden paddle. I managed to chop the snake into four pieces before my shaking knees turned to mush."

Later that year, Chuck and Jamie entered the 1972 Safari, but unfortunately they "hit a wall" midway through the race and dropped out. However, they returned twenty years later and finished in 51 hours and 33 minutes.

In the spring of 2015, Charlie Kouba and his son Coy were determined to complete the race after an unsuccessful attempt the previous year. They were on a practice run along a section of the San Marcos River below Palmetto State Park (mile 60). They had planned to paddle from the park to Gonzales, approximately 26 miles away. They had chosen this stretch of the river because they would likely paddle it at night during the race. As expected, they encountered their first logjam shortly after dark.

They made short work of the first jam and paddled a couple of hours before reaching the second, more formidable one, stopping on the right side of the jam to find the best spot to portage. With straight, muddy banks eight feet tall, tangled with tree roots, they decided that the left bank may be more promising.

After a few maneuvers, which included paddling upstream and getting caught by a tree branch, they reached the left bank, but not before the tree branch knocked their light off the boat and into the San Marcos River. This would undoubtedly make the remainder of their trip much more challenging.

The left bank that was even taller than the right one. Seeing the 22-foot, very steep, muddy bank, exposed rocks, and a tangle of brush and vines, Coy said, "Oh hell no," and they returned to the right bank.

Coy, the bowman, grabbed two sticks and began to stab them, hand over hand, into the slick, muddy banks with the consistency of chocolate pudding.

"As my head crested the top of the bank, my head-lamp made out the distinctive shape of a coiled water moccasin two feet away from my eyeballs. I very gently allowed myself to slowly slide back down the muddy bank into the boat. I told my dad something like, 'No freeking way! Back over to the left bank!'"[1]

During the 2003 Safari, Peter "Fuzzy" Churchman was bitten by a snake somewhere between Gonzales (mile 85) and Hochheim (mile 122). Because Fuzzy Churchman was not certain when he was bitten, his account of the incident is indeed a bit fuzzy (pun

After surviving the encounter with the cottonmouth, Charlie and Coy Kouba finished the 2015 Safari in 95 hours and 43 minutes. (*Left to right*) Tony Kouba (TC), Coy Kouba, and Charlie Kouba. Courtesy of Bob Spain

attempted). Peter said, "I never felt the snake bite me, which led to some confusion later. You would think you would know the instant you were bitten by a snake. In my case, I never saw or felt the bite. It was pieced together after the fact that I had been snake bitten.

"The first possible place it could have bitten me, and where I believe it did—but with no tangible evidence to support the claim—was at one of the small logjams near Gonzales.

"It is my belief that as I was stepping on a log and through trash and sticks, that I was bitten by a water moccasin and didn't think anything of it because you always get a few scrapes and scratches when you are doing that sort of thing."

Peter first started to feel soreness in his ankle near Hochheim (mile 122), but he dismissed it as normal Water Safari aches and pain. "It really started to hurt on the way to Cuero," he said. By the time the team approached the Cuero Dam, the sun had come up and Peter knew he had been bitten when he saw the marks. At that point he received assistance from his team to portage the dam. He felt pain in his ankle, but his support team on the bank had given him a bag of ice to ease the pain and he wanted to continue.

By the time the paddlers reached Cuero 236 (mile 160), there were no more portages, so Peter decided to stay in the boat and keep ice on the ankle. But as they progressed downstream Peter's condition worsened. "I got really bad between loop 175 and the DuPont boat ramp (mile 231)," he said. "I started to hyperventilate and became hysterical." At this point Lee Deviney, who was seated behind Peter, had him blow into a paper bag. I am not sure where they got the bag.

With Peter pretty much out of commission, the team continued to paddle downstream to get help. When they reached DuPont, an ambulance was called and Peter was given oxygen and an IV. While the team went on to finish fifth in 41 hours and 49 minutes, Peter spent three days in the Victoria hospital.

Peter said, "I could not walk for a month without crutches . . . I went to physical therapy and that seemed to help some. It hurt for the first year, especially when I ran. Over the years, it hurts less, but there is internal scarring that bothers me occasionally."

Gar

Over the years, Safari competitors have had numerous encounters with gars. While gars are not aggressive, their large size, armored body, and mouth full of needle-sharp teeth have caused some injuries when they attempt to flee from unsuspecting competitors.

In 1982, Fletcher Anderson and his partner, Gary Lacy, entered the twentieth Texas Water Safari. Both were first timers with little knowledge of what to expect on their way to the finish in Seadrift. On the first day of the race, Fletcher and Gary encountered bad portages with slick clay banks, swam through floating debris filled with spiders, crawled across logjams, and were attacked by swarms of mosquitoes. As the two enjoyed, or endured, their first day on the river, nightfall approached.

According to Fletcher Anderson, "I switched on my headlamp. Instantly a cloud of flying insects honed in on it, blocking my vision.

"'I can see by your light that this must be y'all's first safari,' said the team that had passed us at the hidden portage.

"Finally, we came to a bit of open water, where we could really paddle! With long easy strokes we began eating up the miles—actually beginning to close the two-hour gap between us and the lead boats.

Four species of gar are found in Texas waters: the shortnose, longnose, spotted, and alligator gar. All four species are torpedo shaped with pointed noses. They are primitive fish that are sometimes called "living fossils." All gar have ganoid scales that are bone-like and are covered with an enamel-like substance. The scales provide excellent protection from other predators. The alligator gar (*Atractosteus spatula*) is the largest gar and can reach 10 feet and weigh 300 pounds. Gars are predators that eat fish or waterfowl and mammals that venture into the water.

Gar are found in freshwater streams, estuaries, and bay waters in the southern United States and Mexico. Gar occur in both the San Marcos and Guadalupe Rivers. They are sometimes referred to as "trash fish," but they are eaten by some anglers. Gar are not aggressive to humans. Courtesy of Texas Parks and Wildlife

(At least some spectators at the confluence told us so.) But suddenly with a loud bang the whole boat jumped to one side and a huge fish nearly my own size landed smack in my lap, his tail hanging over the front of the cockpit while his long, pointed snout lay on my stomach. Before I could react, he flipped over, smacked me in the face, knocked my paddle out of my hand, and was gone."[2]

While there were no injuries from the gar, Fletcher and Gary in boat #12 eventually dropped out midway through the race—though not before they began to see imaginary trees in the river and rapids that did not exist.

On the fourth day of the 1996 Safari, canoe #144 was making its way down the river from Victoria.

With only 16 hours until the 100-hour cutoff, the team of three sisters, Marvine and Jackie Cole and Kaki Burruss, were making good time and working well together in pursuit of the Seadrift finish line.

According to Marvine Cole's account of what happened next, "We edged around an inside turn. I was confident that any stumps would have been pushed to the outside, and we were safe to travel the inside. The water seemed deep enough. Then it struck. Like a fist of fire, I was struck in my right rib cage. Instantly I was in the water. I knew I was hurt. And I knew what had done it."

"All I could think of was getting back in the boat. I cried, 'Get me in the boat. Get me in the boat.' Somehow I crawled into the boat, probably with Jackie and

Kaki's help. I could hardly breathe. Jackie and Kaki were both standing in the water at my side, me huddled on my side in the bottom of the boat. I was sure I was injured, but then as I began to get my breath, I thought maybe I wasn't hurt, just stunned. Wrong!

"Our dreams had been dashed—not by our inability, or lack of persistence, or lack of will—but by a fish. Who would believe a tall Texas tale like that?"

Well, it's true, a gar broke Marvine Cole's ribs. The good news is, her sisters took good care of her and her ribs healed. In 1997 the threesome returned and finished the race in 89 hours and 58 minutes.

Coincidentally, in a similar occurrence earlier that morning, another gar jumped into the canoe with Novice paddlers Kelly Covington and Brian Vooletich. Covington reportedly jumped on top of the gar. No injuries were reported, but Covington lost a shoe and hat while recovering Vooletich's headlamp, which had been knocked off in the melee.[3]

In the 2018 race, Chris Stevenson, a six-time Safari finisher, was paddling with four other veterans: Debbie Richardson, Jeff Wueste, R. D. Kissling, and Bobby Smart. They had chosen boat #59, which (if they finished) would be the total number of finishes for the entire team.

On Monday morning, the third day of the race, Chris was not feeling well. He was concerned that he may go downhill and did not want to let the team down. Once he told them his situation, they came to the rescue with candy, caffeine drinks, and fruit to eat and drink.

A little while later, somewhere below 3 O'clock Cut, the team stopped to survey their course. Here is Chris's account of what happened next: "The water was lower than it had been, so things looked different than when we'd been there in training. There were a couple of moments when we were at a stop and looking around to make sure we were on the right track.

During one of those stops, I was holding my paddle and looking to my left when I heard a splash and saw light reflect off something coming up out of the water real fast. Something thudded hard against my chest. At that moment I thought for sure that big momma gator had been lying in wait and had come up out of the water to drag me in. I screamed and threw my paddle and started beating at the thing that was now attached to my chest. I pretty quickly realized that it was a gar. Its teeth were lodged in my shirt and my upper left pectoral. Just as fast as it started, the gar thrashed loose (or I slapped it free) and it disappeared into the water. I turned on my headlamp to survey the damage. At the same time everyone in the boat was shouting, 'What was that?' 'Was it a gar?!' 'Did Chris just get bit by a gar?' I lifted my shirt, which had a few small tears in it, and there were several small cuts in my skin that were bleeding. It wasn't bad, so I didn't

Chris Stevenson, with microphone, tells the story of his encounter with an alligator gar. He is holding a driftwood/gar skull trophy presented to him by his team members: R. D. Kissing and Debbie Richardson (standing behind Chris) and Jeff Wueste and Bobby Smart (not shown). The team finished the 2018 Safari in 53 hours and 19 minutes. Courtesy of Ashley Landis

even treat it. I asked the guys to retrieve my paddle from the water and told them (somewhat proudly), 'Yep, it was a gar and yes, it bit me.'"

After the encounter, Chris perked up some and the team completed the race in 53 hours and 19 minutes—a respectable tenth place overall. Chris also said, "Everyone on the team just thought it was the coolest thing that I had been bitten by a gar, which tells you how depraved this Safari crowd is."

Stingrays

On June 10, the third day of the 1985 Safari, Rocky Harber crossed the finish line at 10:13 p.m. in an aluminum canoe. To the surprise of all the spectators, Rocky finished the race solo. Earlier that evening, Rocky and his partner, Bill, had a mishap in the bay that sent Bill to the hospital.

Rocky said they were having a tough time in the high winds and waves, and to make things worse, Bill, while hallucinating, lost his balance and capsized the canoe. With Bill partially tangled in the canoe cover, Rocky heard a scream that sounded like "I'm hit, I'm hit!" Given Bill's state of mind, Rocky thought that Bill might be having a flashback from his military days.

With water up to his neck, Rocky struggled to get Bill back in the boat. Once he rolled Bill over into the canoe, he could see blood on Bill's ankle and a laceration. Unable to reenter the canoe, Rocky began to swim and wade in the neck-deep water. With no way to paddle the canoe and with the wind and waves crashing against the sides, Rocky, Bill, and the canoe were pushed toward the shore.

Meanwhile, Mike Riley and his partner, Mike Shively, had finished the race in the USCA C-2 Class, and Mike Riley, still on an adrenaline high, decided to drive along the seawall and watch for canoes crossing the bay. After driving a short distance, Mike saw the aluminum canoe and recognized Rocky Harber. Unsure of the severity of Bill's injury and unable to fight the incoming waves with Bill lying in the canoe, Rocky asked Mike to help him get Bill out of the canoe and take him to the hospital. Mike agreed.

A few hours later, Rocky finished, and, knowing that his partner was safe in a hospital bed, he decided to get a few hours of well-earned sleep. The next day Rocky learned that Bill injured his ankle when he stepped on a stingray on the bay bottom. Thinking back on the incident, he remembered that Bill had yelled something that sounded like "I'm hit." What he must have said was "I'm bit." After one night in the hospital, a good dose of antivenom serum, and an IV or two, Bill returned to Seadrift on Tuesday and was able to attend the Texas Water Safari Awards Banquet.

11

Back of the Pack

Most years, the winning team finishes the Safari in under forty-five hours. Those at the back of the pack are less than half way down the course when the leaders finish. Those near the front are able to paddle straight through without sleeping, but spending more time on the course, up to the 100-hour time limit, means those near the back have to sleep several times during the race or else face serious sleep deprivation.

Debbie Sackett (stern) and wife Tina (bow) in 2016. They finished seventy-first and were the third women's team in a time of 78 hours and 2 minutes. Courtesy of Ashley Landis

In many cases, the teams near the back do not make it to the finish line within the time limit. They'll sometimes joke about "getting their money's worth," as compared to the winning teams.

Debbie Sackett had her first taste of the Safari in 1992 when she was team captain for Jeff Wueste and Dale Tilson. Two years later she jumped into the fray and raced in the Women's Tandem Class with Emily "Charlie" Allen. That year they finished thirty-third—in last place—with a time of 98 hours and 16 minutes. Looking back, Debbie said, "I don't care at all about being in the back of the pack. I think finishing in and of itself is a significant accomplishment. The first one was so hard and generally horrible, I swore I would never do it again."

However, like a number of other first timers, she returned for a second try. At the urging of her wife, Tina, Debbie raced again twenty-two years later. This time she and Tina finished in 78 hours and 2 minutes,

cutting twenty hours off her first finish. Two years later in 2018, the pair finished a second time in the Standard Class.

Jason Cade came to Texas from Missouri in 2001. When he met his realtor in San Marcos at Grins Restaurant, he noticed a number of pictures on the walls of the San Marcos River and the Texas Water Safari. Having paddled recreationally in Missouri, he was immediately interested in the race. Two years later, he and a partner from work raced the Safari. Determined to get plenty of sleep, they brought along tents and sleeping bags and slept every night. Like many first-time racers, they bit the bullet, so to speak, and dropped out near Thomaston (mile 177) when they pinned their canoe.

In 2011 Jason began to paddle with a new partner, C. J. Hall, who grew up in Seadrift and had followed the Safari for years. On more than one occasion he had rescued racers stranded in the bay in his

Jason Cade at the low-water bridge in Palmetto State Park. Jason finished last in the 2012 Safari, and only four years later in an impressive performance, he won the 2016 Safari on a six-man team. Courtesy of Ashley Landis

powerboat. While a shoulder problem prevented C. J. from racing in 2011, the pair entered the 2012 Safari.

That year, a record 135 teams started the fiftieth anniversary race, and ninety-four finished, also a record at that time. Jason and C. J. finished last in 99 hours and 27 minutes. While C. J. has not raced since, it was certainly not the last time for Jason: he was just getting started.

In 2014 he raced solo and improved his time to 68 hours and 8 minutes, and in 2015 he finished third overall in 39 hours and 33 minutes with Phil Bowden and Chris Champion. Then, in an amazing effort, in 2016 he finished first overall in 31 hours and 33 minutes with Fred, Kyle, and Logan Mynar, Tommy Yonley, and Phil Bowden. Only four years after finishing last, he had made a remarkable improvement and finished at the top of the field. Jason says, "That year with C. J. was only twice as long as some of my faster finishes, but it easily has three times the memories. It was a good year to finish last. We pulled into Seadrift with a pavilion full of spectators. The awards banquet was held on Wednesday that year because it was the fiftieth Safari." Jason finished his seventh Safari in 2019.

On Wednesday, June 18, 2018, at the fifty-sixth Safari, with time running out, officials, contestants, team captains, family members, and well-wishers gathered at the finish line, waiting for the last competitor. Doug Rhude in boat number #62 had just finished at 10:21 a.m. in 97 hours and 21 minutes, and the last competitor, Norm Thomas, was still out on the course. While I could see several small structures in the distant bay, it was not possible to determine if they were small motor boats, buoys, or Norm. With time running out, someone with binoculars confirmed that the small dot in the distant bay was a canoe. With a mile or more of water between Norm and the finish line, the tension grew. As Norm inched

his way home, I could clearly see that he was walking through the shallow water with his canoe in tow. While some well-wishers clapped and cheered, others walked out along the sea wall to accompany him in.

As he walked the last fifty yards or so to the finish line, I could hear that he was singing a tune. As he took the last few steps to the finish, I was able to make out the familiar hymn, "How Great Thou Art." It was such a joy to see that big smile on his face as he crossed the line. At 11:20 a.m. Norm Thomas in boat #65 finished the fifty-sixth Texas Water Safari in last place, marking his tenth finish, coming forty years after his first Safari race. He has since been inducted into the Texas Water Safari Hall of Fame.

In 1969, Owen West finished his first Texas Water Safari in last place at 125 hours and 56 minutes. Over the next fifty years Owen returned to San Marcos every year and registered for the race. While his dedication is undeniable, he has often struggled to finish. While he finished the first twenty Safaris in a row, over the next thirty-two years he finished only eight times, did not finish (DNF) nineteen times, and failed to start the race five times. During the fifty-two-year period he has the unofficial record of finishing last five times.

In 2019 Owen finished his twenty-eighth Safari in 58 hours and 13 minutes in a four-person team. In doing so, he set a new record of being the oldest competitor to complete the race at eighty-one years and ten months. While finishing at his age is certainly a remarkable accomplishment, I am sure Owen would give a great deal of credit to his partners: Mark Simmons, Chad Keeth, and Linden Welsch.

While Mark Simmons was pleased to have been a part of the team that helped Owen set his record, the race was special to Mark for another reason. Mark carried his brother Mike's ashes in the canoe during the race. Mike was a five-time Safari finisher who

Norm Thomas in 2018. He finished eighty-third overall in last place in 98 hours and 20 minutes. It was his tenth finish, and he became a member of the Texas Water Safari Hall of Fame in 2019. Courtesy of Ashley Landis

Owen West portaging Palmetto low water bridge. He completed his first TWS in 1969. Fifty years later he completed his twenty-eighth TWS and became the oldest finisher at eighty-one years and ten months of age. Courtesy of Ashley Landis

passed away in 2017. In Mike's memory, Mark bid his brother farewell by scattering his brother's ashes at every checkpoint.

When I asked Owen how difficult the 2019 race was, he admitted that he had some problems with his left shoulder and could not paddle on his left side for much of the race. Prior to the race, a doctor had told Owen, "There is good news and bad news. The good news is, I won't operate, and the bad news is, your rotator cuff is shot." Owen would not be deterred and raced anyway.

Owen admitted that he did not paddle during the latter part of the race. In fact, at the insistence of Mark Simmons, Owen lay in the bottom of the boat from the Swinging Bridge / Bloomington Checkpoint to somewhere near the finish. Owen said he felt certain that their canoe slowed down when he stopped paddling. He feared that a number of boats passed them while he lay in the bottom of the canoe.

Given Owen's age and bad shoulder, hanging up his paddle might be a wise thing to do. However, when asked if he had paddled his last Safari, Owen's immediate answer was "NO." At this writing, he is making plans to paddle with his grandsons, Eric and Alex. He said his goal is thirty finishes.

Team #220 portaging Luling Dam in 2019. Team members (*left to right*): Linden Welsch, Chad Keeth, Owen West, and Mark Simmons. They finished the Safari in sixtieth place in 58 hours and 13 minutes. Courtesy of Ashley Landis

PART FOUR
The Rest Is History

At some point during the race, you lose all your mind, body, and spirit,
and somehow, from something within, you keep paddling. Because of that, this
has become more than a race to me. It's an annual cleansing of the mind, body,
and spirit. It depends on the individual, which one gets the cleaning.

—*Matt Sandel, seven-time Texas Water Safari finisher*

12

The Early Years

1964–1972

1964

Frank Brown moved to Waco following the first Texas Water Safari, and San Marcos local Tom Webb took his place as chairman for the second annual race. Unlike the 1963 race, when competitors started in waves, this year all forty boats started together.

The reputation of the Texas Water Safari had spread throughout the paddling community and received national attention in major magazines and newspapers, drawing a number of out-of-state competitors. With this increased notoriety, the array of prizes had grown substantially, now including a moose- and bear-hunting trip to Alaska, two $50 saving bonds from San Marcos Bank, a pickup "sleeper" camper, weekend lodging in Red River, New Mexico, twenty round trip tickets on the Chihuahua Al Pacifico Railroad in Mexico, weekend lodging at an Ingleside marina, a Zebco fishing reel, a rotisserie, three Grumman canoe trophies, the coveted Argosy Adventure Trophy, and $1750.[1]

Leading the field of out-of-state contenders were Frank Havens, a four-time Olympian (1948, 1952, 1956, and 1960) and his partner John Ruckers, a

Forty Safari boats start the 1964 TWS. Competitors in canoe #142 are Robert C. "Bobby" Smith, Willye Waterman, and husband W. J. They finished in 172 hours and 42 minutes. Mrs. Waterman became the first woman to complete the TWS. Courtesy of San Marcos Dailey Record

pentathlete. Professional racers from Michigan also entered the race, including Michigan Canoe Racers Association president Leroy Widing, his partner Ed Adams, and his brother Al Widing with partner Bob Gillings. International kayak champion Ron Bohlender also entered the race, and a four-man

Texas team including the 1963 winners James Jones and Lynn Maughmer and new partners Fred Hurd Jr. and Archie Clark were also vying for the top spot.

Every Safari features unexpected mishaps, and this one was no exception. Near Hochheim, Captain R. Westfall and Captain B. L. Vonkleist in boat #121 lost time when they were delayed by the Texas Liquor Control Board. State officials stopped them because they had a Pearl Beer sign on their canoe in recognition of their sponsors. Apparently, that was against the law. When they were stopped, they were told that they must remove the sign from their boat or drop out of the race. With the blessing of the state Liquor Control Board officers, they painted over the sign and were allowed to continue.

Approximately 5 miles from the mouth of the Guadalupe River, Widing and Gillings in boat #136 were attempting to portage their canoe over some debris in the river. Exhausted and sleep deprived, the two had begun to see apparitions and were unconcerned by an image in the shadows until they heard a metallic "click" that sounded like the breech of a shotgun closing. They made out a man standing in the shadows and heard the word *alto*. While neither of the racers understood Spanish, they did understand that the "click" of the shotgun meant "stop." It turned out someone had been stealing fish from the man's lines, and he had mistaken the Michiganders for the culprits. After inspecting their boat, the man held his growling dogs while the two moved on downriver.[2]

On that same night, upriver near Cuero, Pete McDaniel dropped out of the race and started hitchhiking. He had no money or identification and needed a shave. When he got as far as Shiner, Texas, he found a grocery store and peered innocently through the store window. A passing sheriff patrolling the area saw him and arrested him for vagrancy. Back at the sheriff's office, he was given a chance to make a phone call. Once the sheriff learned his story, he took McDaniel to the local Shiner Brewery where he feasted on food and all the beer he could drink, courtesy of the sheriff.[3]

On the last day of the race, Widing and Gillings, who were leading in boat #136, launched their boat at dawn and covered the last coastal segment in a little over two hours. In fact, they were so fast that the greeting party was not expecting them until noon. On the bank were amphibious cars that were supposed to motor out to meet the winners, but instead, the weary Michiganders jumped in the cars and were escorted out to meet the other boats. They had completed the race in 80 hours and 27 minutes.[4] Of the thirteen teams that finished the course in the allotted time, last but not least was the first woman to finish the Safari. Willye Waterman finished with her husband, W. J., and partner R. C. Smith in 172 hours and 42 minutes. In celebration of the race, the first Miss Texas Water Safari Beauty Contest was held, won that year by Carol Lou Holt, a student at Southwest Texas State University.

The 1964 Safari received national attention in major newspapers and even on TV. One of the winners, Bob Gillings, was featured on the TV show *To Tell the Truth*.

1965

In 1965, the Freeport-Brazosport Chamber of Commerce donated $1,500 to the Safari and partnered with the San Marcos Chamber of Commerce to host the race. In exchange for their support, the San Marcos chamber changed the Safari course. Instead of following the original route to Corpus Christi, the race would turn north from Seadrift and end in Freeport, adding approximately 32 miles to the coastal segment. While the new course would be longer, the prevailing winds would favor the competitors.[5] All competitors would follow the same rules as in the past, with drinking water available in the coastal segments.

Returning was last year's winner Al Widing. Al's younger brother, Patrick, would also be racing with him. Ed Adams also returned for a second year, and Canadian canoe champ Gib McEachern would race with him. All the other teams were from Texas.

Swift water and other obstacles knocked out twelve boats early in the race. Race officials also stopped competitors at the mouth of the Guadalupe River when a raging thunderstorm with fifty-five-mile-per-hour winds blew in.[6]

It came as no surprise when the Michigan team of Widing and Widing took the early lead and held off all competitors from start to finish. The steady pace and methodical paddle strokes of the Widing brothers were too much for the other competitors. The only team to even come close were the other out-of-staters Adams and McEachern. For the second consecutive

1965 TWS winners Al Widing and Pat Widing accept $1,500 check. Standing (*left to right*) David Danheim, president of the Brazosport Chamber of Commerce, Al Widing, Evelyn Stephens, Miss Freeport, and Pat Widing. Courtesy of San Marcos Daily Record

year, Al Widing, with the help of his brother, Patrick, won the World's Toughest Canoe Race—this time in 77 hours and 16 minutes. Adams and McEachren in boat #119 finished 39 minutes back, and two Texans from Seadrift, Robert "Froggie" Sanders Jr. and Charles Hall, came in third. Again, the race had taken its toll, as only ten of the original thirty-one teams were able to finish.[7]

Following the race, Al and Pat Widing were in a serious car wreck in Oklahoma while on their way back to Michigan. Pat broke his back but was able to return in 1967 to race again with his brother.

1966

As the 1966 race date approached, San Marcos Mayor Ellis Serur proclaimed April 24–30 "Texas Water Safari Week."[8] One of the events leading up to the race was the Miss Texas Water Safari Beauty Contest, which was won by Pam Belson, marking the second time a Southwest Texas State University student had won the contest.

Only fifteen boats were entered in the race, none of which were previous winners. All entrants were Texans except for Michael Wolf from Albuquerque, New Mexico. Although teams would not have to face the northern paddlers that had dominated the race for the past two years, they would have to face high river flows that were near flood stage and gale force winds on the coast, making it one of the toughest Safaris in history.[9]

Ten boats were knocked out of the race before reaching the coastal leg. Three of the remaining five boats got lost in the coastal waters and were disqualified for leaving the course and paddling in the Intracoastal Canal. Only boat #123 paddled by Randall Thompson and Robert McGarraugh III and boat #103 paddled by Jay and Harold Bludworth were able to continue on. About 5 miles from Port O'Connor, boat #123 dropped out when McGarraugh had to be hospitalized for exhaustion and hypothermia. That left only team #103, and if they could complete the course, they would be the winners.

Unfortunately, winds were so strong in the bay that the Gulf Coast Emergency Rescue Squadron from Freeport returned their boats to land and were not able to provide support for the last segment of the race. At that point, race chairman Tom Webb decided to give the Bludworth brothers in boat #103 a shuttle by truck to the next checkpoint. While some would argue this was against the rules, Tom Webb said that he would have done it for any of the competitors, this year or in future years, if dangerous conditions prevailed.

On Saturday, May 7, Jay and Harold Bludworth rowed into Freeport, winning the fourth Texas Water Safari. They reached Seadrift in 51 hours and 36 minutes, but a finishing time at Freeport was not recorded. It is presumed that the finishing time was not recorded due to the assistance they received traveling by truck from one checkpoint to the next. Because the Bludworths were the only finishers, they received all the money and prizes. One new prize worth noting was a whitewater raft trip on the Colorado River through the Grand Canyon. The Bludworths were the first team to finish the race in a classic rowing rig, and for the next fourteen years, rowing boats would dominate the field, winning the race ten times.

1967

Lawrence Hagan and Tom Buckner cochaired the 1967 Safari, and several changes were made to the race. Instead of an April start, the race would he held in June. That would give teachers and students a chance to compete. Competitors would now have four days to reach Seadrift instead of five, and there would be classes for "custom made boats" and "store bought" boats. Also, a preliminary canoe race from Cuero to Victoria would be held in May to promote the Safari.

Competitors included last year's winners Jay and Harold Bludworth and Al and Pat Widing, the pro marathon paddlers who had won in 1965. Also returning were Robert "Froggie" Sanders Jr. and Charles Hall, who led the 1966 race but broke their boat in half before reaching the coast. First-time entries included state champions Ben Nolan and Bob

Local students from the San Marcos High School and Southwest Texas State University holding the competitors' boats in place at the start of the 1967 Texas Water Safari. Courtesy of San Marcos Daily Record

Jay (*center*) and Harold (*right*) Bludworth, winners of the 1967 TWS, receiving the Argosy Adventure Trophy from Marilyn Evans, Miss Texas Water Safari. Courtesy of San Marcos Daily Record

Narramore from the Canoe Association of Texas and Tom Goynes and his brother James and Richard Page in a three-man boat. During the next fifty years, Tom would become one of the best-known Safari competitors and an advocate for the conservation of the San Marcos River.

On Saturday, June 17, 1967, forty boats lined up accompanied by a cadre of "Miss Texas Water Safari" pageant contestants that held the boats at the starting line to keep them from floating downstream. At approximately 9:00 a.m. the competitors thrashed through the water in Spring Lake.[10] Over the next three days, low flows, logjams, and other impediments prevented all but six teams from reaching the

Seadrift checkpoint. The Bludworths had taken the lead and were nine hours faster than the next competitors, Robert "Froggie" Sanders Jr. and Charles Hall. For a second consecutive year, high winds and small craft warnings convinced the officials to change the course. All six remaining teams were transported 10 miles on land and reentered the water en route to Port O'Connor.[11]

Despite facing strong winds and waves, all six teams finished the race. While finishing times were not recorded, Jay and Harold Bludworth in boat #103 finished first for the second year in a row. One of the prizes given to the overall winner was half of the airfare and complimentary accommodations in Barcelona, Spain, to race the famous El Descenso del Sella, one of the largest and oldest kayak races in the world.

1968

The race course was changed again in 1968. Instead of finishing in Freeport, competitors would head to Port O'Connor and then turned northwest to the finish at Port Lavaca. Prior to the race, towns along the course held preliminary canoe races to promote the Safari, and the city of San Marcos hosted a number of activities. A parade complete with floats, local politicians, drill teams, fire trucks, and Miss Texas Water Safari contestants passed through the streets. Miss Texas Water Safari contestants also competed in a talent show and swimsuit competition, and a Texas Water Safari Ball was held the week before the race with Astronaut James Lovell, Congressman Jake Pickle, and other dignitaries in attendance.

Unfortunately, the festivities were dampened by the deaths of Richard Page and Paul Beyer two weeks before the race. The two were entered in the race but lost their lives when lightning struck a light pole that fell in the water where they were wading and elec- trocuted them. The two young men were childhood friends of Tom and Jim Goynes, and in fact, Richard Page had raced with Tom Goynes the previous year. As a tribute, a boat with their number was displayed at the starting line, and boat #117 was retired. The race also paid homage to Lynn Maughmer, the 1963 winner who lost his life to cancer.

While no returning winners competed in the sixth Texas Water Safari, Froggie Sanders Jr., who had finished second the previous year, returned with new partner Norman "Buttons" Morgan. After winning

Robert "Froggie" Sanders Jr. (*left*), Joy Simmang, holding Argosy Adventure Trophy (*center*) and Norman "Buttons" Morgan (*right*). Sanders and Morgan won the 1968 Texas Water Safari. Courtesy of San Marcos Daily Record

two years in a row, the Bludworth brothers were sitting this one out. However, Johnny Bludworth, Jay's son, had borrowed his father's rowboat and entered with partner James Patton. It looked as though the race might be a battle between the two rowing boats.

The Froggie Sanders / Buttons Morgan boat, #106, was the first to reach the Seadrift checkpoint, in 41 hours and 12 minutes, a new record. Seven hours and five minutes later, they paddled into Port Lavaca to the cheers of a large crowd of well-wishers. The finishing time of 48 hours and 17 minutes was over five hours faster than the second-place team of Bludworth and Patton. Higher-than-usual flows seemed to have helped the rowing boats, which need more water to move their long oars down the river.

Also worth noting is that Albert Barth in boat #132 became the first solo finisher, with a finishing time of 120 hours and 3 minutes, and Tom Goynes, who finished with his brother Pat, set a record as the youngest finisher at seventeen years, six months, and one day old.

1969

In preparation for the 1969 Safari, both Port Lavaca and San Marcos planned numerous activities leading up to the race. Again, a parade was held in San Marcos, and a carnival-like festival was planned in Port Lavaca to greet the finishers, complete with vendor booths, a go-cart race, and the Miss Texas Water Safari Beauty Pageant. Towns along the Safari route again planned preliminary canoe races leading up to the race. While various teams traded wins, no team dominated. At the start of the Safari, last year's winners, Sanders and Morgan, were the clear front-runners.

A newly manufactured racing canoe called the Sawyer Saber was introduced this year. At 24 feet long and 30 inches wide, the canoe would become the favorite of many racers in the coming years. A new Safari rule also allowed "team captains" for the first time. Team captains were land based and were responsible for tracking the progress of their team throughout the race. Their role would change over the years, with team captains eventually being allowed to provide assistance to competitors during the race.

On Saturday, June 14, at 8:30 a.m., twenty-seven teams lined up for the seventh Texas Water Safari. Fourteen boats reached the finish line, but Buttons Morgan and Froggie Sanders in boat #106 took an early lead and held it all the way to Seadrift. For the second year, the team of two won the race, this time in 49 hours and 2 minutes. Following closely behind were Charlie Hall and Lee Van Sickle, finishing in 53 hours and 3 minutes. Fourteen boats finished that year.

Forty-nine years after he last won the Safari, I had an opportunity to visit with Buttons Morgan at his home in Seadrift—along with Joy and a small group of Safari Board members and their spouses. Morgan talked about that year's race like it was yesterday. The more questions we asked, the more his eyes seemed to light up.

When we entered the house it was immediately apparent that the Safari had been a major event in his life. The pictures on the walls had scenes of the coast, and he even had part of an old Texas Water Safari trophy in his living area. After a short visit indoors, he invited us out back to his outdoor bar, which had a canopy over the top, a concrete floor, and a few easy chairs. The furnishings were modest and the only pictures I saw were old Water Safari photos. It was evident how much the Texas Water Safari meant to him.

1970

The field looked wide open for the 1970 Safari since no past winners were entered. However, competitors would have to contend with Claude Coursol and Luc Robillard, arguably two of the best pro paddlers in Canada. The previous year the pair had won La Classique International Canoe Race, the most competitive canoe race in Canada.

On June 13, 1970, forty-eight Texans, two Floridians, three paddlers from Louisiana, and the two Canadians lined up for the eighth annual race. While river flows were normal, the logjams were the worst ever, particularly between San Marcos and Luling.[12] These jams took their toll on the field, but to the amazement of the spectators and competitors, the Canadians, who were unfamiliar with the course, held the lead all the way down the rivers. Then tragedy struck. Once the two reached the saltwater barrier upstream of Tivoli, they thought they had reached the Gulf of Mexico and were lost. Discouraged, they paddled back upstream hoping to see more competitors. After a couple of hours, the two gave up and paddled back to the saltwater barrier and fell asleep. Little did they know, they were so far ahead of the pack that the other teams were still upriver. Quietly, three teams paddled by the sleeping competitors. After learning their fate from concerned officials, they broke down in tears and never finished the race.[13]

Robert "Bob" Mitchell and John Evans in boat #163 earned their first overall win with a time of 56 hours and 31 minutes. Less than 2 hours back were Tom Goynes and Mike Wooley, finishing in 58 hours and 6 minutes. Don Walls and Owen West finished in tenth place and decided to celebrate by burning their bruised and battered boat at the finish line. The finishers were greeted by 1963 winner Jimmy Jones and newly crowned Miss Texas Water Safari Suzie

Suzie Howard, Miss Texas Water Safari, presenting the Argosy Adventure Trophy to Robert "Bob" Mitchell (*left*) and John Evans (*right*), the 1970 winners. Courtesy of San Marcos Daily Record

Howard, who were on hand to award the Argosy Adventure Trophy. This was the last year the race ended in Port Lavaca.

1971

In 1971, the Safari course changed again, with the finish line moving to Seadrift, and it has remained the same until the present day. The course was publicized as being 416 miles but is actually about 260 miles. No one is sure who did the math. All teams would now have to finish in five days instead of nine, and there would be three classes: rowing, paddling, and amateur.[14] The amateurs would receive no money and would start behind the other competitors. Winners of the competitive classes would receive $2,000 and a complimentary raft trip down the Colorado River.

Returning for a second year, Canadian racer Luc Robillard brought new partner and fellow Canadian Denis Theberge. Also returning was Tom Goynes, who finished second the previous year, and his new partner Pat Oxsheer. Two pro paddlers from

After finishing the 1970 Texas Water Safari, Don Walls (*left*) and Owen West (*right*) burned their canoe. Courtesy of San Marcos Daily Record

Michigan, Jerry Kellogg and Jack Kolka, were also in the mix.

That year the race started on Tuesday afternoon and would end on Saturday, June 12. On the first day, Owen West and Sonny Calloway had a major wreck that knocked the bow off their boat. While that would discourage most competitors, the courageous team simply turned their boat around, taped it up, and paddled on. From the get-go, the Canadians and the Michiganders traded the lead all the way to Hochheim, at which point the Michigan pair dropped out due to exhaustion.

Just when it looked like Luc Robillard would redeem himself after the disappointing race of the previous year, he and his partner capsized below Victoria and lost a couple of hours. The mishap was just enough to give Goynes and Oxsheer a break. Ready for a win, the two Texans double-bladed boat #123 past the northerners. To add insult to more frustration, the Canadians got lost in San Antonio Bay, hitched a ride from a local landowner, and eventually paddled through the Intracoastal Canal to Seadrift only to be disqualified. Goynes and Oxsheer went on to win the race in 57 hours and 38 minutes, more than 9 hours faster than Mike Wooley and Gary Knight in rowboat #114. Only five other teams finished that year.

1972

A strong contingent of forty-four boats, including thirteen in the Amateur Class, entered the 1972 Safari. Darrell Royal, legendary football coach of the University of Texas, was the official starter of the race. Returning were the previous year's winning team of Tom Goynes and Pat Oxsheer, and to no one's surprise, they won again in a record time of 43 hours and

Tom Goynes and Pat Oxsheer carry boat #123 past boat #120 (Morris Mason and Frank Land) at Luling Dam. Tom and Pat were the eventual 1972 winners in 43 hours and 58 minutes. Courtesy of San Marcos Daily Record

55 minutes. Tim Janak and Tom Sofka set a record of 48 hours and 57 minutes in the newly created USCA Amateur Class. Twenty-one boats completed the race, which was the largest number of finishers in its nine-year history.

13

Rowing Boats Are Coming

1973–1982

1973

In 1973, the rowing boats came back with a vengeance. Shut out the past two years by paddlers Tom Goynes and Pat Oxsheer, the rowing boats finished in the top three spots. In a new record time of 43 hours and 17 minutes, Howard Gore and Gary Knight claimed the top place and $1,400. Robert Chatham and Louis "Butch" Hodges finished second for $800, and Richard "Ricky" Carter and Lloyd "Bucky" Chatham claimed third place and $500. This made the seventh time in the eleven-year history of the Safari that a rowing boat had won the race. Only twelve of the thirty-five boats that started the race finished.

1974

In 1974 race chairman Lawrence Hagan had a heart attack and was hospitalized. When it appeared that the Safari would be canceled, Tom Goynes, the 1971 and 1972 winner, volunteered to host an alternate canoe race that would be called the Texas Canoe

Marathon to Corpus Christi. It would commemorate the original, grueling Safari course that finished in Corpus Christi. Only 17-foot aluminum canoes would be allowed and all competitors would use paddles and/or sails.

However, at the eleventh hour, Mike Wooley volunteered to chair the Texas Water Safari. Both races started on June 8, and to avoid any interference between the two, the Safari would start two hours before the Texas Canoe Marathon to Corpus Christi. Unfortunately, the Safari was stopped that year at the Highway 35 bridge near Tivoli due to 44-knot winds and 3- to 6-foot seas. Since Howard Gore and Michael Woolley were in the lead when the race was stopped, they were designated the winners in 46 hours and 46 minutes. This made the seventh time in a dozen years that a rowing boat finished first.

Meanwhile, farther down the coast the Texas Canoe Marathon to Corpus Christi continued on all the way to the finish. Verlen Kruger and Steve Landick handily won the race in 70 hours. Only eight of the original eighteen teams that started the race finished in Corpus Christi.

Eight of the eighteen aluminum canoes that raced the Texas Canoe Marathon to Corpus Christi. This race and the 1974 TWS were held concurrently. Courtesy of San Marcos Daily Record

1975

Good spring rains prior to the 1975 Safari pushed paddlers down the river in record times. On the first day of the race, Jerry Cochran and Tom Goynes set a blistering pace and led the field through Nursery.

Verlen Kruger and Steve Landick (not shown) won the Texas Canoe Marathon to Corpus Christi in 70 hours. Known for his ultramarathon expeditions, Kruger paddled over 100,000 miles in his lifetime, more than any other person, according to the Guinness Book of World Records. Courtesy of San Marcos Daily Record

Then somewhere before Victoria, Mike Wooley and John Nabors took the lead and held it all the way to Seadrift. At 11:05 Sunday night, Nabors and Wooley finished in 38 hours 5 minutes, a new Safari record. The rowing team averaged an amazing 6.83 miles per hour.

For the first time since 1964, a woman, actually two women—Carol Kiernan and Kathie Bellman—raced in the United States Canoe Association Tandem Canoe (USCA C-2) Class. Carol Kiernan and her husband, Jim, were thirteenth overall followed by Kathie Bellman and Peter Derrick in sixteenth place.

Peter and Kathie would later marry, and both became Texas Water Safari Hall of Fame members in 2012. A new record in the USCA C-2 Class of 42 hours and 42 minutes was set by Dennis Borowicz and Johnnie McKee. Pat Petrisky, a future Hall of Famer, and Jim Trimble set a record in the newly created 17-foot Aluminum Canoe Class in 47 hours and 32 minutes. Pat once told a funny story that goes like this: "So, when we were lost above Dupont and kept seeing the same double trunked tree leaning downstream, I suggested that Jim take off his underwear and tie it on the tree so we would know if we were paddling in circles. Well, Jim put his paddle across his lap, turned to me and said 'If you want underwear on the tree … use your own!!!!!!!!" Pat said that was the only time Jim stopped paddling during the race.

Twenty-nine boats started, but only eighteen finished.

1976

With high river flows again in 1976, the conditions were set for a competitive race between the rowing boats. Returning was last year's race winner, Mike Wooley, with a new race partner, Howard Gore, who had won in 1973 and '74. Other hopefuls for an overall win were Louis "Butch" Hodges and Robert Chatham, who had both finished second overall in the past. Jerry Cochran and Tom Goynes, who finished third the past year in a canoe, were back again to challenge the rowers all the way to Seadrift.

Chatham and Hodges in boat #421 took an early lead all the way to Swinging Bridge. Somewhere below the bridge, Wooley and Gore in boat #129 overtook them and rowed down a legal cut that later became their downfall. The cut was clogged with logs, which cost them precious time. Taking advantage

This mural is painted on the wall at Dick's Food Store on Broadway Avenue in Seadrift, Texas. It was painted in 2021 by Joy Emshoff. The rowers in the boat are Robert Chatham and Louis "Butch" Hodges, winners of the 1976 Texas Water Safari in 37 hours and 18 minutes. Courtesy of Joy Emshoff

of the mishap, Butch Hodges and Robert Chatham chose not to follow and rowed into Seadrift in 37 hours and 18 minutes, a new record.

The victory had a special meaning to the hometown boys, who were both from Seadrift. Their rowboat, *Delta Dawn*, was created by Butch Hodges with some help from his partner. The boat was built in Butch's barn and was actually a third-generation rowing boat. Butch had raced two previous times in 1973 and 1974. This year, he made a few modifications, and obviously the third time was the charm. At 24 feet and 3 inches long and 30 inches wide, the boat weighed a hefty 148 pounds.[1] According to Butch, "She was pretty tough. She had to be because we didn't go around anything. We went over it.[2]

To commemorate the victory by the hometown boys, local artist Betty Moone painted a mural of Butch, Robert, and *Delta Dawn* on the wall of Dick's Food Store in Seadrift. After forty+ years the faded, weathered mural was repainted by Austin artist and coauthor of this book Joy Emshoff. If you are ever in Seadrift, drop by to see the mural at Dick's Food Store on Broadway.

Five women finished the race, and finishing for the second consecutive year, Kathie Derrick became the first woman to complete the Safari solo in 76 hours and 13 minutes.

1977

In 1977, Tom Goynes and Pat Oxsheer won the Safari in 38 hours and 43 minutes. This made the third time that Tom and Pat had double-bladed their Sawyer Saber to victory. Only 38 minutes back were John Nabors and Mike Wooley in a rowing scull. Jim Keirnan and Bubba Wood won the USCA C-2 Class in 46 hours and 18 minutes, and Mike Shively and

John Bugge won the Aluminum class two hours back. Mike and John would later become regular partners and Hall of Fame inductees, winning the race overall together five times.

Kathie and Peter Derrick won the Mixed Class in a record time of 49 hours and 19 minutes. Twenty-one boats finished out of the original thirty that started in San Marcos.

1978

Pat Petrisky and Jim Trimble won the sixteenth Safari in an Olympic tandem kayak (K2) in 45 hours and 31 minutes. Pat would go on to complete the race twenty-one times over the next thirty-five years. During this time Pat tried numerous canoes and kayaks. He even raced a USCA C-1 and fitted it with outrigger arms that could be used to row the boat. He could switch from paddling to rowing by simply rotating his seat 180 degrees. Fifteen boats completed the race that year and only one woman, Laura Hanks, and her partner, Edgar Hanks, finished, coming in eighth overall in 62 hours and 30 minutes.

1979

For the second consecutive year, fifteen teams completed the Safari, with Howard Gore and Mike Wooley setting a new record time of 36 hours and 40 minutes. Scott McDonald and Roy Tyrone won the USCA Cruising Class with a new record of 38 hours and 16 minutes, and John Bugge and Bill Yanovich set the aluminum record with 43 hours and 27 minutes. Paula Goynes, racing with her husband, Tom, placed fifth and set a new record in the Mixed Class of 45 hours and 54 minutes.

1980

For the first time in the history of the Safari, a three-person team won the race. Tom Goynes, Pat Oxsheer, and Jim Trimble, all previous winners, won the eighteenth Safari in 43 hours and 40 minutes. Longer canoes with more paddlers would continue to be a trend in future years and turned out to be the key to winning the race.

Owen West completed his eleventh consecutive Safari, finishing in 98 hours and 45 minutes. Over the next forty-one years, Owen would return every year to race. While he often finished near or at the back of the pack, his commitment to the race was undeniable. Since his first race in 1969, he has never failed to enter and eventually became the oldest competitor to finish.

While forty boats started the 1980 race, only sixteen finished—all were men's teams.

1981

Returning for a second year, the trio of Goynes, Oxsheer, and Trimble won again in 40 hours and 41 minutes. Peter Derrick finished his fifth Safari, was fifth overall, and set a record of 50 hours and 35 minutes in the Solo Class. Mike Riley and Mike Shively finished fourth overall and won the Aluminum Class in 48 hours and 24 minutes.

Thirty-eight boats started, but only sixteen finished.

1982

With last year's top team not competing in the 1982 Safari, the field was wide open for a new overall winner. For the first time, a four-person team—John Oertel, Pat Petrisky, Red Motley, and Troy Swift—won the race finishing in 42 hours and 30 minutes. Pat had won the race in 1978, but the other team members were first-time winners. The USCA C-2 Class was closely contested, with two mixed teams racing neck and neck all the way to Seadrift. Finishing first in 49 hours and 46 minutes were Kay Edwards and John Bugge, with Margaret Shelton and Alan Sawyer finishing 15 minutes back. Peter Derrick finished third overall and set a new solo record of 48 hours and 34 minutes. Mike Riley won the Aluminum Class for the second consecutive year with new partner Virgil Poole. He and Virgil finished seventh overall with a time of 52 hours and 40 minutes.

Forty boats started and only eighteen boats finished the race.

14

Unlimited C-2 and Unlimited C-3 Dominate

1983–1992

1983

Fifty-four boats lined up for the 1983 Safari, with three- and four-person teams as clear favorites. The last year's winning team of Troy Swift, John Oertel, Red Motley, and Pat Petrisky made a slight change in personnel. Red Motley opted to paddle with four-time winner Tom Goynes in a 21-foot, International Canoe Federation tandem canoe (ICF C-2) and was replaced by Marty Pribil.

Boat #103 with Troy Swift, John Oertel, Pat Petrisky, and Marty Pribil paddling the 1983 TWS. They finished second overall in 41 hours and 45 minutes. Courtesy of Kevin Bradley

While many expected a win by the three- and four-person canoes, Peter Derrick, team captain for Motley and Goynes, believed otherwise. He thought that "a conditioned and disciplined two-man team in a light-weight racing boat, running 'an intelligent race,' could challenge and even beat the three- and four-person powerhouse gang-boats."[1] Forty-two hours and ten minutes after the start, his opinion proved correct when Motley and Goynes won the race 33 minutes ahead of the four-person team. Mike Riley and Virgil Poole won the Aluminum Class in 50 hours and 30 minutes. This was the third consecutive win for Riley and the second for Poole.

Fifty-four boats started the race, with twenty-seven finishing and an equal number dropping out.

1984

In 1984, forty-three teams started the Safari, and for the first time a solo competitor was considered a contender for a top overall finish. Earlier that year, a solo paddler from Michigan named Steve Landick surprised the entire field of competitors by winning the 40-mile May Safari Preliminary Race. Known up north for his ultramarathon expeditions, Landick had rewritten the record book on long distance paddling adventures. The canoe he paddled was made by the Wabash Valley Canoe Company in Crawfordsville, Indiana. The long, skinny solo canoe was the talk of the Safari crowd. It was specifically designed by the Wabash Valley Company for Landick to compete in the Safari.

While longer multiperson canoes were expected to win, Landick's Wabash Valley "Safari C-1" would certainly be a contender. One month after the preliminary race in May, Steve defied the field with an impressive showing and led all Safari competitors through Cuero Checkpoint (mile 160), at which point

he was passed by Roy Tyrone and Jerry Nunnery in canoe #81. Tyrone and Nunnery held on and won the race, while Landick finished third overall. This was the first time since 1965 that two paddlers had won the Safari while using only single-blade canoe paddles for the entire race.

Roy Tyrone said the 1984 race was certainly one of his favorites, but it was also one of his toughest. Maybe it was the drought-like conditions of the river, the oppressive Texas heat, or the wind that felt like a hair dryer blowing in your face.

Early in the race, Roy got tangled in a fisherman's line, and before he could apologize, the fisherman picked up a revolver, pointed it at him and Jerry, and pulled the trigger. Fortunately, it was not loaded. Later in the race near Victoria, someone began throwing objects (probably rocks) half the size of bricks at their canoe. Luckily, they were unharmed, but their headlamp was smashed. While adverse conditions and unplanned challenges are expected in this race, the one thing that made the 1984 Safari so difficult was the record low flows in the river.

Here is Roy's account: "Jerry in the bow would scan the water carefully, but we still ran aground numerous times. Jerry would run left, looking for a channel, and I would run right. Whoever found water would call out and we would run to the canoe and carry it to the channel. One time we were a bit disorientated. We weren't sure which way was downstream. So, Jerry walked to a sandbar, picked up an oak leaf, and waded into the channel and laid the leaf on the water. It seemed like we watched the leaf for an eternity before it moved ever so slightly. We hopped in the canoe and took off in the direction that the leaf had moved."

The win by Jerry Nunnery from Lake Jackson and Roy Tyrone from Houston was impressive because they paddled a United States Canoe Association

(USCA) C-2. In the past, canoes that won the race were narrower, longer, had a rudder, and/or used double-bladed paddles or oars. All these features make canoes and kayaks faster. But to the amazement of the entire field of competitors, Tyrone and Nunnery single-bladed their USCA C-2 to the overall win in 54 hours. This was the first and last time that a USCA cruiser canoe won the race.

Paula and Tom Goynes finished fifth with a time of 70 hours and 12 minutes. Also making a strong showing was John Dunn. At seventeen years, three months, and twenty-six days old, he became the youngest solo finisher. A total of fifteen boats completed the race that year.

1985

Several previous winners returned to compete in the twenty-third Texas Water Safari. Leading the field were 1983 winners Red Motley and Tom Goynes.

Paddling a four-person boat were previous winners Pat Petrisky, Jerry Cochran, and Troy Swift and new partner Doug Lewis. Also returning was last year's solo sensation, ultramarathoner Steve Landick.

For the second year, Goynes and Motley took the lead at Hochheim with the four-person team in hot pursuit. Steve Landick ran out of gas and pulled out at Cuero, but the four-person long boat continued to chase Goynes and Motley all the way to Seadrift. Motley and Goynes won the race in 43 hours and 10 minutes, with the four-person canoe finishing in second place overall in 44 hours and 22 minutes. Carol Schaefer was the first woman finisher, crossing the finish line with partner John Mark Harras in 81 hours and 10 minutes.

1986

High water provided ideal conditions for a record-breaking year in 1986. With two formidable three-person canoes vying for the overall win, the race proved to be one of the fastest in history. Troy Swift and Pat Petrisky had each won the race in the past, and with the addition of veteran paddler Jerry Cochran, their team was very much in the running. Joe and Brian Mynar had finished second and third overall in the past two years and had recruited Joe's brother, Fred, to paddle with them in a three-person unlimited canoe (C-3). Two former teammates, John Bugge and Mike Shively, had won the Aluminum Class twice in the past and had teamed up in their first attempt in an unlimited canoe.

Once the gun fired, the Bugge and Mynar canoes ran neck and neck at every checkpoint all the way to Cuero. Then at Thomaston, Fred Mynar got sick and left the race and Joe and Brian dropped out at the next bridge. With the Mynar canoe out of the race,

John Bugge and Mike Shively went on to win the race in a new record time of 35 hours and 26 minutes. While this was the first closely contested race between the two teams, it would certainly not be the last. Over the next twenty years the Mynar and the Bugge teams would win the race a combined nineteen times.

The other three-person team of Troy Swift, Pat Petrisky, and Jerry Cochran also had problems when Pat Petrisky withdrew at Cuero. Troy and Jerry continued on and finished second overall in 38 hours and 36 minutes. Peter Derrick finished in 41 hours and 30 minutes, setting a new solo record for the third time. Kevin Bradley and Tom Wilkinson were fifth overall and first Aluminum in a time of 43 hours and 42 minutes. A record number of thirty-eight boats finished the race.

Kevin Bradley (bow) and Tom Wilkinson (stern) won the Aluminum canoe class in 43 hours and 42 minutes in 1986. They were fifth overall. Courtesy of Kevin Bradley

1987

High rainfall and flooding in June caused a postponement of the 1987 race until July 3. Returning for the second year were last year's winners John Bugge and Mike Shively and to no surprise, they set a blistering pace and led all teams from the start. Joe and Brian Mynar, in hot pursuit, fell victim to the floodwaters and had to drop out near Cuero after a boat mishap. For the second consecutive year Mike Shively and John Bugge won the race and set a Tandem Unlimited Class record of 35 hours and 17 minutes that stood for thirty-two years. In a remarkable effort, Rocky Harber and Robert Youens finished second overall and set a new Aluminum record of 42 hours and 54 minutes. The canoe they paddled was a 17-foot Alumacraft Voyager. Weighing only 58 pounds, this voyager model is the lightest, fastest recreational aluminum canoe made. Over the years it has been the choice of canoe racers nationwide and has won the Safari Novice and Aluminum Classes most years. It has won countless other canoe races, including the Texas Canoe and Kayak Association State Championships and the USCA Stock Aluminum National Championships, numerous times.

Sadly, Alumacraft Canoe Company made a marketing decision and stopped making the Voyager sometime around 2003. During this time, Duane Te Grotenhuis owned a canoe livery and boat shop in Martindale, Texas, called T-G Canoes and Kayaks; it repaired and sold Alumacraft canoes. Given the demand for the lightweight Voyager canoes, Duane contacted Alumacraft and made a special order for fifty canoes. While it took several years, he finally received a truckload of the canoes in 2007. He received another standing order in 2010 and a third order in 2017. When I talked to Duane recently, he said his son, Alex, the new owner, had a standing order for yet another truckload. At this point it is hard to predict if and when Alumacraft will make a new batch of Voyager canoes.

A record seven women finished the 1987 Safari, with Carol Schaefer and partner John Mark Harras leading the way and winning the Mixed Class in 48 hours and 32 minutes. Sandy Rinehart and Janet Smith, both from North Carolina, racing a USCA C-2, had a closely contested race with Texans Donna Bugge and Teddy Montgomery. The two North Carolinians eventually won the duel, finishing in 50 hours and 43 minutes. Brian Lisle at seventy-one became the oldest man to complete the race with his younger partner, Sam Thiede.

1988

Returning again for the third straight year were the 1986 and '87 overall winners, John Bugge and Mike Shively. Another strong tandem team vying for the win was Jerry Cochran and Pat Petrisky. Also contending for an overall win were Joe, Fred, and Brian Mynar, who had not been able to finish in the past two years. This year, however, would be a different story.

From the start, the Mynar team took the lead and reached the first checkpoint at Staples slightly ahead of Cochran and Petrisky. At the next two checkpoints, they continued to lead, and by Gonzales, they were nine minutes ahead. Then, just when things were looking good for a win, Joe got sick with stomach cramps. Unable to continue, he got out at Victoria and was taken to the hospital. With a comfortable lead, Fred and Brian Mynar went on to win the race in 39 hours and 31 minutes. Jerry Cochran and Pat Petrisky finished a respectable second in 41 hours and 9 minutes, and John Bugge and Mike Shively finished third in 42 hours and 28 minutes. Mark Finstad and

Grady Hicks (*left*) and Mark Finstad (*right*) at the finish line in 1988. They were fourth overall and first place in the USCA C-2 class. Grady, a future Hall of Famer, would eventually complete the race twenty times. Courtesy of Kevin Bradley

Grady Hicks won the USCA C-2 Class in 47 hours and 19 minutes, and Sandy Reinhart and Janet Smith returned for a second time and won the Women's Class, while Mick Edgar and Hunter Nolan won the Novice Class in 67 hours and 3 minutes. Thirty-one boats completed the race.

1989

The 1989 Safari lived up to its reputation as the "World's Toughest Canoe Race" when low river flows and a rough bay crossing took their toll, knocking out thirty-one of the fifty starting boats. Returning again were last year's winners Brian and Fred Mynar. This year they had chosen a three-man canoe with Joe Mynar filling the third seat. The duo of Cochran and Petrisky were also back, and John Bugge, his wife Donna, and "Uncle" Russ Roberts were competing in the Mixed Class.

As expected, these three teams led the field through the Palmetto Checkpoint when Pat Petrisky suffered chest pains, and he and Jerry Cochran dropped out of the race. After three years with sickness and boats mishaps, all three Mynars were finally able to lead the race from start to finish with a winning time of 45 hours and 45 minutes. Meanwhile, the mixed team of Donna and John Bugge and Russ Roberts finished second in 48 hours and 4 minutes. Donna became the first woman to finish second overall and set a new record in the Mixed Class.

In an impressive effort, Mick Edgar and Hunter Nolan, racing an aluminum canoe, finished sixth overall, winning the Aluminum Class in 64 hours and 35 minutes. Owen West, who had completed twenty Safaris in a row, had his perfect record broken when chest pains and a leaking Unlimited C-1 took their toll. Unable to reach Seadrift in the allotted 100-hour limit, he pulled out at Tivoli.

1990

Returning for the twenty-eighth Texas Water Safari were the previous year's winners Joe, Fred, and Brian Mynar. John Bugge, Mike Shively, and Jerry Cochran were also racing in a three-person canoe. Interest in an overall win had grown throughout the paddling community as sixteen teams were entered in the Unlimited Class. After dominating the USCA C-2 Class for the past three years, Grady Hicks and Mark Finstad teamed up with Grady's brother, Phil, and they were also in the mix for an overall win.

Vying for the USCA C-2 win, John Mark "Lone Wolf" Harras and Bill "Polecat" Stafford would be competing against veteran racer Ted Slaughter with partner Larry Coffey. Competing in the Women's Solo Class, two-time finisher Marie McKay would be racing against newcomer Ginsie Dunn.

As expected, the top Bugge and Mynar canoes raced neck and neck through Gonzales, where Fred Mynar had to drop out. Taking advantage of the mishap, the Bugge/Shively/Cochran team went on

to win the race in 38 hours and 57 minutes. Joe and Brian Mynar continued on, finishing second in 41 hours and 45 minutes. John Mark Harras and Bill Stafford won the USCA C-2 Class, with Marie McKay winning the Women's Solo Class in 81 hours and 28 minutes. Twenty-eight boats finished the race.

1991

In what had become a habit, the Bugge and the Mynar teams were both vying for another win in 1991. While the Bugge team would remain the same as the last year, the Mynar team had a new Spencer-built C-4 and had added two new team members. Fred Mynar would sit out this year but Joe Burns and yours truly, Bob Spain, would complete the team.

When the gun went off, the Mynar canoe took the early lead and was out in front of the entire field. Then just a few minutes into the race, while making a left-hand turn near Thompson's Island, the canoe rudder assembly hung up on a concrete bridge support and the steel rudder cable snapped.

Mike Riley in the canoe with Jim Acker, team captain, on the bank, in 1988. Over a fifteen-year period (1977–1991) Mike finished the race nine times, winning the Aluminum Canoe class three times and USCA C-1 once. Courtesy of Kevin Bradley

With the entire field of canoes approaching, Joe Burns made a quick decision and tied off the snapped cable. With no tools to work with, Joe was able to pull and twist the broken cables together. While the "quick fix" gave our team a chance to continue, the rudder was "kicked to one side" and was only partially functional. Once the team reentered the canoe, only one canoe had passed, and it was the Bugge canoe. Upstream of Staples, the Mynar canoe ran over a rock that knocked the bailer completely out of the boat. After a second stop to try and fix the damaged bailer,

the Bugge canoe had a five-minute lead at the Staples Checkpoint. With the loss of a functional bailer, our team had to manually bail water from the boat for the remainder of the race. From this point on, the front-running Bugge team continued to increase their lead, finishing first in 36 hours and 28 minutes. Fifty minutes later, the Mynar/Mynar/Burns/Spain canoe finished second.

Lone Wolf Harras and Polecat Stafford had a good race, finishing seventh overall in the USCA C-2 Class in 47 hours and 22 minutes. John Maika and Mike Riley won the Aluminum Class in 50 hours and 15 minutes. Donna Bugge, Teddy Gray, and Diana Finstad won the Women's Class in 57 hours and 43 minutes. Twenty-seven boats completed the race.

1992

Heavy spring rains caused near flood conditions in 1992. These conditions pushed Safari competitors down the river in record times. The top two teams from the past year traded places with the four-person Mynar team of Joe, Fred, and Brian Mynar and Joe Burns winning the duel in 31 hours and 2 minutes. The trio of John Bugge, Mike Shively, and Jerry Cochran finished second in 32 hours and 27 minutes.

Returning again was ultramarathon paddler Steve Landick, who had impressed all competitors and spectators in 1984 and '85 when he ran near the front with the lead canoes. This year he finished fourth overall and set a solo record of 36 hours and 8 minutes. The Standard Class record was set by Ron Wilson and Lynn Lightfoot in 38 hours and 18 minutes. Kevin Bradley and Zoltan Mraz won the Aluminum Class and set a record of 39 hours and 55 minutes. Carolyn Stinson and Ron Popp won the Mixed Class in 48 hours and 44 minutes. A record forty-two boats finished the race.

15

Canoes Get Even Longer

1993–2002

1993

For the fifth year in a row, the Bugge and Mynar canoes took the top two spots. This year the winning Mynar trio of Joe, Fred, and Brian had recruited a long, tall Texan, John Dunn, to fill the fourth seat in their canoe. John had finished third the previous year, and with five Safari finishes, he would become a permanent member of the Mynar team. The Bugge team had also changed, with John Bugge and Jerry Cochran returning and new paddlers Roger Myers and Russ Roberts filling seats three and four. With

The winning 1993 Mynar Team at Westerfield Crossing (mile 6). Team members starting in the bow: Joe Mynar, Fred Mynar, John Dunn, and Brian Mynar. They won in 31 hours and 2 minutes. Courtesy of San Marcos Daily Record

"Uncle" Russ Roberts dropping out during the race, the Bugge team finished almost three hours behind the winning Mynar canoe. Donna Bugge finished fifth overall and first mixed along with partners Mick Edgar and Robert Youens in 44 hours and 59 minutes.

The largest class in the 1993 Safari was the Novice Class. One competitor in that class, Roger Zimmerman, also raced the very first 1963 Safari. Returning after a thirty-year hiatus, Roger and his partner, William "Billy" Smith, were vying for the class win. In his first Safari, Roger had dropped out when the rigors of the race and rough coastal water took their toll. That year only two of the fifty-eight boats finished in Corpus Christi. Now thirty years later, Roger, at fifty-five years of age, entered the race again. Sadly, his canoe lodged on a log near Nursery and he was forced to drop out for a second time.

On Tuesday, June 15, the fourth day of the race, Bill Stafford and John Dupont, who finished in fourth place, and John Dunn, who won the race, decided that they had not had enough. With a few hours of sleep, and the Safari still going on, the threesome had another adventure in mind. After attending the Annual Texas Water Safari Banquet and picking up their trophies, they crawled into a bruised and beaten C-3 and set sail (so to speak) for Freeport. The boys had all agreed to commemorate the 1965–67 Safari by paddling to Freeport. Hey, how hard could that be? They had just paddled 260 miles, and 109 more would be a walk in the park. Right? Twenty-seven boats finished the Safari that year and Stafford, Dunn, and Dupont paddled all the way to Freeport.

1994

With eleven finishes to his credit and two overall wins, Jerry Cochran had established himself as one of the strongest paddlers in the field of competitors. While he would normally join a team vying for the overall win, this year he had chosen to race with

Lillie Cochran finished the 1994 TWS along with son Jerry and daughter-in-law Linda in tenth place. She became the oldest woman to complete the race at sixty-six years of age. Courtesy of Kevin Bradley

family instead. Joining Jerry were his wife, Linda, and his mom, Lillie. Jerry and his mom had raced once before in 1987 but dropped out when Lillie became ill. Back for a second effort, Lillie, Jerry, and Linda paddled their way to a tenth-place finish in 54 hours and 4 minutes. At sixty-six years of age, Lillie became the oldest woman to complete the race.

Roger Zimmerman was back again, and the third time was truly the charm. With a time of 59 hours and 25 minutes, Roger and his partner, Billy Smith, won the Novice Class and were thirteenth overall.

For the second straight year the Mynar team won the race, this time in 36 hours and 52 minutes, with Allen Spelce, West Hansen, Jeff Wueste, and Dan Remnitz finishing a distant second in 42 hours and 57 minutes. John Bugge won the USCA C-1 Class in 48 hours and 53 minutes, a new record.

1995

If sleep deprivation, logjams, and miles and miles of river weren't enough to knock teams out of the race, a Sunday morning thunderstorm at the thirty-third Texas Water Safari was. Mike Spencer, race chairman, said, "It was a hard, blowing rain and some people suffered from hypothermia."[1]

While many struggled to finish the race, others shined in the adversity. John Dunn and his wife, Ginsie, both had outstanding races and each won their respective classes. Ginsie set a new record and won the Women's Solo Class in 60 hours and 6 minutes. John, for the third year in a row, won the Unlimited Class and was first overall with partners Joe, Fred, and Brian Mynar.

Donna Bugge finished second overall along with her husband John, Mike Shively, and Robert Youens. Roger Zimmerman, a survivor of the first Safari, recorded his second Safari finish in 69 hours and

5 minutes. In doing so, he became the oldest solo finisher at fifty-seven. Sixty-eight boats started and forty-nine finished—a new record.

1996

Drought conditions in 1996 slowed the competitors in the thirty-fourth Texas Water Safari. For the eleventh consecutive year, either the Bugge or Mynar team finished first overall. In a reversal of last year's two top teams, the five-person team of John Bugge, Mike Shively, Mike Shea, Rich Long, and Jeff Verryp finished first in 41 hours and 20 minutes. The three Mynars and John Dunn finished second overall, 49 minutes back.

The fierce rivalry between these two top teams reached a new high point just below Rio Vista Dam when the boats bumped together. At this point angry words were exchanged. Forty hours later at the finish line, hard feelings persisted.

Cindy Meurer finished fourth overall and first mixed along with team members Jeff Wueste, Jack Kraus, and West Hansen in 51 hours and 46 minutes.

1997

Heavy rain and swollen streams set the stage for a record-breaking 1997 Texas Water Safari. While high flows are the recipe for setting new records, they also increase hazards and risks to the racers.

Two weeks before the Safari, San Marcos police chief Larry Kendrick and his son, Jimmy, were training for the race on the San Marcos River near Ottine Dam. While the dam would normally have to be portaged, at extremely high flows the water flows over the dam unimpeded and the turbulence near and below the dam can cause major hydraulics that can be extremely dangerous.

The water was so high that Larry and Jimmy could not see the submerged dam and paddled right over it. In the high water and turbulence, they were thrown from their boat. While Jimmy was able to swim to safety, his father was caught in the swift water and drowned.

Two weeks after the somber incident, seventy-eight teams—a new record—lined up for the thirty-fifth Safari. Over the next four days, floodwaters pushed competitors down the course in record times. The following are some of the records that were set:

Unlimited—Brian Mynar, Fred Mynar, Jerry Cochran, John Dunn, Steve Landick, and Solomon Carriere—29 hours and 46 minutes

USCA C-2—Allen Spelce and West Hansen— 36 hours and 17 minutes

Aluminum—Donald and Daniel Baumbach— 38 hours and 55 minutes

USCA C-1—Mark Simmons—40 hours and 13 minutes

1998

The Texas Water Safari differs from many other canoe races in that it allows any type of canoe with any number of paddlers, using any type of manpower for propulsion. The "Unlimited Class" has pushed the limits of canoe design, and many competitors have tried every design imaginable to make a faster canoe. In the years following 1998, competitive teams would build longer canoes in order to add additional paddlers. These boats would revolutionize canoe

West Hansen (bow) and Allen Spelce in carbon canoe #394 with Sammy Prochaska and Johnny Prochaska (stern) in cowboy hats. Hansen and Spelce finished the 1997 TWS in a record 36 hours and 27 minutes. The USCA C-2 record still stands today. Courtesy of Kevin Bradley

racing and would win many marathon canoe races across the nation, including the 440-mile Yukon River Quest, the 340-mile Missouri American Water Race, the 135-mile Tour de Teche Canoe Race, and of course, the Safari.

In 1995 the winning Safari canoe had four paddlers. In 1996 there were five, and in 1997 the winning canoe had six paddlers. Again in 1998 a six-person team of Joe, Fred, and Brian Mynar, John Dunn, Tim Rask, and Canadian Mike Vincent won the Safari in 38 hours and 39 minutes. Mike Shively won the Solo Unlimited Class, and Peter and Kathie Derrick won the Mixed Class.

During the Safari, the wild card is San Antonio Bay. Some years it is slick as glass and you can paddle across it in a couple of hours. Other years it can be rougher than the churning water in a washing machine, and a team may spend an entire day and night in the bay. The 1998 Safari was one of the roughest times on record.

One competitor who had a particularly tough time in the bay was Richard Steppe. Richard paddled solo that year and fell out of his boat while crossing the bay. He said, "I fell out and tried to grab the boat, but the next thing I knew, it just blew right away. I took off my life jacket so I could swim faster, but the boat was gone. After a while, I started saying, 'I am going to die out here,'"[2] After floating in the bay for hours, he finally swam to shore and, when he crossed the finish line, to his disappointment, he was disqualified for not finishing with his canoe.

1999

In 1999 a record seventy-nine teams signed up for the thirty-seventh Texas Water Safari. For the third year in a row the Mynar canoe finished first overall, this time in 37 hours and 9 minutes. The six-person team had changed from the previous year, with Donald Baumbach and Chuck Stewart replacing Tim Rask and Mike Vincent. In second place was another six-person team, made up of West Hansen and Allen Spelce, the 1997 USCA C-2 record holders, and four paddlers from California: Mike Shea, Rich Long, Jack Kraus, and Jeff Verryp. John and Donna Bugge and Phil and Mary Jo Gumbert finished third overall and won first mixed. This was the nineteenth consecutive finish for John Bugge. A record fifty-three canoes completed the race.

2000

With swollen streams and higher than normal flows, the field of eighty-four boats was primed for a fast, competitive race in 2000. Returning was 1999's winning six-person Mynar canoe, and to no one's surprise, the competitive team won the race again, improving on their last time by 2 hours and 46 minutes. This made eight times in the past ten years that the Mynar team had won the overall race. When Joe, the eldest of the Mynar clan, was asked about the conditions in the race, he said, "There was some big water. It went a lot faster than normal. Some of the high water covered up places where we normally portage." Chuck Stewart, also on the winning team, said, "It was a lot clearer than we expected. I don't know if winning ever gets easier. But racing on high water was a lot easier because of the experience these guys have had."[3]

Also finishing with a fast time and winning the Mixed and Masters Classes was the six-person team of Donna Bugge, Ginger Turner, John Bugge, Pat Petrisky, Richard Steppe, and Mike Shively. Gary Robinson and Mark Simmons finished eighth overall and won the Aluminum Class in 43 hours and 10 minutes.

Early in the race, Roger Zimmerman, a veteran paddler with two finishes, had a near fatal experience. Roger was paddling a solo canoe on the San Marcos River when a large tree fell into the water. Norman "Norm" Thomas, while paddling behind Roger, saw the entire event. Here is Norm's account of the incident:

> I was 8 to 10 yards behind Roger Zimmerman, just tracking his pace. We had not met yet; he was just some solo guy that I was catching up to and was going to run with for a while. We were coming up on a sharp right-hand turn with a peninsula of bank about the size of 3 pickup trucks, bank 7–10 feet high. It was raining pretty good, but not real loud. The only sound was a little craaack, and the bank slides into the river and a tree, maybe 3 feet in diameter, with it. I got a real good look at it because I was pushed over to the other bank and barely made it under a branch with the second wave. I thought the first wave was big 'til the second wave came up. That's when Roger disappeared. I rode the outside of the wave and looked down into the hole like a doughnut with Roger in it. Then he came up, I came down, and we said our howdies. I remember looking down maybe 3 to 4 feet to see the top of his head in the hole. He got to cheat death—no one would have ever found him, he would have vanished without a trace.[4]

While Roger escaped this close encounter, unfortunately, he dropped out later in the race. A record sixty-seven canoes finished the race.

2001

For the previous four years, six-person canoes were the class of the field and had won the race each of those years. That changed in 2001, when the rival Mynar and Bugge teams paddled eight- and nine-person canoes, respectively. With a woman in both canoes, a heated rivalry was expected for not only the overall win but also the mixed classification as well. When the dust settled, the Mynar team was first overall and won the Mixed Class in 36 hours and 3 minutes, and Fiona Vincent became the first woman to finish first overall. She and Mike, her husband, had traveled all the way from Canada to race. Mike had also won the Safari in 1998. Other members of the team were Donald Baumbach, John Dunn, Chuck Stewart, and Fred, Brian, and Kyle Mynar. This was Kyle's first win but was certainly not to be his last.

Finishing second place overall was another woman, Erin Magee, in a behemoth nine-person canoe. The Bugge C-9 was so long that it had to be hauled in two pieces and assembled at the race site. Other members of the team were John Bugge, Richard Steppe, Vance Sherrod, Jim Pye, John Maika, Rob Wytaske, and Pete and Wade Binion. James DeVoglaer had an outstanding Safari, finishing fifth overall, winning Solo and Masters Classes in 44 hours and 16 minutes. The thirty-ninth Safari was the largest on record with 113 canoes starting and a record sixty-seven finishing the race.

2002

With more than 100 canoes signed up for the 2002 race, the Aquarena Center was buzzing with activity as the 9:00 a.m. start time approached. The banks of Spring Lake were lined with boats and competitors of all shapes and sizes. While some teams had uniforms that matched, others looked like they just got out of bed, long johns and all. One guy wore a hat that looked like an inverted funnel, while others had ball caps fashioned with curtains to keep the sun off. The cowboys were wearing their customary hats, and stern man John Mark Harras, also known as "Lone Wolf," had chosen tights with a colorful psychedelic pattern. (I'm not sure if the tights were chosen to keep the sun off or to keep him awake!)

Just before the race start, Texas State University president Jerome Supple introduced "Big Willie" George, who, along with his partner Frank Brown, had made the initial expedition down the San Marcos River and Guadalupe Rivers to Corpus Christi in 1962. While addressing the racers, Big Willie said, "It's hard to believe that something that started as a canoe ride to the Gulf jetties has turned to something so big."[5]

Once the gun went off, the blue waters of Spring Lake turned to a white froth as the 109 canoes began their 260-mile journey to the coast. Thirty-seven hours and fifty minutes later, the Mynar C-6 touched the seawall in Seadrift. Almost three hours back, the second six-person team of Allen Spelce, Tim Rask, Michael Rask, Jeff Wueste, West Hansen, and Jerry Cochran finished the race. James Devoglaer and California paddler Mike Shea had a strong race, finishing fourth overall and winning the Tandem Unlimited Class in 47 hours and 20 minutes. Erin Magee won the Women's Solo Class in 64 hours and 18 minutes. Seventy-two canoes finished the race that year.

16

C-6s Become the Winning Standard

2003–2012

2003

For the seventh year in a row, the Mynar family fielded a team that won the Texas Water Safari. During the forty-one-year history of the race, no team had dominated the race like the Mynars, and while the team members varied some from year to year, they somehow managed to come out on top. This time Fred and Brian Mynar and Chuck Stewart would be joined by new members Jerry Cochran, Sammy Prochaska, and Allen Spelce.

In an interesting and unusual turn of events, the youngest child record was broken twice in the 2003 race. On Monday, June 15, at 8:34 a.m., James

Jessica Bugge and father John (not shown) running Rio Vista Dam. Jessica, at nine years of age, became the youngest finisher in the forty-one-year history of the race. Courtesy of San Marcos Daily Record

FAMILY MATTERS

During the fifty+ year history of the Safari, a number of paddlers have won the overall race multiple times, but no individual or family of paddlers can match the record of the Mynar family. In all, there are two generations and five family members who have raced: Joe who is the oldest, his younger brother Fred, and Joe's three sons, Brian, Kyle, and Logan, have all won the race multiple times. From 1988 to 2021, a Mynar family member crossed the finish line in first place overall forty-eight times.

In 1983, Joe, the patriarch of the Mynar family, raced his first Texas Water Safari along with his fifteen-year-old son, Brian, finishing seventh overall—an impressive feat for first-time competitors. Over the next two years, Joe and Brian honed their skills and moved up with a second place overall in 1984 and third overall in 1985. Then in 1988 Joe reached out to his brother Fred to race with him. While Joe got sick during

the race and could not finish, Fred and Brian still won the race with an impressive time of 37 hours and 31 minutes.

This was the first in a long line of victories for the Mynars. Whether there were one, two, or three Mynars in the canoe, fans commonly referred to the team as the "Mynar team."

Because the Texas Water Safari's Unlimited Class allowed boats of any size with any number or paddlers, Joe and Brian decided in 1991 to build a longer boat and bring in more paddlers to go even faster. During that time, I raced and trained with the Mynars, so they gave me a chance to race with them. Joe Burns, a Texan, filled the fourth seat and we were off to the races. That year we finished second, with John Bugge, Mike Shively, and Jerry Cochran winning the race in 36 hours and 28 minutes. John and Mike were formidable competitors who won the race three previous times in 1986, 1987, and

(*Left to right*) Fred, Brian, Joe, Kyle, and Logan Mynar holding signs that depict the number of Safaris they have won first overall. Courtesy of Ashley Landis

1990, and Jerry Cochran won once before with John and Mike in 1990.

In 1992 the Mynar boat won the race again, and in 1993 they recruited a tall Texan, John Dunn, to race with them. At six foot seven inches, John holds the unofficial distinction of being the tallest person to win the Safari. For the next twelve years, John was a mainstay in the Mynar canoe. Because either the Mynar team canoe or the Bugge team canoe had won for the past seven years, the two teams established a rivalry that intensified over the coming years and at times became heated.

In 1997 Joe did not race, but Fred, Brian, and John Dunn recruited Jerry Cochran and

John Dunn in the bow of the Mynar team canoe. John raced twelve years on the Mynar team, winning ten times and finishing twice in second place. Courtesy of Kevin Bradley

two "ringers" from up north: Steve Landick, an ultramarathon paddler from Michigan whose long-distance expeditions in a canoe and kayak were legendary, and Solomon Carriere, an elite paddler from Canada. That year the six-man team, aided by high water, set a record of 29 hours and 46 minutes that still stands today. The winning canoe averaged an amazing speed of 8.74 miles per hour, which is unheard of in a paddle-driven canoe.

For the next three years, the Mynar C-6 had consecutive wins, but then in 2001, the boats got even longer. That year the Mynar eight-person canoe won the thirty-ninth Texas Water Safari, and for the first time a woman was in the winning canoe. Fiona Vincent, an elite paddler, and her husband, Mike, also an elite paddler, raced with the Mynars. Vincent, a Canadian, is the only woman to have won the Safari to this day. Joe's son, Kyle, filled a third seat in the boat, and John Dunn, Fred Mynar, Brian Mynar, Donald Baumbach, and Chuck Stewart the other five.

Because the Safari's Unlimited Class had no restrictions on the boat's design, length, or number of paddlers, the boats had gotten so long that navigating the winding upper San Marcos River was extremely difficult. The boats were also so expensive that many competitors could not afford the purchase price. Following the 2005 race, the TWS Board made a tough decision. In an effort to offer a class that more paddlers could participate in, and to create parity in the class, a decision was made by the board that no more than six paddlers would be allowed in a canoe or kayak in the Safari.

In 2004 Joe Mynar won his ninth Texas Water Safari. That was the last year he raced the Safari with his brother Fred or his son Kyle. He returned to race in 2019 with his son Logan but sadly had

(Bow to stern) John Dunn, Fred Mynar, Chuck Stewart, Kyle Mynar, Mike Vincent, Fiona Vincent, Donald Baumbach, and Brian Mynar in 2001. The eight-person team won the Safari in an enormous 46-foot canoe in 36 hours and 3 minutes. Fiona Vincent became the first woman to win the Texas Water Safari. Courtesy of Kevin Bradley

to drop out. Brian Mynar continued to race off and on over the next few years and stopped racing after a second-place finish overall in 2010. Brian won the race an impressive fourteen times. Fred is still racing today and has a record sixteen wins to his credit. Kyle Mynar is an active competitor on the racing scene and currently has seven Safari wins to his credit. Logan Mynar, Joe's youngest son, while attending college and law school, won the race with Uncle Fred and brother Kyle in 2013 and 2016. He and Kyle have become a formidable tandem team with impressive finishes in several pro canoe races up north, including the General Clinton Canoe Race in New York and the AuSable River Canoe Marathon in Michigan.

From 1991 through 2019, the Mynar teams, seeking the overall win, raced with thirty-one different paddlers in the Safari. The majority, twenty-one, either lived in or grew up in Texas, three were Canadians, three were from Belize, two were from New York, one was from Michigan, and one was from California. The accomplishments of this family are second to none, but I would be remiss if I did not mention some of the other outstanding Texas paddlers that raced with them.

John Dunn raced in the Mynar canoe twelve times, winning the race ten times and finishing second two times. He has won the race more times than any other paddler except Fred and Brian Mynar.

Chuck Stewart raced with the Mynars seven times and won the race six times. Jerry Cochran raced with the Mynars seven times, with five firsts and two seconds. He also won the race with the rival Bugge boat two times for a total of seven wins. He is the only Texan to have won the race in both the Mynar boat and the Bugge boat.

Texas Water Safari president Allen Spelce, who raced with the Mynar team in 2003, explained the family's remarkable success: "They have the chemistry, the gel, they've got it all. They're just incredible athletes."[1]

DeVoglaer and his son, James Ian DeVoglaer, finished the race in 47 hours and 34 minutes. Ian became the youngest competitor to finish. Then, less than four hours later at 12:23 p.m., Jessica Bugge and her father, John, finished the race. Jessica was younger than Ian, and at nine years of age, she became the youngest competitor to finish the Safari. This was truly an incredible effort by the two youngsters given the hardships and length of the race.

Pat Petrisky and Mark Simmons, both future TWS Hall of Fame inductees, had an impressive race, finishing third overall with a time of 40 hours and 25 minutes. Their Tandem Unlimited team beat several six-person teams in the process. According to Pat, they purchased an old rowboat hull from perennial competitor Howard Gore. Taking no chances for any type of water or conditions, Pat and Mark rigged the boat to paddle or row. Peter "Fuzzy" Churchman, who was competing on a six-person team, had a bad stroke of luck when he was bitten by a water moccasin during the race. Peter did not know when he was bitten, but as the race progressed, the pain and swelling continued and he finally dropped out at the Swinging Bridge Checkpoint. Eighty-seven canoes finished the race, setting a new record.

2004

In preparation for the 2004 Safari, Lee Deviney recruited Alex Lisbey, Armin Lopez, and Daniel Cruz, three elite paddlers from Belize, to race the Safari. With the addition of these three ringers, he knew that his team would have a good chance for an overall win. Recruiting ringers would become a common practice in future years for teams seeking to win the Safari. Lee also recruited local Texans Jeff Glock and Peter Churchman.

Due to unusually high rainfall and flooding on the rivers, the Safari was delayed not once but twice in 2004. The race was finally held on July 17, although some teams had to find replacements when team members could not reschedule work commitments or other conflicts.

From the starting whistle, Team Mynar took the early lead, with the Deviney canoe close behind. With each successive checkpoint, the Mynar canoe increased its lead. To make things worse for the Deviney team, Peter Churchman got sick and dropped out at Sladen Cemetery Crossing. Later in the race, both Daniel Cruz and Alex Lisbey also withdrew, dashing their hopes of having any chance of a win. With only three paddlers remaining in the Deviney canoe, they faded, finishing sixth overall.

For the eighth consecutive year, Team Mynar won the race, in 33 hours and 8 minutes. A five-person Masters team made up of Vance Sherrod, Pete Binion, John Maika, Jim Pye, and Pat Petrisky finished second and set a new Master's record of 36 hours and 6 minutes. Fred Mynar, paddling alone, finished an impressive fourth in 37 hours and 24 minutes. Kathie and Peter Derrick won the Mixed Class, finishing eighth overall and setting a new record of 39 hours and 27 minutes. Fifty-six canoes finished the race that year.

2005

For the first time in more than a decade, the Mynar team chose not to race the Safari. With the field wide open for a new frontrunner, anticipation was high among several multiperson teams vying for a win in the forty-third Safari. While there were no clear favorites, several teams had a mixture of veterans and up-and-comers. West Hansen and Richard Steppe, both veterans, had teamed with newcomer Tim

Anglin and four "ringers" from Belize: Daniel Cruz, Armin Lopez, Jerry Rhaburn, and Leroy Romero. While their seven-person team led the way at every checkpoint, Pete and Wade Binion, John Maika, Vance Sherrod, Pat Petrisky, and Mark Simmons held on for second place all the way to Seadrift. The winning seven-person team won the race in 36 hours and 56 minutes.

Finishing in fourth place overall were the Cowboys: John Mark Harras, John Dupont, Jerry Cochran, Rob Wytaske, Sammy Prochaska, and Shaun Bain. Regrettably, Bill Stafford, a founding member of the "Cowboys" team and the reason behind the team's name—he always raced in a cowboy hat—did not race. For the first time in twenty-two years, Bill had chosen to sit this one out.

John Jackson had an impressive race, finishing seventh in the USCA C-1 class in 47 hours and 22 minutes, and Holly Nelson, Mary Tipton, and Sandy Yonley finished eighth overall in 48 hours and 31 minutes.

2006

In 2006, a rule change by the TWS Board limited the total number of paddlers per boat to no more than six. This rule change was implemented to help create parity in the race. Returning again after last year's overall win were the three Belize national champs, Armin Cruz, Jerry Rhaburn, and Daniel Cruz. Daniel's cousins, Efrain and Amado Cruz, also joined the team, with John Bugge filling the sixth seat in the Unlimited Class. The strong six-person team would certainly be a formidable opponent for a new Mynar team, back after a one-year absence.

For the first eight hours the two teams ran neck and neck, but then by the Gonzales checkpoint, the Bugge/Belize team began to pull away. By Seadrift, the front boat had pulled farther ahead and finished the race first overall in 38 hours. The Mynar team finished second, 44 minutes back.

2007

With river flows higher than normal, the 2007 Safari was a true record breaker. This year's competitors represented fourteen states, Belize, and the United Kingdom. While a close duel was expected between the six-person canoes, an early boat wreck by canoe #314 occurred just before Staples. To everyone's amazement, the six-person canoe, broken in two pieces, was cobbled together with duct tape and ingenuity and still finished in 58 hours and 50 seconds.

The winning six-man team was made up of four Texans (West Hansen, Richard Steppe, Pete Binion, and Wade Binion) and two of the finest paddlers in Belize (Armin Lopez and Amado Cruz). Finishing in second place overall was Carter Johnson from California, recording the first ever second place finish by a solo competitor. He also set a solo record of 36 hours and 3 minutes. Another Belizean, Jerry Rhaburn, was fourth overall and set a new USCA C-1 record of 37 hours and 7 minutes—truly an amazing time. The mixed record was also broken by Fred Mynar and his wife, Debra Lane, in a time of 39 hours and 45 minutes.

For the first time in the forty-five-year history of the Safari, a woman, Ann Best, completed the Safari in a USCA C-1. In the past women had not attempted the race in this class. Why? Well, a USCA solo canoe is the most difficult boat to navigate down the river. It has no rudder, you are sitting in the middle of a canoe that is difficult to turn, and you have no partner to help steer the canoe.

Jerry Rhaburn, a native of Belize, won the 2007 TWS C-1 class in a record 37 hours and 7 minutes and was fourth overall. He also finished first overall the two previous years (2005 and 2006). He is one of eleven Belizeans who traveled to Texas from 2004 to 2019 to race the Safari. Courtesy of San Marcos Daily Record

2008

On June 14, 2008, ninety boats lined up for the grueling race to the coast. Low flows and warm temperatures took their toll as competitors had to spend more time out in the Texas heat. To make matters worse, the lower coast below Tivoli had a new obstruction—a floating plant called water hyacinth (*Eichhornia crassipes*) was blocking a section of the river. The plant is an exotic that reportedly was brought to the 1884 World's Fair in New Orleans and somehow escaped into Louisiana waters and eventually into Texas. Native to Brazil, the plant flourishes under warm temperatures and had clogged the lower section of the river. Paddlers reaching the section had to pole their way through large rafts of hyacinth to reach open water.

A record number of nine Belizeans entered the 2008 race, and again that year the rivalry between the Bugge canoe #911 and the Mynar canoe #23 continued. While the Mynar boat had all Texans, John Bugge had recruited five paddlers from Belize. Team #314 was also vying for a win with two Texans, William Russell and Andrew Stephens, and four paddlers from Belize in the canoe. The competition between these three teams proved to be one of the closest in years.

At Victoria the Bugge team in canoe #911 dropped out of the race, giving the Mynar canoe the lead, which they held all the way to the end. On Sunday at 12:34 a.m., canoe #23 paddled by Jerry Cochran, Jeff Glock, Tommy Yonley, Mike Rendon, Kyle Mynar, and Logan Mynar, won the forty-sixth Texas Water Safari in 39 hours and 34 minutes. Tommy Yonley said, "It's an indescribable feeling to win. I've been doing this for years, and it was my dream to win it. We just kept pushing ourselves."[2]

Canoe #314 finished second in 41 hours and 15 minutes. The first two women finishers were Mollie

Finishing in sixtieth place with a time of 68 hours and 30 minutes was Zoltan Mraz. At sixty-seven, Zoltan became the oldest competitor to finish the Safari in an Unlimited C-1. Born in Budapest, Hungary, Zoltan took up paddling at an early age. Unlike in the United States, where paddling is a leisure/recreational sport, paddling in Hungary is a way of life. Even though Hungary is smaller than the state of Indiana, Hungarians have won eighty Olympic paddling medals—more than any other country.[1]

Binion and Pauline Tice, along with their father, Pete, and brother, Wade, in 53 hours and 1 minute. Erin Magee was the first woman solo finisher with a time of 65 hours and 28 minutes. In all, fifty-three boats finished the race. Bringing up the rear were the Amelio brothers, John and Jim, in 97 hours and 38 minutes.

2009

The forty-seventh Texas Water Safari was one of the toughest races on record. With low river flows and hot daily temperatures, competitors faced significant hardships en route to Seadrift. While every race is different, the 2009 Safari proved to be the toughest and slowest of the past twenty years.

One team vying for the overall win was made up of five young men from Houston in canoe #3007. While their average age was less than twenty years, all were accomplished canoeists. Stephen Rask was the oldest at twenty-three, his brother Peter was twenty, and his other brother, Philip, was eighteen. Jonathan Yonley was twenty years old, and Max Feaster was the youngest at seventeen. While this was the youngest five-person team ever assembled for the race, they had more paddling experience than many much older teams. All five were homeschooled in Houston, and from elementary school through high school their PE class was canoeing. They were fortunate to have expert teachers/instructors Peter and Kathie Derrick, who had won numerous Mixed and Solo Classes in the Safari dating back to 1976. Both Kathie and Peter would become members of the Texas Water Safari Hall of Fame in 2012.

Returning for another Safari were Belizeans Armin Lopez and Amado Cruz and his cousin Daniel Cruz. They had joined the team of Andrew Stephens,

William Russell, and Kyle Mynar and would certainly be in the running for the overall win. Another team in the Unlimited Class had traveled more than 8,000 miles to compete. The threesome of James Dauman, Jean-Marc Laventure, and Simon Dowker were investment bankers from Abu Dhabi and Dubai, United Arab Emirates. With a fitting name, Abu Dhabi Camels, the team had purchased a Minnesota three (that's a 27-foot touring canoe) and trained for the past seven months in the coastal waters of the Persian Gulf near Abu Dhabi. While the team would not be in contention to win the race, they had an incentive to finish, as they would be donating 50,000 Arab Emirates dirhams (worth about $13,500 dollars) to local charities back home.

On June 13, 2009, at 9:00 a.m., eighty-eight teams paddled across Spring Lake in San Marcos on their way to the coast. The first canoe to reach the Staples Checkpoint, 16 miles downstream, was the six-person Texan/Belizean team in canoe #314. Only five minutes back in second place were the five young men from Houston in canoe #3007. For the next few hours, boat number #314 increased its lead, but then at 11:30 p.m. Saturday night the Houston five in canoe #3007 caught canoe #314 about 85 miles downstream. During the early Sunday morning hours, canoe #314 began to again pull away and continued their lead to Seadrift, finishing at 7:23 a.m. Monday morning. Finishing at 7:53 a.m., only thirty minutes back, was canoe #3007. When the front two boats had safely pulled their canoes on shore in Seadrift, the Abu Dhabi Camels were downstream of Hochheim, less than halfway down the course. Keeping a steady pace, the Abu Dhabi Camels crossed the finish line in forty-sixth place with a time of 91 hours and 36 minutes. Fred Mynar had an outstanding solo race, finishing third overall in 46 hours and 41 minutes.

2010

On July 10 at 9:00 a.m., ninety-four canoes lined up for the forty-eighth Texas Water Safari. For the third time, Sammy Prochaska entered the Solo Class. While Sammy had raced in several different classes in the past, including overall wins in 2003 and 2004, this year he was going to do it alone. With fourteen finishes to his credit, Sammy was obviously a hard-core competitor, but he also took a low-key approach to the race: "Try not to get excited with any obstacle you come up on. Anything can happen, and you do the best you can with it. Some ideas don't work and everybody does things differently. Everyone has their own ideas about how to do stuff, and it will all work. It's all a matter of if you like it or if you can deal with it."[3]

For the seventh straight year, several ringers from Belize entered the race. This year, it was Amado, Daniel, and Efrain Cruz. Also rounding out the six-person team were Sam Ritchie from Virginia and Andrew Soles from Washington, DC. Texan Andrew Stephens filled the sixth seat, and William Russell was their team captain. Also in contention for an overall

World's largest aluminum canoe #1775 passing through Cottonseed Rapid (mile 9). Joe Hunt (stern), his nephew Trey Fly, and four ex-marine buddies finished the race in 60 hours and 50 minutes. Courtesy of Patty Hunt

win were six Texans: Jerry Cochran, Jeff Glock, Wade Binion, Chuck Stewart, and Fred and Brian Mynar.

One canoe entered in the Unlimited Class was much different from the rest. Unlike the long, sleek, carbon/Kevlar six-person canoes vying for the overall win, this canoe was made of aluminum. The history behind the canoe is an interesting one.

In 2009 Joe Hunt, an ex-marine, attended a breakfast meeting of the Blue/Green, an informal group of marines and navy seals that meet monthly. When Joe, a Safari veteran, began talking about the Safari, several of his marine buddies immediately said they wanted to do the race to honor our servicemen and women. Once Mike Riley heard about the effort, he generously donated his time to build the six-man canoe. Mike, a Safari veteran and master metal worker, offered to fabricate the canoe out of aluminum.

First, Mike cut an Alumacraft canoe, made of heavy-duty aluminum, into two equal halves. Next, he welded an aluminum middle section to the bow and stern sections. The resulting massive 30-foot canoe was strong as an ox and weighed about as much.

Shortly before the race, tragedy struck when one of the ex-marine's team members, who worked as a motorcycle cop, crashed his bike and injured is arm and hand. With the team down to five, Joe Hunt recruited his nephew, Trey Fly, to fill the sixth seat.

Once the gun went off at the forty-eighth Safari, the two top teams pushed each other all the way to the finish, with the team of Stephens/Ritchie/Soles/Cruz/Cruz/Cruz winning in 34 hours and 40 minutes. The aluminum C-6 finished in twenty-fifth place in 60 hours and 50 minutes. Sixty-nine canoes finished the race.

2011

On June 11, 2011, the town of San Marcos was buzzing with excitement. For the previous two days, there had been an invasion of cars, vans, and large trucks with long skinny canoes strapped on top. That morning the grounds of the Meadows Center on the Texas State University Campus were overflowing with vehicles, and there were two large tents with several hundred people crowded underneath. At 9:00 a.m., 102 teams launched their canoes en route to Seadrift for the forty-ninth Safari.

There were several six-person teams competing for the overall win, including the top two teams from the previous year. While there were a few substitutions on both teams, all were accomplished paddlers. For the first time in the history, a six-woman team—Holly Orr, Samantha Binion, Virginia Parker, Sandy Yonley, Natalie Taylor, and Jamie Norman—entered the race.

Once the race started, the top two teams from the previous year took the early lead and traded places several times over the first 200 miles. Then somewhere below Victoria Checkpoint, Andrew Stephens, William Russell, Sam Ritchie, Daniel Hammer, and Amado and Daniel Cruz pulled away, holding on for the win in 39 hours and 51 minutes. Gaston Jones, Max Feaster, Jeff Glock, and the three Mynars, Fred, Kyle, and Logan, finished one hour back. The Yonley brothers, Tommy and Jonathan, had an impressive tandem effort, finishing third overall, and the six women in canoe #6 finished in tenth place.

The last canoe crossed the finish line in 98 hours and 56 minutes. After four days on the water, Ben Keating and James Graham paddled their battered, bruised, and leaking canoe across the finish line. Finishing the race had a special meaning to them.

Both were retired US Marines who entered the race to raise money for the Wounded Warriors Project. "There are a lot of needs out there," says Graham. "We're GIs ourselves and we just support them. They need some additional help in different places and we're there to help them."[4] While 102 boats started the race, only 78 finished.

2012

On the fiftieth anniversary of the Texas Water Safari, the TWS Board created the Texas Water Safari Hall of Fame in recognition of all those competitors who had faithfully raced and finished ten or more times.

In celebration of the fiftieth year, a record 135 canoes entered the race. While the celebration and kickoff of the race was a joyous and festive one, the festivities were dampened by an unfortunate turn of events that occurred on June 10.

Approximately 8 miles downstream of the Gonzales Checkpoint 4, early Sunday morning, team #22 was having problems. Thirty-year-old Brad Ellis, a first-time competitor, was feeling bad so he laid down in the canoe while his partner Ian Rolls continued to paddle.

Without warning, Brad fell out of the canoe. Ian entered the water and rescued him. Shortly thereafter, another canoe stopped to give aid. Brad was

Brad Ellis in the bow and Ian Rolls in the stern navigate the dreaded Cottonseed Rapid. Later, on day two of the 2012 Safari, tragedy struck when Brad fell from the canoe downstream of the Gonzales checkpoint #4. Courtesy of Ashley Landis

unresponsive, and a call was made to Life Flight. Brad was flown to a San Antonio hospital for treatment. While a medical staff tried to revive him, he passed away Monday around noon. The cause of death was hyponatremia, a condition that is sometimes called "water poisoning." The condition occurs when sodium levels are extremely low in the blood. This condition can cause nausea, headaches, confusion, seizures, comas, and death.

While the awards banquet would normally be cause for celebration, this year those in the audience of competitors and spectators were saddened by the loss of Brad Ellis. Chris LaRocque, who had trained with Brad, said the following:

> Brad was excited about this. We all practiced and we were doing a logjam together. We spent a lot of time on Google Earth, putting coordinates together, and I did everything I could to make sure I was ready to go. I was really nervous. We did

(Traylor) Cut and we weren't sure what direction to take. And then you look at Brad … and he says, "Oh it's so cool. What an adventure." He looked around and he had the time of his life.[5]

For the first time in the history of the race, a competitor completed the Safari on a stand-up paddleboard (SUP). While many racers felt that it was foolhardy to even attempt the race standing up, Shane Perrin, an elite athlete from St. Louis, finished the race on an SUP in 90 hours and 54 minutes—truly an incredible feat. Even more impressive was the fact that Shane is a kidney transplant recipient, and because of then Safari rules, Shane had to carry all his meds with him on the board during the race. Shane would return in 2019 for an even bigger challenge.

The winning team in 2012 was William Russell, Andrew Stephens, Sam Ritchie, Andrew Soles, Amado Cruz, and Daniel Cruz, with a time of 38 hours and 30 minutes.

17

C-6s Continue to Dominate
2013–2021

2013

The following year, the TWS Board dedicated the fifty-first Texas Water Safari to Brad Ellis and created the Brad Ellis Spirit Award. The award was created to keep Brad's memory alive and would be presented in future Safaris to competitors that exhibit extraordinary acts of sportsmanship. The board also made several rule changes:

- Each team could have one or two team captains.

- In addition to water and ice, team captains could now provide food to competitors during the race.

- Competitors could now receive medical supplies during the race.

While some thought the changes were a good idea, others felt that allowing competitors to take in food defeated the initial mandate of the race, which stated, "Every effort has been made to make it the most rugged event of its kind."

When Safari president Allen Spelce was asked why the changes were made, he said, "Not just from a medical standpoint but from the rules as a whole … how can we make it safer and fun for everyone?"[1]

On Monday, the third day of the 2013 race, Ian Rolls touched the seawall in Seadrift at 9:30 a.m. in fifth place overall. Rolls had been Brad Ellis's partner in the previous year's race. He said, "I was hoping it would be a cathartic deal, and it ended up being just that. Nothing in the race was a downer, and I never felt like I would be better not doing it. It was a good process."[2]

When asked if Brad was on his mind, Rolls said, "I thought about him a lot. I talked to him and he was in my heart the whole time. I asked him to help me and be with me. I had a lot of time to have one-way conversations with him."[3]

Fifty-one hours after Ian Rolls finished the race, Jon Newcomb crossed the finish line. His official time was 99 hours and 52 minutes. While he began the race with partner Andy Toppin, a Wounded Warrior, Andy had to abandon the race in Gonzales when his prosthesis became too painful to continue. Still wanting to finish, Jon paddled the last 175 miles in a heavy

aluminum canoe all alone. Jon Newcomb and Andy Toppin were awarded the first Brad Ellis Spirit Award that year.

The overall winner of the race in 2013 was the Mynar canoe. This time a second generation of Mynars was in the canoe. Kyle and Logan Mynar, their Uncle Fred, Jerry Cochran, Tommy Yonley, and Andrew Condie finished in 39 hours and 45 minutes.

2014

On June 14, 2014, eighty-one teams started the fifty-second Texas Water Safari. With Texas going through a major drought, river flows were down, causing some major logjams in the river. When river flows are low, fallen trees tend to stay in place and logs and other floating debris tend to build up, forming logjams.

Under these conditions, competitors spend more time under the hot Texas sun, and the finishing times are slower.

While the six-person canoes would again be vying for the overall win or a high finish, other teams were looking to win their individual classes. Heather Harrison was going solo for the first time and was looking forward to the challenge. Tommy Yonley would be racing for the eighteenth time and this year in the solo class. He had a string of seventeen consecutive finishes dating back to 1997. John Mark Harras would be racing again with the Cowboys. Each year John Mark and his perennial partner, John Dupont, recruited other paddlers to fill their six-man team. This year they recruited several "ringers" from Belize. Charlie and Coy Kouba, father and son, would be racing their first TWS, and their goal was simply to finish. Roger Zimmerman, with four finishes to his credit, would attempt to become the oldest finisher at seventy-six years of age.

Once the gun went off, the six-person team of Ian Rolls, Clay Wyatt, Gaston Jones, Andrew Condie, Wade Binion, and Jeff Glock led the field at every checkpoint, finishing in 40 hours and 3 minutes. Tommy Yonley finished his eighteenth Safari third overall in a solo boat. John Mark Harras finished fifth overall in the six-person Cowboys canoe. It was his twenty-ninth time to finish the race. Heather Harrison finished solo at 3:33 p.m. on Tuesday and, ironically, her canoe number was #333. While she had hoped to finish much faster, the rigors of the race had taken their toll: "Doing it solo was way more difficult than I could have anticipated or than anyone could have told me."[4] Roger Zimmerman, Santiago Marroquin, John Valdivia, and Kenneth Startz finished

the race in 74 hours and 52 minutes. Zimmerman fulfilled his goal and became the oldest finisher at seventy-six years of age.

2015

Better rainfall prior to the fifty-third Safari gave competitors hope of a faster race. While higher flows are a welcome sight to the racers, fast moving water also presents new challenges, especially when competitors are paddling at night. Canoe wrecks and injuries are a legitimate concern, and teams have to exercise caution in the fast-moving water. Rhett Stuman, five-time finisher, cautioned that, "It's faster, so you hurt less, but there's some danger because of the currents. Normally, when you tip over here you can stand up in the water. But we tipped over on a training run and we were out for thirty minutes."[5]

Tommy Yonley paddling in the 2014 Safari. He finished his first Safari in 1997 and has completed and finished every year since. He finished third overall in 2014 making it eighteen consecutive finishes. Courtesy of Ashley Landis

Returning again was the previous year's six-person canoe, and to no surprise to the field, for the second consecutive time, the team finished first overall in 35 hours and 2 minutes. The tandem team of Max Feaster and Jonathan Yonley had an impressive race also, finishing second overall and winning the Tandem Class in 38 hours and 22 minutes.

While several teams had impressive times, the fifth-place team was the talk of the race. At 2:39 a.m. on Monday, July 15, Virginia Condie (formerly Parker) and Kaitlin Jiral set a new record in the Women's Unlimited Class. While the tandem team, "Martindale Mamacitas," certainly deserve a lot of credit for their effort, they credited their support team for making it all possible. They were on a record pace early in the race and Kyle Mynar, Kaitlin's boyfriend (and now husband), purposely underestimated their progress; the team broke the existing record by more than two hours. Kaitlin said, "He was doing that so that we would stay motivated, which I appreciated for

sure. I would lie to my team too. So that was kind of fun."[6] Eighty-one boats finished the race that year.

2016

High flows in 2016 made the Texas Water Safari one of the fastest and most competitive races in years. The top two six-person teams pushed each other all the way to the finish, with the winning team of Fred, Kyle, and Logan Mynar, Tommy Yonley, Phil Bowden, and Jason Cade finishing in an impressive 31 hours and 33 minutes. Jason Cade, who finished in the winning canoe, said, "Oh my gosh, it was too intense. All night long they were like just right there. I think it made us race faster for sure. We went harder than we would have gone."[7] Virginia Condie also set a new women's solo record with an impressive time of 40 hours and 17 minutes. Veteran competitor Mac McCann, at seventy-eight years of age, set a new record for the oldest competitor to finish the

Mac McCann (white shirt) and partner Kenneth Startz complete the 2016 Safari in 72 hours and 35 minutes. At seventy-eight years of age, Mac became the oldest competitor to complete the Safari. Courtesy of Ashley Landis

race along with his partner Kenneth Startz. While completing the race at age seventy-eight would be truly remarkable for anyone, McCann also suffers from Parkinson's disease and has arthritis and kidney issues. This made his effort even more impressive. His clinical massage therapist said, "It has been phenomenal to see how far he has come from lying in bed to being out on the water. He never wanted to give up and you could see that he was in good spirits the whole time."[8]

Also worthy of recognition was the solo effort by Robert Briggs. Instead of a canoe or kayak, Robert paddled a stand-up paddleboard (SUP) in an outstanding time of 71 hours and 41 minutes. It hurts my legs and ankles to think about it.

Chelsea Keenam and Joseph Lyon were the last team to finish, in 98 hours and 45 minutes. While they had not expected to have a cheering section at the finish, to their surprise, a crowd of fans awaited. Here is Chelsea's reaction: "It was great to see people here cheering us on when we got to the finish line. I honestly thought no one was going to be here, and it felt great to be back on land."[9] That year, 102 canoes finished the race.

2017

With interest in the Safari at an all-time high, a record 143 teams lined up for the race start. The race had always been a male-dominated event, with the men outnumbering the women about ten to one. However, the number of women participants had grown exponentially in the past ten years, and women had certainly made an impressive showing. In fact, over the past ten years, twenty-five women had finished in the top ten places overall. In 2017, a record forty women signed up for the race.

Two teams were vying for top spot in the Women's Class. Returning again after a fifth place overall in 2015 were Virginia Condie and Kaitlin Jiral, with Shannon Issendorf making the team a threesome that would be challenging the men's teams. Their major competition in the class was a five-woman team of Holly Orr, Debbie Richardson, Melissa James, Amy Boyd, and Rebekah Feaster. While both teams had some seasoned competitors, both had some newcomers that would be tested. Generally speaking, a five-person team would be favored over a three-person team, but the length and obstacles of the race can change all that.

The five-woman team made an impressive showing, finishing fifth overall with a time of 43 hours and 13 minutes. One hour and seven minutes back, the three-woman team finished an impressive seventh overall.

The Yonley brothers, Tommy and Jonathan, teamed up again and had an outstanding race, finishing second overall. Kyle Mynar and Belizean Henner Cruz paddled a USCA C-2 to third place overall in 39 hours and 26 minutes. The winning team of Andrew Condie, Chris Issendorf, Clay Wyatt, Gaston Jones, Ian Rolls, and stern man Jay Daniel finished in 36 hours and 49 minutes. A new record 109 boats finished the fifty-fifth Safari.

2018

The 2018 Safari was the most closely contested race for the overall win in its fifty-six-year history. While canoe #150, with Andrew Condie, Nick Walton, Tommy Yonley, William Russell, Ian Rolls, and Amado Cruz, took the early lead, twenty-six hours later at the Victoria Checkpoint (mile 200), they were only four minutes ahead of canoe #123 (Clay Wyatt,

Michael and Ben Schlimmer, and Fred, Logan, and Kyle Mynar). Eager to increase their lead, they picked up the pace and paddled over the saltwater barrier (mile 248) with a 13-minute lead. They reached the bay first, but their boat capsized in the rough waters and the team swam for 30 to 40 minutes.

When the team finally reentered the canoe, they were uncertain if they still held the lead. Waves crashed against their canoe and water poured over the sides, causing them to capsize again. After about 10 minutes, they washed closer to shore and were finally able to reenter the canoe. With the finish line in sight, they paddled frantically toward the lights of the pavilion, not knowing if they were still in first place. Once they reached the seawall and heard the congratulatory cheers of the crowd, they learned that they had won the race. On Sunday, June 11 at nine forty-five at night, Andrew Condie, Nick Walton, Tommy Yonley, William Russell, Ian Rolls, and Amado Cruz won the Texas Water Safari in 36 hours and 45 minutes. Finishing only five minutes later, Clay Wyatt, Michael and Ben Schlimmer, and Fred, Logan, and Kyle Mynar were second overall. Solo paddler Erin Magee completed the Texas Water Safari for the twentieth time, more than any other woman. It was also her fifteenth solo finish, which is more than any other competitor—man or woman.

2019

The fifty-seventh Texas Water Safari had the largest turnout in the history of the race. On June 10 at 9:00 a.m., a record 176 teams lined up for the grueling 260-mile race to the coast. Four days later, 142 teams finished—also a record. First-time racers reached a new high as well, with thirty-nine teams entering the Novice Class.

One of the most impressive records that fell that year was the Women's unlimited record. With a time of 37 hours and 31 minutes, Virginia Condie, Kaitlin Jiral, Morgan Kohut, and Mary Schlimmer shattered the old record of Virginia and Kaitlin of 41 hours and 29 minutes, set in 2015. The team placed fourth overall. Mary Schlimmer, the only non-Texan in the canoe, traveled all the way from Michigan to compete. Mary, "a ringer" by anyone's standard, is one of the finest women marathon racers in the United States. While it's true that most people expect the men's team to be the fastest, these four women are changing that.

After a seven-year hiatus, Shane Perrin returned again to race the Safari on a stand-up paddle board (SUP), but this time, he brought five other paddlers and a six-person stand-up paddleboard. Actually, the SUP looked like a stand-up outrigger. The board was twenty-nine feet and six inches long, weighed 97 pounds, and had an "ama" just like an outrigger canoe. Because the board was four feet wide, the team had to remove the ama on some portages. According to Shane, the board took a terrible beating during the race, and he had to use six or seven rolls of Gorilla Tape to make repairs. On Tuesday, June 11, 2019, at 7:55 p.m., the team finished the race in 82 hours and 55 minutes.

The winning six-person team from the previous year returned with five of the original paddlers, but Bill Torongo, an elite paddler from Michigan, replaced the Belize phenom Amado Cruz. To no one's surprise, the new team won again in an impressive time of 34 hours and 27 minutes. Lillian Jones and Gaston, her father, had a great race in the Adult/Youth Class, finishing in 45 hours and 47 minutes. In a gallant effort they missed the record by only two minutes; that record was set in 2015 by Cecili and

Shane Perrin (bow) and members of the six-person SUP Team, including: Chip Walker, Justin Brooke, Jessica Kiefer, Jerico Lefort, and Kyle Patrick. The team completed the 2019 Safari in 82 hours and 55 minutes—an incredible effort. Courtesy of Sandy Yonley

John Bugge. Tommy and Jonathan Yonley had an outstanding race, finishing second overall, only 29 minutes behind the six-man winning team.

2020

Many large gatherings, including sporting events, were postponed or canceled during 2020 as COVID-19 emerged and became a global pandemic. Numerous canoe races and especially the larger ones up north chose to cancel their annual competitions.

While a number of factors had to be considered before hosting the Safari, the obvious one was the health effects of the virus, which was rapidly spreading in Texas and across the nation. Hosting the race could potentially spread the virus to competitors and spectators alike. Other considerations included gaining access to checkpoints that could be closed to public gatherings and recruiting enough volunteers to host the race. Given the various concerns, the Texas Water Safari Board made a tough decision and canceled the 2020 race.

Following last year's cancellation of the Texas Water Safari, marathon paddlers were eager to once again compete in the race. The Safari Board faced several challenges, including not only the coronavirus but also higher than normal rainfall, moderate flooding on the lower Guadalupe River, muddy roads leading to Safari checkpoints, and closure of public lands near the river. Fortunately, rainfall declined in early June, the water levels dropped, muddy roads leading to checkpoints became passable, and Victoria City Park was opened to the public, allowing the race to be held on schedule.

On June 12, 138 boats lined up for the fifty-eighth Texas Water Safari. Unlike previous years, two elite teams chose to race in C-4s instead of the traditional C-6s that had won the race for the past fourteen years straight. One month prior, two C-4s (canoes #1 and #123) had placed first and second overall in the qualifying 35-mile Texas River Marathon and would certainly be in contention for the win.

On race day, C-4 (canoe #1) and C-3 (canoe # 123) and the leading C-6 (canoe #407) were the first three teams to reach the Staples Checkpoint (mile 16). Canoe #1, paddled by Tommy Yonley, Kyle Mynar, Tim Rash, and Nick Walton, took the lead at the Luling Highway 90 Bridge checkpoint (mile 39) and held it all the way to Seadrift, finishing in 35 hours and 46 minutes. Canoes #407 and #123 pushed each other all the way to Seadrift. Canoe #407, paddled by Phil Bowden, Brad Daniels, Ryan Martinez, Dylan Mchardy, Ryan Slebos, and Wes Wyatt, finished second in 37 hours and 1 minute. The third place canoe (#123), paddled by Andrew Condie, Clay Wyatt, and Danny Medina, had an unplanned handicap. While the team had originally planned to paddle with Mike Schlimmer, a New Yorker, he was injured the week

Adelaide Rolls with dad Ian Rolls (not pictured), swimming the boat under the Palmetto checkpoint bridge in 2021. They won first mixed tandem unlimited and first adult-child. Adelaide was thirteen. Courtesy of Ashley Landis

Lilly Jones (*right*) and her dad Gaston Jones (*left*) at the Palmetto checkpoint in 2021. Lilly was seventeen years old. They won first Aluminum in 52 hours and 28 minutes. Courtesy of Ashley Landis

before the Safari. So, the team, with only three paddlers, placed third in a gallant effort.

Mollie Binion, Cecili Bugge, Lydia Huelskamp, Melissa James, and Holly Orr in canoe #357 placed fifth overall in 41 hours and 41 minutes. This was the second consecutive year that a women's team placed in the top five overall. Top father/daughter teams of Adelaide and Ian Rolls and Lillian and Gaston Jones won the Mixed Tandem Unlimited Class and Aluminum Class, respectively. Both teenagers, Adelaide, at thirteen years of age, and Lillian, seventeen, will be pushing their competitors for years to come.

Adding to the grueling nature of the race, a Monday (day three) mid-afternoon squall dumped heavy rains, and 50+ mile-an-hour winds pounded the Seadrift area. The squall capsized canoes in the bay, stranded team captains on muddy roads leading to the Swinging Bridge Checkpoint, and collapsed the tents at the finish line. Several competitors were rescued in the bay, stranded vehicles were towed to firm ground, and the finish line tent was repaired Monday night, paving the way for the banquet on Tuesday afternoon. Ninety-nine of the original 138 boats finished the race.

Epilogue

While all Safaris have their challenges, the 59th race was one of the most difficult in years. Low rainfall in the spring greatly decreased river flows in the San Marcos and Guadalupe and unusually high 100-degree temperatures slowed the racers. Many were unable to meet mandatory time checkpoints along the way.

Once racers reached San Antonio Bay, 20 mph headwinds greeted them. Some attempted to cross the bay, risking swamping their boats and having to swim until they could find shallow water to climb back aboard. Others waited along the shore, or on spoil islands, for the winds to subside. All these conditions knocked out 67 of the original 138 boats that started the race.

For the 21st time over the past twenty-five years, a six-person canoe won the race. The winning elite 6-person crew (canoe #2) included five Texans, all previous winners, and one first-timer from Michigan. They took the lead somewhere below the Luling Checkpoint 2 (mile 39) and held it all the way to Seadrift, finishing in 40 hours and 52 minutes.

"This year's race was one of the hottest I can remember," said Clay Wyatt, stern man of the winning team. "There was absolutely no cloud cover on day two. We were getting buckets of ice water at every stop to stay cool."

"I think around Cuero it became pretty apparent that we were pulling away and we would most likely take the river portion of the course if we stayed healthy and continued racing smart. I never once had it in my head that we had the race won until we crossed the finish line. I have a lot of respect for the guys in the boat we were up against and anything can happen in the bay." Other members of the winning team were Andrew Condie, Gaston Jones, Logan Mynar, Ian Rolls, and Weston Willoughby, who traveled from Michigan to compete.

The race saw stiff competition in the Mixed Tandem Unlimited Class with several previous winners vying for the title. Last year's solo winner, Keifer Mauldin, and six-time finisher, Brenda Jones, were fresh off a Mixed Class win in the Texas River Marathon in May. Vance Sherrod, a Hall of Famer with twenty finishes, teamed up with Samantha (Sam) Binion. They won the class in 2017 and would be vying for the class win.

Once the gun went off, the Jones/Mauldin team (canoe #5961) took the early lead and held it all the way to the Palmetto Checkpoint 3 (mile 60). The Binion/Sherrod team (canoe #216) took the lead somewhere below the Palmetto Checkpoint and held it all the way to Checkpoint 10, the Saltwater Barrier at mile 248.

The Binion/Sherrod team had a comfortable lead of approximately 2 hours, and with only 12 miles to the finish, they were the odds-on favorite for the class win. However, two mother/son mixed teams (canoe #333 and canoe #357) had methodically moved up to second and third, respectively.

After 2 1/2 days of paddling, with little sleep, and facing stiff headwinds and a rough bay, several of the top mixed teams decided to stop and get some rest, while one mother/son decided to continue on.

Making their move, canoe #357, paddled by Holly Orr and son William, picked up the pace, passing all the class contenders and finishing the race in 64 hours and 16 minutes. Their bay crossing was the eighth fastest of the seventy-one boats that completed the race. Even more impressive is the fact that William is a first-timer and he is only thirteen years of age.

"The hardest thing was staying awake at night and the heat of the day during the long boring sections," William said, "I could not keep my eyelids open. They kept closing even while I was paddling."

William's mother, Holly, added a funny story. "As we approached Nursery Bridge Sunday night, William was sound asleep in the back of the canoe. He was leaning on the side, about to flip us. I pulled over and attempted to wake him—called his name and shook him. The only response I got was, 'Stop it Matthew' [his younger brother's name].' He would randomly sit up and begin paddling—only he didn't have a paddle in his hands—then tell me good night and lay back down."

When asked about beating the adults in his class, he said, "Winning didn't mean a whole lot to me, other than beating the other mother/son team [Heather and Cameron Harrison, boat #333]. But it was still pretty cool passing all the people in the bay."

All Safaris have their mishaps, boat wrecks, hallucinations, and unplanned debacles, and this one was no exception. The heat, low river flows, and high winds slowed the pace, causing an unusually high rate of DNFs.

Most novice competitors choose to race an aluminum canoe, and some race the Aluminum Class in successive years. However, most experienced racers move on to lighter, faster racing canoes, because they finish faster, avoiding long hours in the Texas heat. Hoyt Moss is the exception.

In 2001 Hoyt Moss finished his first Safari in an aluminum canoe—the only canoe he has raced over the past twenty-one years. With nineteen aluminum canoe finishes to his credit, no one can come close to this achievement. While he planned to complete his 20th Safari in 2022, his hopes were dashed by an unplanned action of his own doing.

"We made it through the logjams, just before dark," he said. "Now just on the other side of the jams with daylight fading, my eyes could not transition to the dark and all the flashes of light from our bow and headlights. The glow from underneath the boat was calming but it felt like we were high in the air on a flying carpet, and I was able to make ripples in the air with my fingers.

"Most people would have stopped and slept, let the hallucinations slow down and then gotten back in the race. We decided to push on past the saltwater barrier—after all it was only two hours more to the wooden bridge. I would like to call the next stretch of river 'The Village of the Damned.'

"The mirrored effect from the small river cabins was tough to get through. My eyes were all over the place and my partner in the bow had grown tired of me explaining what I was seeing in the lights. Long story short, by the time we reached the wooden bridge, I had positioned myself in the middle of our 17-foot aluminum boat. I was anxiously waiting for an opportunity to get over to the bank. Before the boat stopped, I jumped like a cat, some say, with my paddle, and headed toward a group of parked cars.

"I woke up to my team captain telling me, 'Better luck next year.' Finishing the Texas Water Safari has to be one of the most incredible feelings I have ever experienced in my life; getting in that car and being told it was over with only 8 miles to go is one of the worst. 'Better luck next year!' Ouch. Hut!"

While every safari finish is special, the tenth entitles a competitor to a place in the Texas Water Safari Hall of Fame. Myla Weber in canoe #34 had nine finishes. A finish in the 2022 Safari would be her tenth. A fiasco by her team near the end almost wrecked her chances.

Months before the race a team came together to support Myla's Hall of Fame run. Her husband, Jim, said, "Bobby Smart started the plan to get a big boat together to celebrate Myla's 10th finish. Training was always fun and we performed well."

He also said, "We had a smooth run the first day down the San Marcos River and were right where we expected to be. As in any race, paddlers have their ups and downs, and we experienced that as well. We made it to the bay and past the Cowboy's [team] as they skirted up. More high expectations brewed. However, the bay had other ideas. The high winds and big waves mixed with no sleep for almost 60 hours took its toll on us. Hard to say but true, five paddlers at that time have not one brain between them. We paddled and walked all night until we were almost to the original finish when our pumps failed and we had to put the boat up on the seawall."

At his point in the race, Tuesday morning, I was standing on the second-floor porch of the Seadrifter Inn, in Seadrift. To my surprise, I looked down Bay Avenue and saw safari canoe #34, named "Naut Normal," and five paddlers staggering along the road. Some paddlers were carrying the canoe while others held hands, supporting each other. I immediately recognized Jim and Myra Weber, Bobby Smart, Edoh Amiran, and Luke Parker. Speechless by the site, I kept quiet and watched them pass the hotel, then turn right at the boat basin and disappear. I knew it was a good three miles by road, versus just 3/4 of a mile by water, and I wondered if they planned to carry their boat all the way to the finish.

A few minutes later, Joy, my wife, and I jumped in the pickup and drove over to the area where the five-person boat had gone. There they were—Jim and Bobby carrying and floating the canoe and the trio of Luke, Myla, and Edoh holding hands and wading in the shallow water.

I had expected to see the team in canoe #34 paddle in to the finish several hours later, but instead, Bobby Smart came floating in all alone. The other four "Naut Normal" team members were still out in the shallow water. Over the next 45 minutes or so, the foursome floated, swam, and staggered like drunk sailors through the muck and mud along their shore. Once all five team members passed the finishing buoy, it was official. Team #34, Naut Normal, finished the race in 73 hours and 52 minutes in 30th place.

Two weeks after the race, I called Jim Weber to talk about their race experience and learn why they walked so much near the end. Maybe it was the hours with no sleep, sweltering Texas heat, or the rough bay crossing, whatever the reason, as he said earlier, they "had not one brain between them." His only explanation was, "A subtle suggestion of lightening the boat by removing gear ended up meaning we should get rid of our paddles. So from then on we were forced to walk or carry the boat." They truly were in a boat without paddles.

Jim also expressed how proud he was of his wife's finish and that they were only the third husband/wife team in the Texas Water Safari Hall of Fame. He also said, "We were out there as a team and determined to get a finish no matter what the race put before us. Through all the adversity we encountered no one ever said QUIT!"

I think we can all agree that team #34 and the canoe was "Naut Normal."

1. Other class winners were:

2. 1st Solo Unlimited, 1st Masters—Andrew McEwan—48:30 (4th overall).

3. 1st Tandem Unlimited—Brian Jones and Nate Tart- 51:46 (5th overall).

4. 1st Aluminum—Joe and Libby Geisinger —64:54 (10th overall)—An impressive feat by a father/daughter team racing against male teams.

5. 1st Solo Unlimited Woman—Salli O'Donnell —65:46 (11th overall)—This was the third consecutive win for Sally, who is also the most senior woman to ever complete the race solo.

6. 1st USCA C-2—Bill and Brandon Stafford —68:12 (15th overall)—This made Bill's 30th finish.

7. 1st Standard—Chris Champion and Wendell Smith—68:48 (16th overall).

8. 1st Novice—Trent Lowry and Bren Rose— 72:58 (22nd overall).

9. 1st Unlimited Women—Katie Bee and Kim Kaiser—77:38 (34th overall)

See the results for all fifty-nine Texas Water Safaris at https://www.texaswatersafari.org.

Appendix 1

The Texas Water Safari Hall of Fame

In recognition of paddlers' dedication to the race, the TWS Board created the Texas Water Safari Hall of Fame in 2012. To be inducted, a competitor had to complete the race at least ten times. On the fiftieth year of the race in 2012, oddly enough fifty competitors had completed at least ten Safaris.

Texas Water Safari Hall of Fame Plaque. Courtesy of Ashley Landis

Completing ten Safaris is indeed an impressive feat, but some competitors have completed twenty, thirty, or more. Consequently, the board created three levels of recognition: a 2,600-mile Club for all those who had at least ten finishes, a 5,200-mile Club for those who had competed at least twenty Safaris, and a 7,800-mile Club for those who had completed thirty or more Safaris. Each year, new honorees are inducted when they attain ten, twenty, or thirty finishes. Since the initiation of the Hall of Fame, eighty-five paddlers have completed at least ten Safaris.

Two competitors who have completed thirty or more Safaris are John Mark Harras (thirty-five) and John Dupont (thirty-two). In fact, John and John Mark have finished in the same boat twenty-seven times, which is more finishes than any other two competitors racing together. John Mark also finished the race for thirty consecutive years, which is the longest streak by any competitor. Both John Mark and John DuPont are permanent members of the well-known "Cowboys" team, which has gained notoriety over the years. The team has been featured on the cover of *Texas Parks and Wildlife* magazine, written up in the *New York Times*, included in a Blue Bonnet Electric Cooperative calendar, and pictured on the first page of the Texas Water Safari website.

John and John Mark are an impressive pair, but no individual can match the forty-two finishes of John

Some of the Texas Water Safari Hall of Fame Inductees: front row (sitting) Kathie Derrick, Ginsie Stauss, Joe Hunt, and Jim Pye. Standing (*left to right*) Stacy Greer, Ken Startz, Holly Orr, Mike Dross, Bobby Smart, Robert Youens, Phil Bowden, Ted Slaughter, James Ward, Jeff Wueste, Chris Paddack, Tommy Yonley, Tim Curry, Jay Daniel, Erin Magee, John Mark Harras, Grady Hicks, Peter Derrick, and Zoltan Mraz. Standing on table (*left to right*) Vance Sherrod, Hoyt Moss, John Dupont, and Jonathan Yonley. Courtesy of Ashley Landis

John Bugge, Hall of Famer, on his way to his forty-first TWS finish in 2019. His time was 52 hours and 39 minutes. Courtesy of Ashley Landis

Bugge. Forty-two finishes is equal to approximately 10,920 miles, roughly equivalent to traveling by air from New York City to Melbourne, Australia. Not only has John completed seven more Safaris than any other individual, he has also finished first place twenty-seven times in the following classes: Aluminum (four times), USCA C-2 (five times), Tandem Unlimited (twice), Solo (twice), Mixed (five times), Unlimited (four times), Parent/Child (once), Standard (three times), and USCA C-1 (once), and he has been an overall winner six times.

In recognition of John's accomplishments, the Texas Water Safari Board created a fourth level of recognition in 2019, the 10,400-Mile Club. John is the only member.

When asked why he continues to compete year after year, John said, "It's a little hard to put into words, but I'll try. The Safari is like the worst thing that happens to me every year and that's because it makes the other things so much better—like bumps in the road. Secondly, all the adversities that we go through, the different things that happen, and the perseverance that we have to maintain to get through these throughout the year, prepare us, and I think that's the reason I keep coming back. It prepares us for all those bumps in the road."

An important group within the hall of fame is the Mynar family, with a total of eighty-seven finishes to their credit. Joe, the patriarch, has eighteen; Brian, his oldest son, has twenty-two; and Kyle, his middle, son has fourteen finishes. His youngest son, Logan, has eight finishes, and Fred, Joe's younger brother, has twenty-five finishes. Since four Mynars are still racing, who knows how many finishes they may record in the future.

Several inductees have had a long string of consecutive finishes, but few can match the record of Pete Binion, who finished the race for twenty-eight consecutive years. During this time he has raced with a number of partners, including his son, Wade, and daughters, Pauline and Mollie. In 2017 he made it a total family affair when he raced with Mollie and Wade, his two children, and three grandchildren: Payton, Daniel, and Tristin. The streak ended in 2018 when his four-man team capsized in San Antonio Bay and had to be rescued. While Pete's incredible string of finishes is over, he finished in 2019 and in 2021 he finished his thirtieth Safari with his son, Wade, in 53 hours and 26 minutes. Pete's son, Wade, also has an impressive record of finishes. Beginning in 1995 he has raced every year except 2009 and the COVID year, 2020. He has twenty-five finishes to his credit.

When the Hall of Fame was established in 2012, Owen West was inducted with twenty-seven finishes. Since his first finish in 1969, he has registered for the race every single year. His 2019 Safari finish was Owen's twenty-eighth, and he became the oldest finisher at eighty-one years and ten months.

There are six women in the Texas Water Safari Hall of Fame: Kathie Derrick, Erin Magee, Holly Orr, Debbie Richardson, Ginsie Stauss, and Sandy Yonley.

Kathie Derrick was the first woman to finish ten Texas Water Safaris, and she was also the first woman to finish the race solo. The woman with the most finishes is Erin Magee. She has finished the race twenty-one times with sixteen solo finishes, which is more solo finishes than any other competitor, man or woman. In 2008, Debbie Richardson raced her first Texas Water Safari, and eleven years later she finished her twelfth consecutive Safari. Sandy Yonley has eleven finishes, Ginsie Stauss has twelve, and Holly Orr has finished thirteen times. A complete list of Water Safari Hall of Fame Inductees follows.

Pete Binion and son Wade, both TWS Hall of Fame inductees, and other family members in 2017. Pictured (*left to right*): Pete, Daniel Tice (grandson), Mollie Binion (daughter), Tristin Tice (granddaughter), Payton Binion (grandson), and Wade Binion (son). Courtesy of Patty Geisinger

Erin Magee, twenty-one finishes.
Courtesy of Ashley Landis

Debbie Richardson, twelve finishes.
Courtesy of Ashley Landis

Holly Orr, thirteen finishes.
Courtesy of Ashley Landis

Ginsie Stauss, eleven finishes.
Courtesy of Patty Geisinger

Sandy Yonley, eleven finishes.
Courtesy of Ashley Landis

Kathie Derrick, ten finishes.
Courtesy of Ashley Landis

Texas Water Safari Hall of Fame

2,600 Mile Club

2012—Wade Binion, Phil Bowden, Larry Coffey, Jay Daniel, Kathie Derrick, Peter Derrick, John Dunn, Jack Elvig, Mark Elvig, Gib Hafernick, West Hansen, Joe Hunt, Daryl Jiral, Jim Keirnan, Erin Magee, John Maika, Hoyt Moss, Zoltan Mraz, Joe Mynar, Johnny Prochaska, Sammy Prochaska, Timothy Rask, Mike Riley, Vance Sherrod, Mark Simmons, Robert Smart, Allen Spelce, Ginsie Stauss, Richard Steppe, Charlie Stewart, Chuck Stewart, James Ward, Jeff Wueste, Sandy Yonley, Tommy Yonley, Robert Youens

2013—Gaston Jones, Jim Pye, Jon Schoepflin

2014—Stacy Greer, Michael Rendon

2015—Holly Orr, Jeff Glock

2016—Max Feaster, Jonathan Yonley, Ken Startz

2017—Tim Curry, Mike Drost, Kyle Mynar, Chris Paddack, Liam Price

2018—John Hoffart, Randall Kissling, Debbie Richardson, Brandon Stafford

2019—Shawn Boyett, Andrew Condie, Benjamin Duckett, Kent Harlan, Norm Thomas, Jim Weber, Clay Wyatt

2021—Karim Aziz, Mark Hellinger, Chad Keeth, Michael "Mike" Martin, William Mitchell, John Qualls, Doug Rhude, Andrew Stephens, Don Zeek

5,200 Mile Club

2012—Pete Binion, Jerry Cochran, John Dupont, Tom Goynes, John Mark Harras, Grady Hicks, Brian Mynar, Fred Mynar, Pat Petrisky, Mike Shively, Ted Slaughter, Bill Stafford, Owen West

2013—John Dunn

2016—Wade Binion

2017—Tommy Yonley

2019—Erin Magee, Vance Sherrod

2021—West Hansen

7,800 Mile Club

2012—John Bugge

2016—John Mark Harras

2019—John Dupont

10,400 Mile Club

2019—John Bugge

Appendix 2

Race Results and Records (1963–2021)

Top three boats and top three boats with women (red) competitors

Year (Boats Finished)	Place	Competitors Names	Time (hr:min)
1963 (2)	1st Overall	James "Jimmy" Jones Lynn Maughmer	110:35
	2nd Overall	Sam Hare Fred Hurd Jr	145:00
1964 (14)	1st Overall	Robert "Bob" Gillings Albert "Al" Widing	80:27
	2nd Overall	Edward "Ed" Adams Leroy Widing	82:08
	3rd Overall	Harold Bludworth Jay Bludworth	83:44
	14th Overall	Bob Smith, Jim Waterman Willye Waterman	172.42
1965 (14)	1st Overall	Albert "Al" Widing Patrick "Pat" Widing	77:16
	2nd Overall	Edward "Ed" Adams Gib McEachern	77:55
	3rd Overall	Charles Hall Robert "Froggie" Sanders	missing
1966 (1)	1st Overall	Harold Bludworth Jay Bludworth	missing
1967 (6)	1st Overall	Harold Bludworth Jay Bludworth	missing
	2nd Overall	Charles Hall Robert "Froggie" Sanders	missing

Year (Boats Finished)	Place	Competitors Names	Time (hr:min)
	3rd Overall	Karl Lee Reddell Paul Sanders Jr	missing
1968 (14)	1st Overall	Norman "Buttons" Morgan Robert "Froggie" Sanders	48:17
	2nd Overall	John "Johnny" Bludworth James Patton	53:27
	3rd Overall	Don Dixon Patrick "Pat" Oxsheer	53:58
1969 (14)	1st Overall	Norman "Buttons" Morgan Robert "Froggie" Sanders	49:02
	2nd Overall	Charles Hall Lee Van Sickle	54:03
	3rd Overall	John "Johnny" Bludworth James Patton	55:32
1970 (13)	1st Overall	John Evans Robert "Bob" Mitchell	56:31
	2nd Overall	Tom Goynes Mike Wooley	58:06
	3rd Overall	Gary Knight James "Buddy" Mitchell	60:33
1971 (5)	1st Overall	Thomas "Tom" Goynes Patrick "Pat" Oxsheer	57:38
	2nd Overall	Gary Knight Michael "Mike" Wooley	66:55
	3rd Overall	Frank Land Morris Mason	76:07
1972 (21)	1st Overall	Thomas "Tom" Goynes Patrick "Pat" Oxsheer	43:55
	2nd Overall	Howard Gore Gary Knight	46:17
	3rd Overall	Tim Janak Tom Sofka	48:57
1973 (12)	1st Overall	Howard Gore Gary Knight	42:17

Year (Boats Finished)	Place	Competitors Names	Time (hr:min)
	2nd Overall	Robert Chatham Louis "Butch" Hodges	45:22
	3rd Overall	Richard "Ricky" Carter Lloyd "Bucky" Chatham	51:09
1974 (9)	1st Overall	Howard Gore Michael "Mike" Wooley	46:46
	2nd Overall	Terry Braun Louis "Butch" Hodges	47:53
	3rd Overall	Dennis Borowicz Perry Pauley	56:40
1975 (19)	1st Overall	John Nabors Michael "Mike" Wooley	38:05
	2nd Overall	Lloyd "Bucky" Chatham Robert Chatham	40:17
	3rd Overall	Jerry Cochran Thomas "Tom" Goynes	41:28
	5th USCA	Carol Keirnan James "Jim" Keirnan	65:46
	6th USCA	Kathie Derrick Peter Derrick	75:05
1976 (18)	1st Overall	Robert Chatham Louis "Butch" Hodges	37:18
	2nd Overall	Howard Gore Michael "Mike" Wooley	37:36
	3rd Overall	Dennis Borowicz Peter Derrick	41:47
	3rd USCA	Nova Hall Carol Keirnan	65:05
	5th Aluminum	Joe Hunt Nancy Wattner	66:10
	5th USCA	Edgar "Shorty" Hanks Laura Hanks	68:20
	5th Solo Unlimited	Kathie Derrick *** 1st Woman Solo Finisher	76:13

Year (Boats Finished)	Place	Competitors Names	Time (hr:min)
1977 (21)	1st Overall	Thomas "Tom" Goynes Patrick "Pat" Oxsheer	38:43
	2nd Overall	John Nabors Michael "Mike" Wooley	39:21
	3rd Overall	Chuck Lyda Carl Toeppner	43:20
	2nd USCA	Kathie Derrick Peter Derrick	49:19
	5th USCA	Edgar "Shorty" Hanks Laura Hanks	61:16
	4th Aluminum	Yvonne Bellmear Joe Hunt	69:15
1978 (15)	1st Overall	Pat Petrisky James "Jim" Trimble	45:31
	2nd Overall	John Nabors Michael "Mike" Wooley	46:39
	3rd Overall	James "Jim" Keirnan Merrill "Bubba" Wood	51:36
	3rd USCA	Laura Hanks Edgar "Shorty" Hanks	62:30
1979 (15)	1st Overall	Howard Gore Michael "Mike" Wooley	36:40
	2nd Overall	Scott McDonald Roy Tyrone	38:16
	3rd Overall	Jerry Cochran, Richard Miller Doug Lewis	39:45
	2nd USCA	Paula Goynes Thomas "Tom" Goynes	45:54
1980 (17)	1st Overall	Thomas "Tom" Goynes, Patrick "Pat" Oxsheer James "Jim" Trimble	43:40
	2nd Overall	Red Motley, Pat Petrisky Robert "Bob" Smith	46:34
	3rd Overall	Howard Gore Michael "Mike" Wooley	47:45

Year (Boats Finished)	Place	Competitors Names	Time (hr:min)
1981(16)	1st Overall	Thomas "Tom" Goynes, Patrick "Pat" Oxsheer, James "Jim" Trimble	40:41
	2nd Overall	John Oertel, Troy Swift David Young	46:45
	3rd Overall	John Bugge Bill Yonavich	46:56
	6th USCA	Cynthia Rogers Ray Rogers	98:45
1982 (18)	1st Overall	Red Motley, Pat Petrisky John Oertel, Troy Swift	42:30
	2nd Overall	Jerry Cochran, Doug Lewis Randall Lewis, Mike Shively	45:14
	3rd Overall	Peter Derrick	48:34
	1st USCA C2	Kay Edwards John Bugge	49:46
	2nd USCA C2	Margaret Shelton Alan Sawyer	50:02
1983 (27)	1st Overall	Thomas "Tom" Goynes Red Motley	42:10
	2nd Overall	John Oertel, Troy Swift Pat Petrisky, Marty Pribil	42:43
	3rd Overall	Jerry Cochran, Patrick "Pat" Oxsheer Mike Shively	44:37
	4th Aluminum	Lisa Frederick Lynn Poole	77:17
1984 (15)	1st Overall	Roy Tyrone Jerry Nunnery	54:00
	2nd Overall	Brian Mynar Joe Mynar	58:53
	3rd Overall	Steve Landick	59:02
	4th Overall	Thomas "Tom" Goynes Paula Goynes	70:12

Year (Boats Finished)	Place	Competitors Names	Time (hr:min)
	13th Overall	Marlane Angle Lelia Knight	94:02
1985 (26)	1st Overall	Thomas "Tom" Goynes Red Motley	43:10
	2nd Overall	Jerry Cochran, Doug Lewis Pat Petrisky, Troy Swift	44:22
	3rd Overall	Brian Mynar Joe Mynar	47:09
	6th Unlimited	John Mark Harras Carol Schaefer	81:10
1986 (38)	1st Overall	John Bugge Mike Shively	35:26
	2nd Overall	Jerry Cochran, Troy Swift Pat Petrisky (DNF)	38:36
	3rd Overall	Jerry Nunnery Roy Tyrone	40:18
	4th Unlimited	Carol Schaefer John Mark Harras	50:22
	lst Women's	Teddy Montgomery, Celeste Wilkinson Donna Bugge (DNF)	72:00
	1st Women's Solo	Marie McKay	85:05
1987 (30)	1st Overall	John Bugge Mike Shively	35:17
	2nd Overall	Rocky Harber Robert Youens	42:54
	3rd Overall	Mark Finstad Grady Hicks	45:41
	1st Mixed Unlimited	Carol Schaefer, John Mark Harras	48:32
	3rd USCA C2	Janet Smith Sandy Reinhart	50:43
	4th Unlimited	Teddy Montgomery Donna Bugge	50:54

Year (Boats Finished)	Place	Competitors Names	Time (hr:min)
1988 (31)	1st Overall	Fred Mynar, Brian Mynar Joe Mynar (DNF)	39:31
	2nd Overall	Jerry Cochran Pat Petrisky	41:09
	3rd Overall	John Bugge Mike Shively	42:28
	1st Mixed	Donna Bugge Jim Keirnan	55:33
	1st Women's	Sandy Reinhart Janet Smith	59:11
	2nd Mixed	Carol Taylor, John Mark Harras Corky Collier	61:29
1989 (19)	1st Overall	Fred Mynar, Brian Mynar Joe Mynar	45:45
	2nd Overall	Donna Bugge, John Bugge Russ Roberts	48:04
	3rd Overall	Mark Finstad, Grady Hicks	56:20
	2nd Mixed	Athanasee Swift Chris Paddack	59:10
	3rd Mixed	Dianna Finstad John Wilson	88:27
1990 (28)	1st Overall	John Bugge, Jerry Cochran Mike Shively	38:57
	2nd Overall	Brian Mynar, Fred Mynar (DNF) Joe Mynar	41:45
	3rd Overall	Mark Finstad, Phil Hicks Grady Hicks	42:53
	1st Mixed 1st Masters	Mary Ellen Keirnan Jim Keirnan	62:58
	1st Standard	Judy Haney Sam Thiede	65:46
	1st Women's	Debbie Brown Judy Hallmark	80:56

Year (Boats Finished)	Place	Competitors Names	Time (hr:min)
1991 (27)	1st Overall	John Bugge, Jerry Cochran Mike Shively	36:28
	2nd Overall	Joe Burns, Brian Mynar Joe Mynar, Bob Spain	37:18
	3rd Overall	Mark Finstad, Phil Hicks Grady Hicks	41:38
	1st Mixed 7th Unlimited	Ginsie Dunn John Dunn	49:43
	8th Unlimited	Donna Bugge, Dianna Finstad Teddy Gray (Montgomery)	57:43
	9th Unlimited	Mary Ellen Keirnan, Martha Koslosky Jim Keirnan, Ed Koslosky	61:50
1992 (42)	1st Overall	Joe Burns, Brian Mynar Joe Mynar, Fred Mynar	31:02
	2nd Overall	John Bugge, Jerry Cochran Mike Shively	32:27
	3rd Overall	Phil Bowden, John Dunn Roger Myers	34:33
	1st Mixed	Carolyn Stinson Ron Popp	48:44
	1st Women's Solo	Marie McKay	69:42
	3rd Mixed	Mary Wilson John Alexander Bob Brooks	74:13
1993 (27)	1st Overall	Brian Mynar, Fred Mynar Joe Mynar, John Dunn	34:31
	2nd Overall	John Bugge, Jerry Cochran, Roger Myers, Russ Roberts (DNF)	37:22
	3rd Overall	Grady Hicks, Jon Nilsestuen Chris Paddack	42:37
	1st Mixed	Donna Bugge, Mick Edgar Robert Youens	44:59
	2nd Mixed	Kay Coffey, Larry Coffey Sam Thiede	50:43

Year (Boats Finished)	Place	Competitors Names	Time (hr:min)
	3rd Mixed Aluminum	Cindy Alford Bob Nicol	71:31
1994 (33)	1st Overall	John Dunn, Brian Mynar Fred Mynar, Joe Mynar	36:52
	2nd Overall	West Hansen, Dan Remnitz Allen Spelce, Jeff Wueste	42:57
	3rd Overall	Donald Baumbach, Tom Dornak, Grady Hicks Jon Nilsestuen, David Thielman	45:54
	1st Mixed	Erin Bowden, Phil Bowden, Ron Henk	51:21
	2nd Mixed	Linda Cochran, Lillie Cochran Jerry Cochran	54:04
	3rd Mixed	Kay Coffey Larry Coffey, Bill Fiala	62:18
1995 (49)	1st Overall	John Dunn, Brian Mynar Fred Mynar, Joe Mynar	34:49
	2nd Overall	Donna Bugge, John Bugge Mike Shively, Robert Youens	38:23
	3rd Overall	West Hansen Jeff Wueste	42:38
	1st Women's Solo	Ginsie Dunn	60:06
	2nd Mixed	Teddy Gray (Montgomery) Jim Keirnan	63:15
	4th Standard	Patricia Bayers Lewis Bayers	75:32
1996 (27)	1st Overall	John Bugge, Rich Long, Mike Shea Mike Shively, Jeff Verryp	41:20
	2nd Overall	John Dunn, Brian Mynar Fred Mynar, Joe Mynar	42:09
	3rd Overall	Jerry Cochran, Pat Petrisky Allen Spelce, Troy Swift	47:51
	1st Mixed	Cindy Meurer, West Hansen Jack Kraus, Jeff Wueste	51:46

Year (Boats Finished)	Place	Competitors Names	Time (hr:min)
	2nd Mixed	Marie McKay, Lee Deviney, Robert Youens	56:26
	3rd Mixed	Paula Goynes, Sandy Goynes Tom Goynes	83:18
1997 (46)	1st Overall	Solomon Carriere, Jerry Cochran, John Dunn Steve Landick, Brian Mynar, Fred Mynar	29:46
	2nd Overall	John Bugge, Jack Kraus, Rich Long Mike Shea, Jeff Verryp	31:53
	3rd Overall	West Hansen Allen Spelce	36:27
	1st Mixed	Susan Cowan, Steve Ayers, Grady Hicks Rob Rojas, Robert Youens	36:41
	2nd Mixed 1st Masters	Kathie Derrick Peter Derrick	43:09
	1st Women's	Ginsie Dunn, Teddy Gray (Montomery) Cindy Meurer	47:35
1998 (37)	1st Overall	John Dunn, Brian Mynar, Tim Rask Fred Mynar, Joe Mynar, Mike Vincent	38:39
	2nd Overall	John Bugge, Phil Gumbert, West Hansen Mike Shea, Allen Spelce, Robert Youens	40:41
	3rd Overall	Donald Baumbach, Tom Dornak Johnny Prochaska, Sammy Prochaska	46:53
	1st Mixed	Kathie Derrick Peter Derrick	54:02
	1st USCA C2	Cindy Meurer Grady Hicks	56:38
	2nd Mixed	Sandy Goynes Tom Goynes	59:18
1999 (53)	1st Overall	Donald Baumach, John Dunn, Brian Mynar Fred Mynar, Joe Mynar, Chuck Stewart	37:09
	2nd Overall	West Hansen, Jack Kraus, Rich Long Mike Shea, Allen Spelce, Jeff Verryp	41:31
	3rd Overall	Donna Bugge, John Bugge Mary Jo Gumbert, Phil Gumbert	42:40

Year (Boats Finished)	Place	Competitors Names	Time (hr:min)
	2nd Mixed	Kathie Derrick Peter Derrick	50:15
	3rd Tandem Unlimited	Sandy Goynes Tom Goynes	54:31
	1st Women's Solo	Erin Magee	73:42
2000 (68)	1st Overall	Donald Baumbach, John Dunn, Brian Mynar Fred Mynar, Joe Mynar, Chuck Stewart	34:23
	2nd Overall	Larry Coffey, Butch Loller, John Maika, Vance Sherrod, Rob Wytaske	36:36
	3rd Overall	Donna Bugge, Ginger Turner, John Bugge Pat Petrisky, Mike Shively,Richard Steppe	36:49
	2nd Mixed	Mollie Binion, Pete Binion, Wade Binion, Jim Pye	40:52
	2nd Tandem Unlimited	Sandy Goynes Tom Goynes	46:23
	1st Women's	Cindy Meurer Ginsie Stauss	46:55
2001 (76)	1st Overall	Fiona Vincent, Mike Vincent, Donald Baumbach, John Dunn, Brian Mynar, Fred Mynar, Kyle Mynar, Chuck Stewart	36:03
	2nd Overall	Pete Binion, Wade Binion, John Bugge, Erin Magee, Jim Pye, Vance Sherrod, Richard Steppe, Rob Wytaske, John Maika	38:35
	3rd Overall	Ian Adamson, West Hansen, Allen Spelce Jeff Wueste	41:53
	3rd Tandem Unlimited	Sandy Goynes Tom Goynes	51:24
	3rd Mixed	Julie Morgan Colin Grimshaw	61:45
	1st Women's Solo	Ginger Turner	81:10
2002 (72)	1st Overall	Donald Baumbach, John Dunn, Brian Mynar Fred Mynar, Kyle Mynar, Chuck Stewart, Dave Jensen	37:50

Year (Boats Finished)	Place	Competitors Names	Time (hr:min)
	2nd Overall	Jerry Cochran, West Hansen, Tim Rask Michael Rask, Allen Spelce, Jeff Wueste	41:10
	3rd Overall	Pete Binion, John Maika, Johnny Prochaska Vance Sherrod, Mike Shively	45:09
	1st Mixed	Kathie Derrick Peter Derrick	50:46
	2nd Mixed	Mary Jo Gumbert Phil Gumbert	51:47
	4th USCA C2	Sandy Goynes Tom Goynes	61:28
2003 (87)	1st Overall	Jerry Cochran, Brian Mynar, Fred Mynar Sammy Prochaska, Allen Spelce, Chuck Stewart	36:15
	2nd Overall	Wade Binion, John Dupont, John Mark Harras Tim Rask, Bill Stafford, Tommy Yonley	40:04
	3rd Overall	Pat Petrisky Mark Simmons	40:25
	4th Unlimited	Gwyn Hayman, Marc Coppedge, Lee Deviney Jimmy Harvey, Peter Churchman (DNF), Bob Vincent (DNF)	41:49
	1st Mixed	Lori Yonley, Jonathan Yonley	49:15
	1st Women's Solo	Erin Magee	51:19
2004 (56)	1st Overall	Jerry Cochran, Sammy Prochaska, John Dunn Joe Mynar, Brian Mynar, Chuck Stewart	33:08
	2nd Overall	John Maika, Pete Binion, Vance Sherrod Pat Petrisky, Jim Pye	36:06
	3rd Overall	John Mark Harras, Jay Daniel, Jonathan Zeek Jonathan Yonley, Jeremiah Jackson, Bill Stafford	37:02
	4th Unlimited	Cindy Meurer, Mike Drost, Phillipe Blouin, Grady Hicks Jeff Wueste, Marc Coppedge, Jimmy Harvey	37:33
	1st Mixed	Kathie Derrick Peter Derrick	39:27
	1st Tandem Unlimited	Erin Magee Richard Steppe	39:47

Year (Boats Finished)	Place	Competitors Names	Time (hr:min)
2005 (70)	1st Overall	Tim Anglin, Daniel Cruz, West Hansen, Richard Steppe Armin Lopez, Jerry Rhaburn, Leroy Romero	36:56
	2nd Overall	Pete Binion, Wade Binion, John Maika Pat Petrisky, Vance Sherrod, Mark Simmons	38:06
	3rd Overall	Jay Daniel, Jim Pye, Tim Rask Jonathan Yonley, Tommy Yonley, Jonathan Zeek	40:06
	1st Women's	Holly Nelson, Mary Tipton Sandy Yonley (Goynes)	48:31
	2nd Mixed	Cindy Meurer Grady Hicks	54:47
	3rd Mixed	Rebekah Zeek Don Zeek	61:10
2006 (51)	1st Overall	Armin Lopez, Jerry Rhaburn, Efrain Cruz Amado Cruz, Daniel Cruz, John Bugge	38:00
	2nd Overall	Jerry Cochran, Fred Mynar, Brian Mynar Sammy Prochaska, Mike Vincent, John Dunn	38:44
	3rd Overall	Pat Petrisky, Tim Rask, Michael Rask Stephen Rask, Jonathan Yonley, Tommy Yonley	42:20
	1st Mixed	Kathie Derrick Peter Derrick	56:02
	1st Women's	Sandy Yonley (Goynes), Sarah Walliser Holly Nelson	59:20
	1st Women's Solo	Erin Magee	72:51
2007 (81)	1st Overall	Pete Binion, Wade Binion, Amado Cruz West Hansen, Armin Lopez, Richard Steppe	34:09
	2nd Overall	Carter Johnson	36:03
	3rd Overall	Tim Anglin, Andres Cobb, Felix Cruz John Dupont, John Mark Harras, Rob Wytaske	36:47
	1st Mixed	Debra Lane Fred Mynar	37:45
	2nd Mixed	Abigail Rask Tim Rask	39:48

Year (Boats Finished)	Place	Competitors Names	Time (hr:min)
	1st Standard	Meagan Yeager John Bugge	40:06
2008 (53)	1st Overall	Jerry Cochran, Jeff Glock, Tommy Yonley Mike Rendon, Kyle Mynar, Fred Mynar	39:34
	2nd Overall	Andrew Stephens, William Russell, Armin Lopez Amado Cruz, Leroy Romero, Felix Cruz	41:15
	3rd Overall	John Qualls, Rob Wytaske, Richard Ameen John Hoffart, John Maika, Sammy Prochaska	48:02
	6th Unlimited	Mollie Binion, Pauline Tice, Pete Binion Wade Binion	53:01
	1st Women's	Jamie Norman Stephanie McFerren	61:02
	1st Women's Solo	Erin Magee	65:28
2009 (50)	1st Overall	Kyle Mynar, Andrew Stephens, Amado Cruz William Russell, Armin Lopez, Daniel Cruz	42:55
	2nd Overall	Stephen Rask, Peter Rask, Philip Rask Jonathan Yonley, Max Feaster	43:31
	3rd Overall	Fred Mynar	46:41
	1st Women's	Holly Orr (Nelson) Debbie Richardson	71:35
	1st Women's Solo	Erin Magee	73:22
	2nd Women's Solo	Rebekah Zeek	77:00
2010 (69)	1st Overall	Andrew Stephens, Amado Cruz, Daniel Cruz Andrew Soles, Sam Ritchie, Efrain Cruz	34:40
	2nd Overall	Jeff Glock, Fred Mynar, Chuck Stewart Jerry Cochran, Brian Mynar, Wade Binion	35:23
	3rd Overall	Tommy Yonley Tim Rask	38:11
	1st Mixed	Meagan Yeager John Bugge	46:00
	5th Unlimited	Sheila Reiter, John Maika, Jeff Wueste	47:25

Year (Boats Finished)	Place	Competitors Names	Time (hr:min)
	1st C2	Sarah Kittle Jonahan Kittle	53:56
2011 (78)	1st Overall	Amado Cruz, Sam Ritchie, Daniel Cruz Daniel Hammer, William Russell, Andrew Stephens	39:51
	2nd Overall	Gaston Jones, Fred Mynar, Max Feaster Jeff Glock, Kyle Mynar, Logan Mynar	40:54
	3rd Overall	Jonathan Yonley Tommy Yonley	48:52
	1st Women's	Jamie Norman, Samantha "Sam" Binion, Holly Orr (Nelson) Sandy Yonley (Goynes), Natalie Taylor, Virginia Parker	55:42
	1st Mixed	Rachel Thompson Stephen Rask	67:42
	2nd Mixed	Melanie Hof Paul Cox	69:18
2012 (94)	1st Overall	William Russell, Andrew Stephens, Sam Ritchie Andrew Soles, Daniel Cruz, Amado Cruz	38:30
	2nd Overall	Philip Rask, Peter Rask, Stephen Rask Jonathan Rask, Michael Rask, Jeremiah Jackson	41:49
	3rd Overall	Clay Wyatt Logan Mynar	42:12
	1st Mixed	Sandy Yonley (Goynes) Tommy Yonley	43:05
	2nd Mixed	Erin Magee Jerry Cochran	45:23
	3rd Mixed	Samantha "Sam" Binion Wade Binion	48:32
2013 (81)	1st Overall	Fred Mynar, Kyle Mynar, Logan Mynar Andrew Condie, Tommy Yonley, Jerry Cochran	39:45
	2nd Overall	Mike Rendon, Clay Wyatt, Jeff Glock Bobby Smart, Sammy Prochaska	44:46
	3rd Overall	Jay Daniel, Mike Vandeveer, Brandon Stafford John Dupont, John Mark Harras, Andres Cabb	45:12
	1st Women's	Virginia Parker Morgan Kohut	49:30

Year (Boats Finished)	Place	Competitors Names	Time (hr:min)
	1st Mixed	Meagan Yeager John Bugge	50:46
	5th Unlimited	Kaitlin Jiral, Darryl Jiral Karim Aziz	51:46
2014 (77)	1st Overall	Gaston Jones, Clay Wyatt, Wade Binion Andrew Condie, Jeff Glock, Ian Rolls	40:03
	2nd Overall	Jay Daniel, Sammy Prochaska, Brandon Stafford, Shawn Boyett, Mike Vandeveer, Steve Bis	44:55
	3rd Overall	Tommy Yonley	45:58
	1st Mixed	Erin Magee Jerry Cochran	47:40
	4th Unlimited	Kaitlin Jiral, Darryl Jiral Landen Jiral	50:53
	2nd Mixed	Debbie Richardson Phil Bowden	51:00
2015 (67)	1st Overall	Gaston Jones, Clay Wyatt, Wade Binion Andrew Condie, Jeff Glock, Ian Rolls	35:02
	2nd Overall	Jonathan Yonley Max Feaster	38:22
	3rd Overall	Chris Champion, Phil Bowden Jason Cade	39:33
	1st Women's	Virginia Condie (Parker) Kaitlin Jiral	41:29
	1st Mixed	Debbie Richardson Shawn Boyett	43:33
	1st Standard	Cecili Bugge John Bugge	45:45
2016 (81)	1st Overall	Kyle Mynar, Logan Mynar, Fred Mynar Tommy Yomley, Phil Bowden, Jason Cade	31:33
	2nd Overall	Chris Issendorf, Wade Binion, Clay Wyatt Gaston Jones, Ian Rolls, Andrew Condie	31:55
	3rd Overall	Amy Boyd, Debbie Richardson Bobby Smart, Jeff Wueste	39:02

Year (Boats Finished)	Place	Competitors Names	Time (hr:min)
	1st Women's Solo	Virginia Condie (Parker)	40:17
	1st Women's	Morgan Kohut Kaitlin Jiral	42:10
	5th Unlimited	Jeannette Burris, Charlie Stewart, Chris Paddack John Qualls, John Hoffart, Mike Dey	42:48
2017 (107)	1st Overall	Andrew Condie, Chris Issendorf, Clay Wyatt Gaston Jones, Ian Rolls, Jay Daniel	36:49
	2nd Overall	Tommy Yonley Jonathan Yonley	38:58
	3rd Overall	Hener Cruz Kyle Mynar	39:26
	1st Women's	Amy Boyd, Debbie Richardson Holly Orr (Nelson), Melissa James, Rebekah Feaster	43:13
	2nd Women's	Kaitlin Jiral, Shannon Issendorf, Virginia Condie (Parker)	44:20
	4th Unlimited	Jeannette Burris, Mike Tecci, Chris Paddack John Qualls, John Hoffart, Max Hambly	45:06
2018 (83)	1st Overall	Andrew Condie, Nick Walton, Tommy Yonley, William Russel, Ian Rolls, Amado Cruz	36:45
	2nd Overall	Clay Wyatt, Logan Mynar, Kyle Mynar, Fred Mynar, Michael Schlimmer, Ben Schlimmer	36:50
	3rd Overall	Jason Cade, Phil Bowden	45:46
	1st Mixed Tandem Unlimited	Shannon Issendorf, Chris Issendorf	52:37
	4th Unlimited	Debbie Richardson, R. D. Kissling, Jeff Wueste, Chris Stevenson, Bobby Smart	53:19
	6th Unlimited	Brenda Jones, Ed Jones, Brian Jones	54:51
2019 (142)	1st Overall	Bill Torongo, Nick Walton, Andrew Condie, William Russell, Wade Binion, Ian Rolls	34:27
	2nd Overall	Jonathan Yonley, Tommy Yonley	34:56
	3rd Overall	Brad Daniels, Michael Matthews, Dylan Mchardy, Phil Bowden, Michael Cade	35:30
	1st Unlimited Women	Mary Schlimmer, Virginia Condie (Parker), Morgan Kohut, Kaitlin Jiral	37:31

Year (Boats Finished)	Place	Competitors Names	Time (hr:min)
	3rd Unlimited	Holly Orr (Nelson), Luke Zolnierowski, David Kaiser, Alex Leonard, Mark Schattenberg	38:33
	4th Unlimited	Debbie Richardson, Joel Truitt, Zach Elkins, James Green, Jeff Wueste	40:11
2020		Canceled due to COVID	
2021 (99)	1st Overall	Tim Rask, Kyle Mynar, Nick Walton, Tommy Yonley	35:46
	2nd Overall	Ryan Siebos, Wes Wyatt, Brad Daniels, Phil Bowden, Dylan Mchardy, Ryan Martinez	37:01
	3rd Overall	Andrew Condie, Clay Wyatt, Danny Medina	37:28
	4th Unlimited	Rebekah Feaster, Jonathan Kittle, Dave Walliser, Rachel Rask, Stephen Rask, Jonathan Rask	40:46
	1st Women's	Melissa James, Holly Orr, Mollie Binion, Cecili Bugge, Lydia Huelskamp	41:41
	5th Unlimited	Jay Daniel, Morgan Kohut, Michael Tecci, Wayne Thorp (DNF)	44:43

Notes

Chapter 1

1. Frank Brown, "River Voyage," *Southwest Holiday*, November 1962, 9.

2. West Hansen, "The Texas Water Safari," unpublished manuscript, Austin, TX, 1997.

3. Frank Brown, "River Voyage," *Southwest Holiday*, December 1962, 10.

4. Brown, "River Voyage," 11.

5. Brown, "River Voyage," 28.

6. Brown, "River Voyage," 29.

7. Frank Brown, "River Voyage," *Southwest Holiday*, January 1963, 15.

Chapter 2

1. San Marcos Chamber of Commerce, "Texas Water Safari, 'The Toughest Boat Race, in the World,' Race Application," San Marcos, TX, 1963, 7.

2. Texas Water Safari Archives, unpublished materials, 1963, 19 and 20.

3. Bob Brister, "The World's Toughest River Race," *Argosy*, July, 1963, 74.

4. Brister, "World's Toughest River Race," 78.

5. Fred W. Strong, "Outdoors," *Victoria Advocate*, May 1, 1963.

6. Brister, "World's Toughest River Race," 78.

7. Curtis Carpenter, "Trial by Water," *Texas Game and Fish*, Austin, July 1963, 18.

8. Brister, "World's Toughest River Race," 78.

9. *Life*, June 7, 1963, 110.

10. Bill Manning, "Race to the Sea!" *Texas Parade*, June 1963, 10.

11. Carpenter, "Trial by Water," 30.

12. Brister, "World's Toughest River Race," 78.

13. Carpenter, "Trial by Water," 30.

14. Brister, "World's Toughest River Race," 80.

15. Brister, "World's Toughest River Race," 81.

16. Bob Brister, "Exclusive, Timed Photos Reveal How Houstonians Won World's Toughest Boat Race," *Houston Chronicle*, May 12, 1963, 6.

17. Texas Water Safari Archives, unpublished material, 1963–2019.

Chapter 3

1. West Hansen, The Texas Water Safari, unpublished manuscript, Austin, TX, 1997.

2. Craig H. Roell, Handbook of Texas online, "Hochhein, TX," Texas State Historical Association, Austin, June 15, 2010, http://tshaonline.org/handbook/online/articles/hnh34.

3. Amber Aldaco, "Remembering the Small Community of Cheapside, Now a 'Ghost Town,'" Victoria, TX, October 30, 2018.

4. Craig H. Roell, Handbook of Texas online, "Thomaston, TX," Texas State Historical Association, Austin, TX, June 15, 2010, http://tshaonline.org/handbook/online/articles/hnt18.

5. Craig H. Roell, Handbook of Texas online, "Nursery, TX," Texas State Historical Association, Austin, TX, June 15, 2010, http://tshaonline.org/handbook/online/articles/hln29.

6. The *Gonzales Inquirer*, April 3, 2005.

Chapter 4

1. Thad Sitton, "Texas Unlimited! San Marcos to the Sea by Fair Means or Fowl," *Canoe*, August 1987, 32.

Chapter 5

1. Tom Taylor, "Texas Water Safari 1984," *Canoe*, September/October 1984, 70.

Chapter 7

1. Chris Stevenson, "50th Texas Water Safari Edition," Official Newsletter of the Texas Canoe and Kayak Racing Association, June 2012, 3.
2. Bob Spain, *Bob Spain's Canoeing Guide and Favorite Texas Paddling Trails* (College Station: Texas A&M University Press, 2018), 170.

Chapter 8

1. Wes Bloomquist, "Stay Connected," *Victoria Advocate*, June 2009, C1, C2.
2. Bloomquist, "Stay Connected," C2.
3. Bloomquist, "Stay Connected," C2.

Chapter 9

1. Robert Smith, "Inability to Accept Defeat or Self Torture Can Be Fun," *Texas Water Safari Magazine*, June 5–9, 1982, 22.
2. Tom Goynes, *The Splash King and His Mermaid Queen*, unpublished manuscript, 2022.

Chapter 10

1. Charlie Kouba, *Still Crazy—The Adventure of a Lifetime*, self-published, Victoria, TX, 2019, 81.
2. Fletcher Anderson, "Tackling the Texas Water Safari," Nors/Currents, Sylva, NC, July 1982, 20.
3. Kevin Sherrington, *Dallas Morning News*, June 16, 1996.

Chapter 12

1. *San Marcos Record*, April 16, 1964, 1.
2. Bob Brister, "500-Mile Marathon," *Argosy*, August 1964, 118.
3. Brister, "500-Mile Marathon," 118.
4. Brister, "500-Mile Marathon," 122.
5. West Hansen, The Texas Water Safari, unpublished manuscript, Austin, TX, 1997.
6. Hansen, Texas Water Safari, unpublished manuscript.
7. Texas Water Safari Archives, unpublished material, 1963–2019.
8. Hansen, Texas Water Safari, unpublished manuscript.
9. Texas Water Safari Archives, unpublished material, 1963–2019.
10. Henry Wolff Jr., "Dallas Pair Leading Safari on First Day," *Victoria Advocate*, June 1967.
11. Tom Buckner, "Defending Champs Own Large Margin in Safari," *San Marcos Record*, June 1967, 1.
12. Hansen, Texas Water Safari, unpublished manuscript.
13. Hansen, Texas Water Safari, unpublished manuscript.
14. Texas Water Safari Archives, unpublished material, 1963–2019.

Chapter 13

1. Pat Hathcock, "Seadrift's Water Safari Warriors," *Victoria Advocate*, May 21, 2006, 8A.

2. Hathcock, "Seadrift's Water Safari Warriors," 8A.

Chapter 14

1. Tom Taylor, "Texas Water Safari 1984," *Canoe*, September/October 1984, 57.

Chapter 15

1. Louise Popplewell, "49 Canoeists Brave Storm to Finish the Race," *Victoria Advocate*, June, 16, 1995, 10A.

2. Wes Bloomquist, "This Year's TYWS One of the Toughest Ever," *Victoria Advocate*, June 17, 2008, C2.

3. Mike Foreman, "Mynar Crew in Water Safari Race," *Victoria Advocate*, June 2000, 1B, 2B.

4. Norm Thomas, Texas Water Safari Archives, unpublished material, 1963–2019.

5. Jason Gordon, "More Characters Than Canoes at Texas Water Safari," *San Marcos Daily Record*, June 9, 2002, 1B and 5B.

Chapter 16

1. Chris Stevenson, "50th Texas Water Safari Edition," Official Newsletter of the Texas Canoe and Kayak Racing Association, June 2012, 3–5.

2. Wes Bloomquist, "This Year's TYWS One of the Toughest Ever," *Victoria Advocate*, June 17, 2008, C2.

3. Stephen Hawkins, "Solo Trip to Seadrift," *Victoria Advocate*, July 10, 2010, C1, C4.

4. Jennifer Preyss, "Paddling for a Cause," *Victoria Advocate*, June 14, 2011, B4.

5. Will Brown, "Many Paddlers Hear Tragic News at Water Safari Finish Line," *Victoria Advocate*, June 14, 2012, 1 and 4.

Chapter 17

1. Taylor Mitchell, "Safer Safari," *Victoria Advocate*, June 9, 2013, A6.

2. Taylor Crowe, "He Was on My Heart the Whole Time," *Victoria Advocate*, June 12, 2013, A1.

3. Crowe, "He Was on My Heart the Whole Time," A6.

4. Julie Garcia, "One-Woman Team," *Victoria Advocate*, June 18, 2014, A4.

5. Taylor Mitchell, "High Water Leads to Fast Times at Texas Water Safari," *Victoria Advocate*, May 3, 2015, C1 and C4.

6. Chris Derritt, "Finish Line," *Victoria Advocate*, July 15, 2015, C1.

7. Mike Forman, "Close as It Gets," *Victoria Advocate*, June 27, 2016, 1C.

8. Marcus Gutierrez, "Buddy System," *Victoria Advocate*, June 29, 2016, C4.

9. Gutierrez, "Buddy System," C1.

Bibliography

Aldaco, Amber. "Remembering the Small Community of Cheapside, Now a 'Ghost Town.'" Victoria, TX, October 30, 2018.

Anderson, Fletcher. "Tackling the Texas Water Safari." Nors/Currents, Sylva, NC, July, 1982, 18–21.

Bloomquist, Wes. "Stay Connected." *Victoria Advocate*, June 2009, C1, C2.

———. "This Year's TYWS One of the Toughest Ever." *Victoria Advocate*, June 17, 2008, C1, C2.

Bondurabt, Matt. "Texas Water Safari." *Texas Monthly*, October 2014.

Brister, Bob. "Exclusive, Timed Photos Reveal How Houstonians Won World's Toughest Boat Race." *Houston Chronicle*, May 12, 1963, 6.

———. "500-Mile Marathon." Argosy, August 1964, 17–23 and 118–22.

———. "The World's Toughest River Race." Argosy, July 1963, 74–81.

Brown, Frank. "River Voyage." *Southwest Holiday*, November 1962, 8–19, 28 and 30.

———. "River Voyage," Part II." *Southwest Holiday*, December 1962, 10, 11, 26, 28–30.

———. "River Voyage." *Southwest Holiday*, January 1963, 8, 9, 14, 26.

Brown, Will. "Many Paddlers Hear Tragic News at Water Safari Finish Line." *Victoria Advocate*, June 14, 2012, 1 and 4.

Buckner, Tom. "Defending Champs Own Large Margin in Safari." *San Marcos Record*, June 1967, 1.

Carpenter, Curtis. "Trial by Water." *Texas Game and Fish*, July 1963, 14, 18, 30.

Chilton, W. Earl. *Freshwater Fishes of Texas*. Austin: Texas Parks and Wildlife Press, 1997.

Conant, Roger. *A Field Guide to Reptiles and Amphibians*. Boston: Houghton Mifflin, 1958.

Crowe, Taylor. "He Was on My Heart the Whole Time." *Victoria Advocate*, June 12, 2013, A1 and A6.

Derritt, Chris. "Finish Line." *Victoria Advocate*, July 15, 2015, C1 and C3.

Dixon, James R., John E. Werler, and Michael R. J. Forstner. *Texas Snakes: A Field Guide*. Austin: University of Texas Press, 2000.

Eid, Ron. "Tough Enough." *Spirit*, May 1994, 36–42, 114–16.

———. "A Year-Round Race." *Spirit*, May 1994, 42, 117, 118.

Fly, W. Lamar. Handbook of Texas online. "Cheapside, TX." Texas State Historical Association, Austin, 2010. http://tshaonline.org/handbook/online/articles/hnc50.

Forman, Mike. "Close as It Gets." *Victoria Advocate*, June 27, 2016, 1C.

———. "Mynar Crew in Water Safari Race." *Victoria Advocate*, June 2000, 1B, 2B.

Garcia, Julie. "One-Woman Team." *Victoria Advocate*, June 18, 2014, A1 and A4.

Garza, O. C. "The Great Texas Water Safari." *Texas Highways*, June 1982, 28–35.

Gordon, Jason. "More Characters Than Canoes at Texas Water Safari." *San Marcos Daily Record*, June 9, 2002, 1B and 5B.

Gutierrez, Marcus. "Buddy System." *Victoria Advocate*, June 29, 2016, C1 and 4.

———. "Last Call." *Victoria Advocate*, June 30, 2016, C1.

Hansen, West. "The Texas Water Safari," unpublished manuscript, Austin, TX, 1997.

Hathcock, Pat. "Seadrift's Water Safari Warriors." *Victoria Advocate*, May 21, 2006, 1A and 8A.

Hawkins, Stephen. "Solo Trip to Seadrift." *Victoria Advocate*, July 10, 2010, C1 and C4.

Kouba, Charlie. "Still Crazy—The Adventure of a Lifetime." Self-published, Victoria, TX, 2019.

Langley, Ricky L. "Alligator Attacks on Humans in the United States." *Wilderness and Environmental Medicine* 16 (2005): 118–24.

Lohse, Jon C. "Underwater Archaeology at 41HY147, the Terrace Locality at Spring Lake." Index of Texas Archaeology: Open Access Gray Literature from the Lone Star State, Center for Archaeological Studies, Texas State University, San Marcos, vol. 2013, 137.

Manning, Bill. "Race to the Sea!" *Texas Parade*, June 1963, 8–10.

Marcee, Clarisa. "Scared Springs." *Outdoor Magazine of Texas*, June 1999.

Mitchell, Taylor. "High Water Leads to Fast Times at Texas Water Safari." *Victoria Advocate*, May 3, 2015, C1 and C4.

———. "Safer Safari." *Victoria Advocate*, June 9, 2013, A1 and A6.

Montier, Don. "Don Montier—Texas Water Safari 1967." Montier Family Stories, www.grannyfkgil.com/indes38.html.

Popplewell, Louise. "49 Canoeists Brave Storm to Finish the Race." *Victoria Advocate*, June 16, 1995, 10A.

Press Release. "GBRA Officials Conduct Tour of Guadalupe's Lower Basin." *Gonzales Inquirer*, April 5, 2005, 5.

Preyss, Jennifer. "Paddling for a Cause." *Victoria Advocate*, June 14, 2011, B1 and B4.

Robinson, Alice. "Canoeists Face Race with Thrill and Trepidation." *Victoria Advocate*, June 13, 2003.

Roell, Craig H. Handbook of Texas Online. "Hochhein, TX." Texas State Historical Association, Austin, June 15, 2010. http://tshaonline.org/handbook/online/articles/hnh34.

———. Handbook of Texas Online. "Nursery, TX." Texas State Historical Association, Austin, June 15, 2010. http://tshaonline.org/handbook/online/articles/hln29.

———. Handbook of Texas Online. "Thomaston, TX." Texas State Historical Association, Austin, June 15, 2010. http://tshaonline.org/handbook/online/articles/hnt18.

"Safari Race Starts This Weekend." *San Marcos Record*, April 16, 1964, 1.

San Marcos Chamber of Commerce. "Texas Water Safari, 'The Toughest Boat Race in the World,' Race Application." San Marcos, TX, 1963, 1–12.

San Marcos Record. Staff photo, June 22, 1967, 5.

Sherrington, Kevin. *Dallas Morning News*, June 16, 1996.

Sitton, Thad. "Texas Unlimited! San Marcos to the Sea by Fair Means or Fowl." *Canoe*, August 1987, 30–32.

Smith, Robert. "Inability to Accept Defeat or Self Torture Can Be Fun." *Texas Water Safari Magazine*, June 5–9, 1982, 22–25.

Spain, Bob. *Bob Spain's Canoeing Guide and Favorite Texas Paddling Trails*. College Station: Texas A&M University Press, 2018.

Spezia, Mark. "The Old Man and the River." *My City Magazine*, September1, 2014, 21–23.

Stevenson, Chris. "50th Texas Water Safari Edition." Official Newsletter of the Texas Canoe and Kayak Racing Association, June 2012, 1–13.

Strong, Fred W. "Outdoors." *Victoria Advocate*, May 1, 1963.

Taylor, Tom. "Texas Water Safari 1984." *Canoe*, September/October 1984, 56–58, 70–73.

Texas Parks and Wildlife Department. "Paddling Race: A Long Way to Seadrift." 1994. www.youtube.com/watch?v=YCxFOs9QNao&authuser=O.

Texas Water Safari Archives, unpublished material, 1963–2019.

Texas Canoe and Kayak Racing Association Board. "50th Texas Water Safari Edition." Official Newsletter of the Texas Canoe and Kayak Racing Association, June 2012, 1–13.

Thompson, Edward K., ed. "57 Boats Started a Rugged 12-Day Race in Texas, Only Two Finished." *Life*, June 7, 1963, 107–13.

Victoria Advocate editorial board. "Congratulations for Finishing Tough Race. *Victoria Advocate*, June 19, 2014, A7.

Wolff, Henry, Jr. "Dallas Pair Leading Safari on First Day," *Victoria Advocate*, June 1967.

Index

Folbot, Watermans', 69–70
Freeport, 17, 142, 164
Frey, Brian, *22*
Frey, Sarah, *22*

gar, 89, 129–33
Geisinger, Joe, 194
Geisinger, Libby, 194
General Clinton Canoe Regatta, 62, 65, 173
George, Big Willie, 169
Georgia, alligator fatalities, 126
Gillings, Bob, 53, 141, 142
Glock, Jeff, 46–47, 66–67, 116–19, 174, 176, 179, 184
Glos, Janie Mize, 80, 83–84
Gonzales checkpoint, 29, *30*
Gonzales Dam, 29
Gore, Howard, 38, 39, 150, 152, 153, 174
Goynes, James, 145
Goynes, Jim, 94, 146
Goynes, Pat, 146
Goynes, Paula, 39–40, 78, 94, 95–98, 116, 153, 157
Goynes, Sandy (later Yonley), 76, 78–80, 94, 120–21, 175, 179, 197, *199*
Goynes, Tom: overview of role in Safari, 39–40, 94–98; alternate canoe race plan, 150; hallucinations story, 115–16; races during the 1960s, 145, 146; races during the 1970s, 38, 78, 147, 148–49, 151, 152, 153–54; races during the 1980s, 154, 155–56, 157
GPS trackers, 110
Graef, Joe, *80*
Graham, James, 179–80
Gray, Teddy, *72, 73,* 88
Greer, Stacy, *196*
Grimshaw, Colin, 119–20
Grumble, Clarence "Shorty," 24–25
Guadalupe-Blanco River Authority, 33
Guadalupe River, 29, 123–26. *See also* race course, current route
Guiness World records, 59, 60, 62
Gumbert, Mary Jo, 167
Gumbert, Phil, 167
gun encounters, 142, 156

Hafernick, Gib, *105*
Hagan, Lawrence, 116, 144, 150
Halbert, Kevin, 22
Hall, C. J., 135–36
Hall, Charles, 143, 144–45, 147
Hall, Charlie, 38
Hall, Nova, 70
Hallmark, Jamie, 100, 126–27
Hallmark, Judy, 100
Hall of Fame, overview, 195–200
hallucinations, 90, 92, 113–15, 119–22, 133, 192–93
Halstead, Ryan, 62
Hambly, Max, *80*
Hammer, Daniel, 179
ham operators, overview, 108–10
Hanks, Edgar, 153
Hanks, Laura, 70, 153
Hansen, West: Hall of Fame membership, 200; races during the 1990s, 72, 73CAPTION, 165, 166, 167; races during the earliest 2000s, 46, 58, 59, 169, 174–75; races during the 2010s, 91, 183–84
Harber, Rocky, 133, 159
Harle, Lee, *30*
Harle, Rob, *30*
Harras, John Mark: Hall of Fame membership, 195, *196,* 200; mentoring comment, 88; races during the 1980s, 157, 159; races during the 1990s, 161, 162; races during the earliest 2000s, 169, 175; races during the 2010s, 183–84
Harrison, Cameron, 192
Harrison, Heather, 91–93, 183, 184, 192
Harvey, Jimmy, 91, 118
Havens, Frank, 141
Henk, Ron, 74CAPTION
Herbert, Richard, 102–103
Hicks, Grady, 72, 160, 161, *196*
Hicks, Phil, 161
Highway 20, 25
Highway 59 Bypass, 32
Highway 90A bridge, 28
Highway 183 bridge, 29–31
Highway 236 bridge, 31–32
Highway I-35, 19

Hippie Chicks Team, 83–84
Hoch, Valentine, 31
Hochheim checkpoint, 29–31, 104–105
Hodges, Louis "Butch," 38, 150, 152–53
Hoffart, John, *80*
Holt, Carol Lou, 142
Hopkins Street Bridge, 18
Howard, Suzzie
How Winning Works (Benincasa), 60
Hudgins, Nathan, 83CAPTION
Huelskamp, Lydia, 190
Hunt, Joe, *178, 179, 196*
Huntington Harbor, California, 60
Hurd, Fred Jr, 141
Hwy 90 Bridge checkpoint, 25–27, 100–101, 109, *138*
hyacinth rafts, 176
hyponatremia, 181

ICF C-2 design, 40, *41*
Imua Canoe Club, 56
International Dragon Boat Federation Championships, 65
Invista Corporation, 32
Ironman Hawaii World Championships, 60
Issendorf, Chris, *95,* 186
Issendorf, Shannon, 186

Jackson, John, 175
James, Melissa, *77,* 82–83, 186, 190
Janak, Tim, 149
Jiral, Kaitlin, 65, 85, 185, 186, 187
Johnson, Carter, 60–62, 175
Johnson, Milton "Skip," 42, 43, 45, *47*
Jones, Brenda, 89–91, 191
Jones, Brian, 194
Jones, Donna, 89–91
Jones, Gaston, 179, 184, 186, 187, 190, 191
Jones, James, 141
Jones, Jimmy, 147–48
Jones, Lillian, 187
Jones, Lilly, 190

Kaiser, Kim, 194
Kancewick, James, 20
kayak winner, 38
Keating, Ben, 179–80

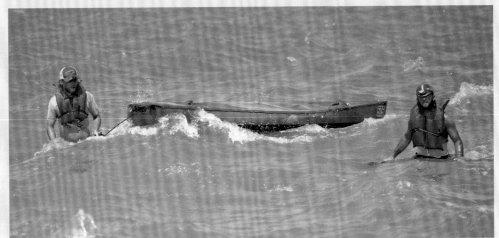